Lost Technologies
of the
Great Pyramid

Lost Technologies
of the
Great Pyramid

How the Great Pyramid was Built!

By

Steven Myers

CreateSpace
2010

Cover design by Mark Sampson, www.markstechservice.com
Back cover photo courtesy of Tammy Myers

ISBN: 1449916155
EAN-13: 9781449916152

To order additional copies, please visit:
www.thepump.org

Also by Steven Myers
The Great Pyramid Prosperity Machine

Printed in the U.S.A.

10 9 8 7 6 5 4 3 2 1

Contents

Dedication

To my parents: Charles and Bell Myers
For showing me the way
To my wife: Tammy Myers
For showing me the way
To my savior: Jesus Christ
For showing me The Way
To the researcher: Edward Kunkel
For showing me the way

Acknowledgments

No man is an island and no book is created solely by its author.

I want to acknowledge some of the people who helped to make this book possible. This list includes present and past board members of the nonprofit foundation I founded, as well as technical advisors, scholars, consultants, fellow researchers and supporters.

Special thanks go to Dr. P. H. Robinson whose help was instrumental in making this book a reality.

Additional people who have helped me with this book include the following.

Pat Smith, Mitch Walton, Dr. Sarah Ward, Stephanie Myers, Amy May, Sidney Christensen, Tim Powell, Ron Brittian, David Glawson, Sidney Christensen, Dr. Tammy Marino, Nick Spano, Jim Peart, Mark Sampson, Harlan Ray Cooley, John Sbarbaro, Bruce Smith, Jordi Lindegren, Jeff McKee and Dr. James Sinnott.

I also want to thank the numerous people who had the courage to help me with this book and related research but did not wish to be listed here.

Special Notes

The illustrations created specifically for this book are not copies of the original architectural drawings used in the construction work of the Great Pyramid. The style of these illustrations is intended to be as simple as possible and still convey the intended information. Each illustration does not depict every detail of this complex building. This is not a sign of inaccuracy but an attempt for clarity.

All dimensions provided in this book are only approximations. In describing the construction procedure and original function of the Great Pyramid approximate dimensions are more than sufficient. To be involved in the endless debate as to ultra-exact dimensions is unnecessary and detrimental to understanding how the Great Pyramid was assembled and used by its builders. The exact angle of the face of a hydroelectric dam has nothing to do with understanding how the dam was built and how it operated to serve its intended purpose. Therefore this author will not be caught up in the unresolved and unnecessary debate concerning exact dimensions, exact angles and the original unit of measure.

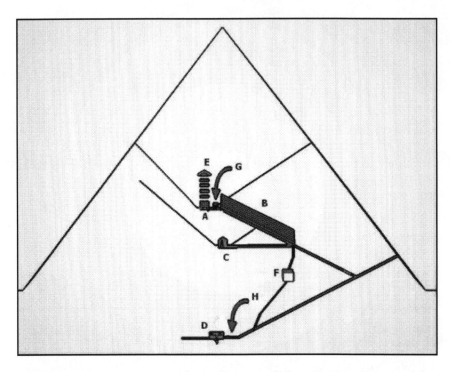

Fig. 0.1 Important Chambers of the Great Pyramid

- A. King's chamber
- B. Grand Gallery
- C. Queen's chamber
- D. Subterranean chamber
- E. Relieving chambers
- F. Grotto
- G. Antechamber
- H. Lesser Subterranean chamber

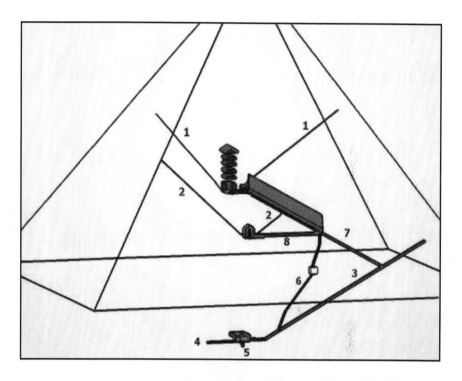

Fig. 0.2 Important Passages of the Great Pyramid

1. King's chamber vents
2. Queen's chamber vents
3. Descending passage
4. Dead End Shaft
5. The "Pit"
6. The Well Shaft
7. Ascending passage
8. Horizontal passage

Preface

Because there is much to discuss and many issues to address it is difficult to know where to start. While some people are most interested in knowing how the massive stones of the Great Pyramid were moved and set in place, others want to know where this radical theory came from. Many are interested in knowing why the massive effort was expended by the ancient builders to construct the Great Pyramid. Still others are concerned first and foremost with credentials and peer review. Other people's interest and focus is solely in mummies and burial treasure. There are also readers whose interest is how this theory fits into the context of the conventional understanding concerning the historical flow of the assent of mankind. Other people want to know how the information in this book could affect the future in a positive way.

These subjects will be thoroughly addressed, along with many other aspects of this understanding of the Great Pyramid. We all have different priorities, and the order in which these issues are addressed may not suit every reader. All of the above subjects and the issues they bring to mind are important and I intend to address every relevant aspect of the building and purpose of the Great Pyramid to the best of my ability as independent researcher, antiquities scholar, and author. Everything is interrelated and the discussion of these varied interests are intertwined, and addressed throughout the book.

When anyone—professional or layman alike—learns something, it becomes integral to that person. No matter what the subject, anything one has learned is a component of who they are. To use a computer analogy, every time we learn something it is recorded on the hard drive of our minds. All learned information, to follow the analogy, is like programming and affects our subsequent learning, opinions and actions. Humans are a synthesis of all they know.

This book is about a subject about which most readers already know a great deal. We all have opinions regarding mountainous research the Great Pyramid has inspired in the last 1,000 years. However the information in these pages and the direction of this research will be unfamiliar to most. This book presents information and interpretation of direct physical evidence which is contradictory to what most readers have already accepted as fact.

The hurdle of this book is not the acceptance of the material in its pages. The hurdle this book presents is whether or not you, the reader, have the ability to consider the possibility that the information you already accept as fact may be incorrect and then to find a different set of facts, a truer set of facts which is consistent with reason, the laws of physics, and the available remaining direct physical evidence. People tend to be subservient to their acquired knowledge instead of its master. Few, indeed, can put aside what they have accepted as fact to embrace newfound understanding.

To change what we know is to change who we are. With computers one can write over old, outdated information with ease. This is the nature of computers. The computer analogy breaks down when dealing with the human mind. The mind of the species of mankind has never been well equipped at discarding old data and replacing it with new information. For most of us it is our nature to resist change. Not only are old habits hard to break, accepting new ideas contrary to what one has already learned and accepted as true, presents a tremendous challenge.

Real learning can only take place when resistance to change is transcended. Some readers will have opinions about the Great Pyramid that are immutable, etched in stone. The hurdle mentioned above will be a stumbling block for readers with insurmountable conceptual rigidity. It does not matter what subject is involved: to unlearn something once accepted as true and then accept something else to take its place is one of the most difficult tasks to ask of anyone. Yet it is this very task I ask of the reader. It is for this reason, I have addressed in this book how we as humans learn and accept knowledge. The purpose, for including information on various aspects of how we acquire and process information, is that unlearning an accepted truth is more difficult than original learning has ever been. There is much you will have to unlearn to accept what this book has to offer.

Young people, who do not yet have an entrenched opinion as to what the Great Pyramid was for or how it was built, have been very receptive to the ideas presented in this book. To them, this understanding has an equal footing with all other explanations. They have the advantage of not having to unlearn one interpretation of evidence to accept another. I wish we all had this same advantage of freedom from preconceived notions as young people have.

Don Marquis said, "If you make people think they're thinking, they'll love you; but if you really make them think they'll hate you." It is not my interest how you feel about me. This book is not about me. I would like you to really <u>think</u> about the fundamental inadequacies of currently accepted conventional explanations of the Great Pyramid as well as to give consideration of this alternative explanation of how and why the Great Pyramid exists.

Edwin Schlossberg said, "The skill of writing is to create a context in which other people can think." This is my intent in writing this book. If you already "know" everything you need to know; then you won't have to trouble yourself with learning something new. Harriet Martineau said, "Readers are plentiful, thinkers are rare." I hope this book attracts a very rare class of reader who is also a thinker.

According to Dr. Samuel Johnson, "The two most engaging powers of an author are to make new things familiar and familiar things new." My goal is to present something as familiar and well known as the Great Pyramid in an entirely new way. To examine the contents of this book and consider it as the answer to how and why the Great Pyramid was built is the challenge I pose to you, the reader. My job as author is to present the plethora of information about this research in as cohesive and inclusive presentation as I can. In other words it is my job as author to tell the story of how the Great Pyramid was built and why.

Your job and responsibility as reader is to absorb the totality of this information, ponder it, and come to your own conclusion as to the relative merits of this research, compared to other theories about the Great Pyramid. As the author of this book, I have high expectations of you. The philosopher Herbert Spencer said, "Reading is seeing by proxy." I wrote this book in hopes you see what I see.

Galileo said, "You cannot teach a man anything, you can only help him find it within himself." He knew what he was talking about. It is my desire that you find the information in this book a viable explanation of how and why the Great Pyramid was built. In your inquiry into this theory of understanding of the Great Pyramid I wish you well. I also wish you good fortune in your own quest of understanding, whatever it may be.

Edward Abbey, naturalist and author, wrote, "May your trails be crooked, winding, lonesome, dangerous, leading to the most amazing view. May your mountains rise into and above the clouds."

It is my hope this book will help you proceed on your journey for understanding.

Sincerely,

Steven Myers
    Author of:
    Lost Technologies of the Great pyramid
    The Great Pyramid Prosperity Machine
Founder, Pharaoh's Pump Foundation   www.thepump.org

Introduction
To Read or Not to Read?

From the title of this book and a cursory glance at the illustrations, it is immediately apparent this treatise is a total departure from the diverse multitudes of books already available about the Great Pyramid. The subject of the Great Pyramid has held the interest and attention of thinkers throughout recorded history and across the globe, inspiring the creation of countless books and a multitude of theories on this greatest of mankind's ancient structures. This book is set apart from all other books written on the Great Pyramid in two distinct regards.

The first distinction this book has from other books on the same subject is for whom this book was written. Most books are written to be read by any reader. Not this book. The book in your hands is definitely not intended for everyone, rather, it was purposefully written to be read only by a select few. In determining if you are or are not among the select few for whom this book is written, I have listed a number of characteristics and attributes describing who should and should not read this book.

If your primary interest is in the qualifications and credentials of the person presenting this information instead of the information itself, then this book is not written for you. Pivotal aspects of what is presented in this book are not currently supported by any discipline of science. There are no college degrees currently available or university departments supporting everything presented in this book. That does not worry me, I have faith they will catch up some day. This book is not for those who seek comfort and reassurance in official-sounding titles over information.

For many readers the essential and critical imperative is: by what authority does the author validate what is written in this book? If this is the case with you, please close the book and put it down. This book is written for minds who feel authentic information is self-validating and stands on its own merits. The information in this book is not validated or invalidated on the basis of any kind of educational title.

If your contention is unanimity of opinion is evidence, then this is the wrong book for you. There is, in fact, no unanimity of opinion regarding the Great Pyramid even though currently the most prevalent story being told is: it was a tomb, built using ramps. If unanimity of opinion is the determining factor in your mind as to what is true or not, then there was a time when you would have "known" heavier than air machines could not fly. It was the experts who scoffed and ridiculed the research responsible for these and most other major revolutionary advancements in scientific understanding. If you are excessively uncomfortable with ideas which are radically opposed to current conventional thought, then this book is not for you.

If you lived in the 1920's and thought unanimity of expert opinion somehow validates expert assertions then you would have "known" the Piltdown skull was legitimate evidence of a valid missing link. Experts are just people who are quite often simply wrong. Galileo Galilei said, "In questions of science, the authority of a thousand is not worth the humble reasoning of a single individual." If you oppose what Galileo said then this is not the book for you.

If your idea of learning is to have information fed to you like pabulum, doled out by a high priest of the exalted religion of Science, then this book is not written for you. If you cannot think and reason for yourself and make your own conclusions as to the validity of anything you encounter then this book will be a difficult and disturbing read. This book was written for those who will not shirk their responsibility.

If you will not expend the effort to do the open-minded research necessary to understand what you accept as true, then this book was not written for you. If you can swim all day in the sea of knowledge and never get wet, then instead of reading this book, I suggest you jump into a different pond. True learning takes energy, passion and a burning desire on your part, not just believing what you are told by one expert and disregarding what you are told by another expert.

James Baldwin says, "The purpose of education is to create in a person the ability to look at the world for himself, to make his own decisions." If this does not describe you then you are not educated or prepared to read this book.

If you, the reader, are unable to bear the burden of the responsibility of being the final determiner of what is right, true and beautiful, then I suggest you close this book. To subjugate yourself by relegating this ultimate responsibility to the opinion of "experts" is to take the lazy way out. If this describes you, instead of reading this book to become informed and make up your own mind, simply pick out any of the contradictory experts and believe whatever their opinion may be. This will save you from being inconvenienced by finding out for yourself. It is said, "For every expert, there is an equal and opposite expert."

If it is of the utmost importance to you that the information in these pages "fits in" with current traditional explanations of our species distant past, then this book will not comply with your preconceived paradigm. What is presented in this volume does not comply with any contemporary traditionally accepted explanation. This book does not "fit in" to the prevailing historical world view we have all been taught concerning how the Great Pyramid relates to the assent of mankind.

The information presented in this book does not fit into the generally accepted contextual constraints in which the Great Pyramid has been pigeonholed by the experts. It is absolutely imperative any historical contextual world view fits all the direct physical evidence, instead of the other way around. Evidence is always of a higher priority than its conceptual interpretation. This book is an alternative explanation of the same direct evidence available to everyone.

If to you, often repeated but never demonstrated explanations by traditional Egyptologists about the Great Pyramid's construction make perfect, logical sense then this book is not written for you. There is no point in reading on. If you cannot transcend the stories you have already been taught as fact about the Great Pyramid, then this book is beyond you. The obsolete notions about the Great Pyramid must be set aside to embrace the new understandings of this ancient structure. To do this is difficult but it is a requirement to the process of learning. This has always been true whenever a newer truth replaces an obsolete invalidated interpretation.

If you want to read yet another book about the Great Pyramid which rehashes the same tired undemonstrated stories of sweat soaked ramps, Pharaoh's tomb, golden treasures, esoteric knowledge, symbolism, aliens or prophesy, then you will have to read another book. This book is a fresh alternative to all of these well-worn concepts. If you are adverse to, or reject ideas simply because they are new, then you are not yet ready for the information in this book. Isaac Asimov tells us, "Man's greatest asset is the unsettled mind." If your mind is already settled about ancient mankind and his achievements there is no reason for you to read this book.

If you feel it is necessary for this research to be validated by peer approval from Egyptologists then there is a problem. There are no Egyptologists who consider me their peer, so peer approval is impossible. I am proud to say that no Egyptologist is my peer either. As this book has been published, the information on its pages is available to any Egyptologist who may dare to become familiar with it.

If you have a vested interest in maintaining the current paradigm of understanding about ancient Egypt or are eagerly intent in character assassination of myself as

Robert M. Schoch suffered after his research became public about the age of the Sphinx please do not bother with your efforts. (Joseph Davidovits suffered a similar fate after the publication of his book: The Pyramids: an Enigma Solved.) To ponder and debate the ideas presented in this book (or any book) is one thing, but life is too short to worry about personal attacks. It is said in the realm of intelligencia people defend their positions so viciously because the stakes are so small! Linus Pauling said, "Science is the search for truth - it is not a game in which one tries to beat his opponent, to do harm to others." I do not advocate, initiate or participate in any type of intellectual bullying. I am above that.

If you are a debunker who is not bothered by fully understanding the concepts you are debunking, then why bother yourself with reading this treatise? My experience with debunkers is they almost universally simply parrot whatever the mainstream paradigm happens to be. They read books espousing conventional yet unrepeatable building methods and quote from them like scripture. Debunkers, more often than not, are just another group inhibiting as best they can any fundamental change in our understanding of the distant past.

Debunkers have taken the role of modern day naysayers. Their positive contribution to the world is extremely diminutive; their primary activity apparently is simply to criticize, unable to offer any fundamental research or experimentation of their own. The British philosopher Herbert Spencer said, "There is a principle which is a bar against all information, which cannot fail to keep a man in everlasting ignorance—that principle is contempt prior to investigation." If he is describing you, don't bother yourself with reading this book.

If you are interested in reading a book focusing on diverse subjects such as King's Lists, clothing, furniture, jewelry, hieroglyphics, battles, language, customs, religion, gods, embalming, art or lifestyles of the ancient peoples of the Nile valley, this is not the book for you. If your burning desire is to know about amulets and idols, which have been shoved up mummies, you will have to select another book. These diverse areas of interest are not the focus of this book. The focus of this book is not broad but extremely narrow. This book's focus is on how the stones were moved to build the Great Pyramid and to reveal the purpose of this enigmatic structure. Although this book's focus is narrow the implications of what is presented in this volume are extremely broad.

If you are comfortable with the destructive, expensive and polluting forms of energy systems our culture has devised, this book is not for you. If you are convinced the energy systems we use today are the best our species has or can create, please select another book. If you need to believe the power system used by the builders of the Great Pyramid was the sweat saturated backs of multitudes harnessed as beasts of burden pulling stones up dirt ramps in the blazing hot sun, then this book is not written for you.

If you want to debate angles to the nearest second and dimensions of the features of the Great Pyramid to the nearest ten-thousandth of an inch, then this is the wrong book for you. That is like debating the height of the Seattle Space Needle to the nearest micron. To fret and worry about angles and dimensions to such a ridiculous degree of accuracy is both unnecessary and detrimental to understanding the Great Pyramid's construction method and purpose.

If the fairytale notion of "unbiased science" is a necessary component of your belief system, then this book was written for people other than yourself. If in your mind, the realm of Science has become deified and exalted in an ivory tower then this book will be sacrilegious to your cult. George Bernard Shaw said "All great truths begin as blasphemies." If your religion is to worship Science and if

Science is your God, please stop reading now. If to you, Science is anything other than the pursuit of truth, then I ask you not to read this book or become involved in the controversy of this material. Dr. Thomas Gold tells us, "Science is like religion. Heresy (in science) is thought of as a bad thing, whereas it should be just the opposite."

If your mind is closed, please close this book. If it is your contention you already "know" then why read this or any other book for that matter? Those who already "know" (or think they do) are in a very precarious predicament when faced with the prospect of learning. If you are an intellectual Pharisee I see no reason for you to read this book. William James wrote, "A great many people think they are thinking when they are merely rearranging their prejudices." If he is describing you, there is no use in reading on. It is interesting that the Pharisees were the professionals and experts as recorded in the New Testament. Yet the vast majority of this group never changed their minds nor comprehended or acknowledged the Truth in front of them. If you have eyes to see but do not see, you have my sincere condolences.

If you want to maintain the status quo of the current understanding of the Great Pyramid long after the quo has lost its status then this book is not for you. If your comfort zone is clinging to the trailing edge of outdated ideas instead of riding high on the leading edge of new discoveries and understanding, then stay away from this book. Dr. Martin Luther King Jr. tells us, "The soft-minded man always fears change. He feels security in the status quo, and he has an almost morbid fear of the new. For him, the greatest pain is the pain of a new idea." If you prefer to maintain the security of being sheathed in the cocoon of antiquated explanations of the Great Pyramid; then that is your prerogative. This book will not support those efforts.

If any of the above describes you, then book in your hands was not written for you. What follows are the attributes of those for whom this humble book was written.

xxiv   Lost Technologies of the Great Pyramid

This book was written expressly for those who stand in absolute awe and are sincerely humbled by the magnificent accomplishments of ancient mankind—unduplicated to this day. If your mind is open to new ideas and you *want* to know them, this book was written for you. Aristotle wrote, "The high-minded man must care more for the truth than for what people think." If you have a craving for knowledge and understanding from whatever source, I cordially invite you to read this book.

If, to you, knowledge and understanding are separate from and of a much higher priority than any type of ordained or proclaimed authority, then this book was written for you. If, to you, authority and credentials do not validate assertions as fact, then I am privileged if you will read this book. Knowledge and understanding always stand on their own ground, high above any exalted qualifications of those who advocate or oppose new ideas. If you consider yourself to be the final and ultimate authority as to the validity of ideas you are exposed to, then please read on.

If the convoluted explanations of the Great Pyramid's construction and purpose offered by traditional Egyptologists do not ring true in your mind, do not square with your intuition, seem unsupportable by valid demonstration, or do not fit the available physical evidence, then this alternative explanation is for you. If, to you the traditional descriptions of how the stones of the Great Pyramid were quarried and moved do not comply with logic or reason, you have the right book in your hands. If the assumptions of undemonstrated construction techniques, convoluted Bible-confirming prophecy, secret symbolism, sweat drenched ramps, outer-space alien intervention, power plants that do not generate power or the bizarrely designed tomb for a despotic, mind-changing Pharaoh are unacceptable and you seek a different explanation of the evidence, read this book, because it was written for you.

If you are interested in learning about the new cutting-edge paradigms, transcending the outdated notions presented by traditional Egyptologists about the Great Pyramid and human antiquity, then this book is for you. If you are fed up with the intellectual pabulum associated with the Great Pyramid but have a genuine hunger and thirst for knowledge on this subject, then this book will offer you a full plate! Oliver Wendell Holmes wrote, "Man's mind stretched to a new idea never goes back to its original dimension." If you have a desire to stretch your mind, read this book.

If to you, the only purpose of Science is the pursuit of truth, and you genuinely pursue truth, then as far as I am concerned, you are a scientist. If the above sentence describes you, your inquiry into this understanding of the Great Pyramid would be considered by the author as peer review. This author is not an intellectual elitist inhibiting pursuit of truth in any way and I bar no one who pursues truth from reviewing this publication.

Friedrich Nietzsche said, "In the mountains of truth you never climb in vain." Truth is not determined by popular or majority vote. Truth is not acquired by democratic process. New ideas, which transcend outdated ideas, are always first the opinion of the minority. This has always been so. If you understand unanimity of expert opinion is not evidence, then I wrote this book for you. Spinoza wrote, "Be not astonished at new ideas; for it is well known to you that a thing does not therefore cease to be true because it is not accepted by many."

If your interest is not in ancient clothing, religion, Pharaoh's hats or the amulets thrust into the bowels of mummies, then this is the book for you. If the focus of your interest is to know about the construction procedure and purpose of the greatest surviving achievement of ancient mankind, I offer this book to you. If your interest is focused on the technical aspects of the Great Pyramid, then you are about to read some compelling material.

If you are open to the idea of ancient mankind utilizing their deep understanding of physics, which are not now fully understood in our time, then this book is for you. If you are interested in the development of the same energy systems utilized by the ancients to improve the world we live in, I commend you on your genuine interest in mankind's antiquity and your desire to improve today's world!

If you are aware we are in the midst of a revolution in understanding in every scientific discipline, then this book is for you. Sir William Osler wrote, "The philosophies of one age have become the absurdities of the next, and the foolishness of yesterday has become the wisdom of tomorrow." If you want to know about tomorrow's truth, please continue to read this book.

This book is not directed exclusively to highbrow, erudite, academic eggheads. This book was specifically written to be read and understood by anyone, including high school students and above. It is both young people and those with an open-minded interest for whom I have penned this book. The unverifiable opinion of antiquated experts is subordinate to the understanding of this material by young people and the public at large.

Decide for yourself which of the attributes best describes who you are and what you bring to the experience of reading this (or any) book. One's frame of mind as much as anything else will determine the value of the experience of becoming familiar with the information this book has to offer. Many feel they can conquer the Great Pyramid by understanding it. This book is about a mountain of stone and we cannot conquer this mountain by understanding it. We can only understand this mountain of stone by first conquering the hurdle of transcending antiquated ideas! The great mountain climber, Edmund Hillary said, "It is not the mountain that we conquer but ourselves." Because of the mountain of misinformation about the Great Pyramid, to understand this book you will have to conquer, subdue and transcend that formidable obstacle. The mountain of misunderstanding is the enemy to conquer, not the theory proposed in this book.

The second distinction this book has over other books about the Great Pyramid is the explanation offered regarding both the construction methods of the Original Builders and the purpose of their fantastic structure. This book is written to examine the mainstream assertions about the Great Pyramid, which have been presented as fact, and to offer an alternative explanation. After becoming familiar with this radically new and controversial interpretation of the same evidence available to all, it is the obligation of the reader to ponder and then decide for himself or herself which (if any) of the diverse theories of the Great Pyramid best complies with the evidence provided by the Great Pyramid itself.

No one in the world really knows how the Great Pyramid of Giza was built: that is, of course, except for myself! This is how I often start a lecture or presentation on this controversial subject. As an attention grabber, it works well, but it is nothing compared to the subject matter at hand.

The Great Pyramid is more than just the only remaining example of the Seven Wonders of the ancient world; it is probably the world's greatest historical architectural enigma. This magnificent, mysterious marvel has captured the hearts and minds of many great thinkers. No other structure of human creation has invoked more conjecture and supposition than the Great Pyramid.

There have been more books written, both published and not, on the subject of the Great Pyramid than any other ancient building ever created. Why, then, would the world need another volume added to this mountain of material? What could be added to the monumental body of work on this subject? Is there more that can be known and if so, what new knowledge can be mastered? Is there a higher wisdom that can be gained by investing the time to read yet another book on the greatest known achievement of the ancients? Is the information presented in these pages esoteric and of interest to only the study of distant antiquity or is there any relevance to improving today's world?

This book will answer these issues by answering one specific question. This question comprises nothing less than the Riddle of the Ages! That question is:

How was the Great Pyramid constructed?

A simple question indeed, but the answer has eluded mankind since the beginning of recorded history. The answer to the question above proposed in this volume is a complete departure from, and contradictory to, all other theories. These pages will describe how the ancients transported and set into place the massive stones and will reveal the Original Builder's purpose of the features of the interior of the Great Pyramid.

I make but one request of the reader. Because this material is such a quantum leap of understanding from current thought, and in part quite technical, please read the entire work before passing judgment on the validity of this interpretation of the direct physical evidence. Embracing this theory will require one to put away the myth and mythology taught as facts that we have all been subjected to our entire lives. This is a difficult task for most of us and for some it is an impossibility. Aristotle tells us, "It is the mark of an educated mind to be able to entertain a thought without accepting it." I assume the reader has this ability. My only request of the reader is an open mind for the evening or two it takes to read this book and to ponder the information it presents.

This book contains a large amount of material and concepts which are unfamiliar to many in this day and age. This theory is such a shift from conventional thought; everything cannot be explained at once. This is a technical explanation of a technological wonder. Reading these pages will often create more questions than answers. Those very questions are often not answered immediately but are addressed in much greater detail as the explanation of the Great Pyramid unfolds. It is the intent of the author to address those questions with answers representing the fullest extent of the most recent ongoing research regarding this understanding of the Great Pyramid.

To read this book is to travel from the familiar to the realm of new and unfamiliar intellectual territory. This journey is best traveled without any excess baggage. Mark Twain wrote, "Travel is fatal to prejudice, bigotry, and narrow-mindedness." To be encumbered with the baggage of preconceived notions, biases, prejudices and inclinations towards any predisposition or paradigm will reduce the value of your journey.

For most readers, this book will be covering new ground. For some this may invoke apprehension on their journey of discovery, but it will be worth it. J.G. Holland observed, "Who never walks save where he sees men's tracks makes no discoveries."

We have entered into a new age, a new era, a new century, and a new millennium. We are in the midst of a revolution of new understandings, shaking the very foundations of every aspect of science. This new era will be a paradigm shift away from the ideas of outdated past understandings of the Great Pyramid, replacing them with a new and more accurate understanding of this monumental building and our species' distant past.

Obviously this book and this theory about the construction of the Great Pyramid are unorthodox. That in itself does not make it inaccurate. Carl Sagan warns us all by saying, "If you are only skeptical, then no new ideas make it through to you. You become a crotchety old person convinced that nonsense is ruling the world. But every now and then, a new idea turns out to be on the mark, valid and wonderful. If you are too much in the habit of being skeptical about everything, you are going to miss or resent it, and either way you will be standing in the way of understanding and progress." I do not object to anyone's skepticism, but I just hope you are not among those who stand in the way of progress. If you want to be truly skeptic, direct your skepticism to what you accept as irrefutable. Only then will revolutionary learning take place.

You will encounter experts of several disciplines of science who dismiss this research as total folly. Arthur C. Clarke's First Law states, "When a distinguished but elderly scientist states that something is possible, he is almost certainly right. When he states that something is impossible, he is very probably wrong." Keep that in mind when you encounter the opinion of experts in regards to this research.

T.H. Huxley gives us important advice and I hope you take it to heart; I certainly have. "Sit down before facts like a child, and be prepared to give up every preconceived notion, follow humbly wherever and to whatever abysses Nature leads, or you shall learn nothing."

As you follow the pages of this book you will be a participant in the unfolding of a new understanding of how the Great Pyramid came to be and what it was for. The twin veils of misinformation and misinterpretation will be lifted from your eyes. To read this book is to take part in an exploration into the lost technologies of the Great Pyramid.

Soon, you too will know the answer to the Riddle of the Ages. You will know HOW the Great Pyramid was built!

Chapter 1
When the Mystery was Not a Mystery

There was a time, when there was not a "Mystery of the Ages" as we know it. It is strange to us in our day and age to realize at one time in humanity's distant past there was no endless debate or continuous conjecture as to the construction methods or purpose of the Great Pyramid. There was no need for the thousands of mutually contradictory books and theories which grope for some now hidden meaning or true understanding of this enigmatic structure. Both the Great Pyramid's reason for existence and how it was built were at one time well known, undisputed and widely understood.

Those humans who were of the civilization, which conceived and created this enduring monument, witnessed firsthand the Great Pyramid's construction or may have been active participants in the many aspects of creating this wonder. The fabrication techniques and daily progresses were observed firsthand and were topics of conversation by those who watched the Great Pyramid slowly and systematically rise to the sky.

Once the capstone (some feel that the Great Pyramid never had a capstone and was left unfinished for symbolic reasons) was set in place and the work was complete, this ancient civilization celebrated and rejoiced for they knew the value of their accomplishment. This great achievement was the shining glory of their fine culture and was the high point or capstone of their advanced society and high technology. This ancient civilization saw the Great Pyramid not as a mystery as we do but as a wonderful achievement.

The Great Pyramid was not a source of backbreaking oppression. Its construction was labor efficient, not labor intensive. This building was built as an investment. It was an investment not for the spiritual enrichment of people

4,000 years later, nor as an elaborate object built to tell us in our age the builders knew Pi, nor even as a gigantic grave marker to show robbers where the treasure was but a tangible investment for the Original Builder's own lives and the enrichment of their children. For the Original Builders knew their achievement would change their lives for the better! The completion of the Great Pyramid meant toil was transformed into leisure and hardship transformed into prosperity.

Times change. The ancient civilization, which constructed the Great Pyramid, rose to majestic heights then ultimately fell into anarchy. Flourishing cities were turned to ruins. Order became chaos. Productive expanses of farmland returned to barren desert. Life supported by high technology was replaced by subsistence living. An urban society regressed to hunter-gathers. Barbarians burned libraries. The vast wealth of acquired knowledge was lost, replaced by ignorance and confusion. The knowledge, technology and enlightenment that embodied the once high civilization which built the Great Pyramid became entombed and concealed by the sands of time.

After the passage of eons, a new, different civilization emerged and developed. This new civilization is our civilization which developed and progressed becoming advanced but in different ways than the ancient civilization responsible for building the Great Pyramid. Our ideas, technologies, manufacturing processes, education, medicine, art, communication and energy systems are all sophisticated but different from the civilization that created the Great Pyramid.

From our civilization arose generations of thinkers, seers, theologians, historians, archeologists, Egyptologists, technologists and independent researchers who have pondered the Great Pyramid and all of its implications. These great thinkers have lacked the resources that were common to the everyday people who were there when the

Great Pyramid was built. Our civilization is devoid of eyewitnesses who saw how the Great Pyramid was built and used.

Modern man cannot ask someone who actually quarried and shaped a casing stone how it was done. Modern man cannot visually observe how the massive stones were moved and set in place. Modern man cannot see the Great Pyramid as it was when first built and put to use as the Original Builders intended it to be. The working people who built this structure or watched this structure being assembled knew and understood how this structure was built. The average people of this ancient advanced society who utilized the Great Pyramid for its original purpose understood both how and why the Great Pyramid was created.

The civilization, which built the Great Pyramid and used it as they intended did not have a Riddle of the Ages because they experienced the answer. It has been different for modern mankind. Our thinkers, seers, theologians, historians, archeologists, Egyptologists, technologists and independent researchers have had to evaluate the remaining evidence and attempt to develop an answer to the Riddle of the Ages.

From these modern minds arose the plethora of conjecture and supposition on the subject of the Great Pyramid's construction methods and purpose. Our understanding is lacking in eyewitness accounts and must rely solely on the opinions of those who offer solutions to these modern day riddles.

There are about as many proposed methods of construction, as there are people who propose theories on the subject, with the informed reader aware of most. Our civilization has created a concept of this marvel of construction based on what information was available.

Just as relevant as the information available are the preconceived notions of the minds contemplating this massive structure. In the history of the study of the Great Pyramid, it is the predispositions, preconceived notions and biases which have established various "expert" conflicting opinions to explain the Great Pyramid. The "conclusions" of these early researchers have shaped many of the prevailing ideas swaddling the Great Pyramid in legend and misinterpretation.

Many of the early researchers and authors from Europe were devoutly religious. Their religions varied but were based on the Holy Bible. The Bible mentions huge buildings in Egypt and the pyramids are huge buildings in Egypt. These Middle Age researchers knew the huge buildings mentioned in the Bible were granaries therefore the huge buildings in Egypt (pyramids) were (to them) granaries. This information was taught as fact for centuries. In the prestigious universities of medieval Europe, the Great Pyramid was understood by many experts, authors and professors to be the ancient granaries of Joseph's day. A famous mosaic in the San Marco church in Venice depicts this once mainstream idea.[1] Generations of people lived and died knowing this was true.

Many other ideas were formed about the Great Pyramid, which were based on the preconceptions of early researchers much more than on any type of direct evidence. Early religious researchers knew the Jews were enslaved in Egypt. It has been assumed slaves were used to build the Great Pyramid. Therefore, it has been asserted by numerous researchers, Jewish slaves built the Great Pyramid.[2] This was the nature of early devoutly religious researchers of the Great Pyramid.

The passing of millenniums has been very hard on the Great Pyramid. It and its surroundings have been ravaged by barbarians of all the Ages. Fortune hunters, amateur and professional thieves, vandals and other exploiters came not to gain understanding but to take from the Great Pyramid anything they could. In their wanton, blinding greed they ravaged this structure and destroyed as much as they could. The Great Pyramid was used as a quarry with the removal of over ninety nine percent of the precision crafted casing stones.3 Through the eons, had the scavengers possessed sufficient power to tear down what the ancients had build up, the Great Pyramid would have ceased to exist long ago.

Early archaeologists and Egyptologists studied every aspect of the Great Pyramid in vain hopes of revealing its secrets. Their motivation was to find "hidden apartments" and burial chambers rich with golden treasures and amulet stuffed mummies. Most of these men employed primitive and destructive methods of research, causing much more damage, destruction, and harm than good. Explosive black powder was their tool of choice.4 However, they did leave their writings, journals, books, observations, measurements and drawings, many of which describe features of the Great Pyramid destroyed by these early "researchers" and others to follow.

The body of work created by these early researchers of the 18th and 19th centuries brought an era of different understanding of the Great Pyramid. A paradigm shift took place away from the granaries of Biblical Joseph's day to a different understanding. The information gathered and brought back by Napoleon's savants made an immense contribution to this change in understanding.5 It took years (actually generations) for the widely held concept of granary, to entirely give way to the new and different theories about the Great Pyramid. These theories too were based on the preconceived notions of the researchers and limited understanding of available physical evidence. The Great Pyramid was no longer generally thought to be a granary but the tomb (or even to some, "symbolic tomb") for the mummy of a dead Pharaoh. Even to this day; this is the prevailing thought of traditional Egyptologists.

During the early years of the study of Ancient Egypt the researchers who professed to be Egyptologists were not much more than treasure seekers and grave robbers. Their exploits are infamous. The way in which they financed their rampages was to find graves containing mummies or other treasure and sell those artifacts to either rich investors or rich museums anywhere in the world. They took everything of value they could and destroyed whatever was necessary in the process.

Later the method of funding became much more genteel, but the results remained exactly the same. A museum would finance a research dig with the "understanding" the museum would get the booty. Patrons of the museum would pay admission to see the artifacts and the whole process was financially self-perpetuating. This has left a dark and sad legacy.

Even to this very day there are efforts to return priceless items which should have never been removed from Egypt.[6] A joke I have heard which is tragically funny is this. What is the difference between an Egyptologist and a grave robber? One has a college education, and the other one doesn't!

Early Egyptologists who were busily removing items from every grave they could find were confronted by the Great Pyramid. Abraham Maslow said, "People who are only good with hammers see every problem as a nail." If your preoccupation and interest is to remove items from graves for financial reward then what is the Great Pyramid? Your preconceived notions are a bias dictating the Great Pyramid is also a giant grave. If your understanding of pyramids is they are ALL big pointed markers to show where mummies can be removed then your understanding of the Great Pyramid is: it was built to be a tomb.

Why was there no mummy and treasure in the Great Pyramid? Egyptologists, inexorably bound by the contextual presupposition of the Great Pyramid as a grave maintain the coveted burial treasure was removed in antiquity. They contend thieves long ago stole the treasures from the Great

Pyramid before the Egyptologists could. No evidence or historical account supports this assertion.

Another ideology emerged about the Great Pyramid's purpose from the realm of the devoutly religious researcher. With leather bound Holy Bible in hand these 18th and 19th century researchers dropped the centuries old teaching of pyramids as granaries to another purpose for the Great Pyramid. Proponents of Pyramidology conducting absurdly precise measurements of passages and chambers concluded the original purpose of the Great Pyramid was to be a stone testament and monument (or altar to the Lord) confirming Bible prophecy. Pyramidology maintains that by using the same unit of measure as was thought to be used by the ancients the Great Pyramid could prophetically reveal and confirm the scriptural destiny of mankind.7 This theory still has many proponents even in our contemporary world.

Books on Pyramidology are full of charts and illustrations showing the passages and chambers to be constructed with the symbolic purpose of revealing divinely inspired prophecy. Their thought is that the millions of stones were set in place so the Holy Bible could be substantiated by confirming scriptural prophecy in our "end times."

Currently the most widely accepted stories about the Great Pyramid are those offered to us by Egyptologists. They tell the tale of countless human beasts of burden hauling massive payloads up some configuration of colossal ramp.

Recently new age influences have dominated the thoughts of many concerning how the Great Pyramid was built and why. The impetus for much of the new age alternative ideas is the inability or unwillingness of the science of Egyptology to demonstrate any pivotal aspect of their story of construction. Egyptology's total abandonment of the scientific method and abhorrence of demonstrations has brought rise to a fantastic collection of concepts on how the Great Pyramid was built and why.

These concepts of the Great Pyramid include theories relating to mind over matter: alien beacon or transport, built by the hand of technically advanced "gods" or intervening alien cultures, pyramid power, mental levitation, sonic levitation, antigravity devices, elite secret societies imbued with some form of higher wisdom or enlightenment. To many of new age thought, the Great Pyramid was built to serve as a sacred temple to initiate members into obscure secret ancient societies replete with ritual and regalia.

To most who inquire into the mysteries of the Great Pyramid all of these ideas, concepts and notions fail to pass the test of open-minded inquiry. Although there are elements of all disciplines which seem to shed some light on this monument's mysteries not one type of understanding seems to ring true. This is what makes the Great Pyramid the great enigma! Even though there are those who adamantly ascribe to one theory or another, be it tomb, pyramid power, Bible prophesy, secret societies, aliens, unique energy source, etc. a large contingent of inquiring minds cannot accept any of the various explanations offered to the public. To the vast multitudes none of the popular, well known theories seem to fit the most important criterion, parameter, or guideline.

The most crucial yardstick or guide, regular people in the real world use to evaluate any theory on how or why the Great Pyramid was built is that the explanation must make sense. For an idea to make sense it must be doable. My experience is that regular people feel if the Original Builders did it modern man should be able to show how it was done. Traditional Egyptologists who tell *their* story have a difficult time demonstrating the feasibility of their ideas. Missouri is the "Show Me State" and most people are of that state of mind. This mindset of regular people is perfectly consistent with the scientific method.

In the scientific world (except for Egyptology) it is generally required that any discovery or theory must be verifiable. Verification in the form of repeatable and reliable experimentation is expected and demanded. This is the essence of the scientific method and is the manner in which the general body of scientific knowledge grows. In researching subjects like Evolution or the Big Bang theory it is obviously difficult to make fundamental types of valid demonstrations. In researching the Great Pyramid most every aspect of the construction process should be subject to some form of valid demonstration. It is not necessary to recreate an entire exact full sized replica of the Great Pyramid to demonstrate the pivotal aspects of the construction techniques used by the original builders.

It is very interesting to note information and discoveries involving the Great Pyramid have not been required to meet the fundamental scientific requirement of verifiability. A researcher, Egyptologist or historian, (some with official sounding credentials, some without) make a claim or offer a thesis or write a book about the Great Pyramid. However none seem to offer any demonstrable proof to support their hypothesis. No demonstrable proof is offered and in the realm of this subject matter none is expected! This and other factors, has caused the tremendously diverse and conflicting theories about the Great Pyramid. Contrary to the norm, the author is the founder of an organization whose purpose includes demonstrations to substantiate the information in this book.

Although it is not necessary to construct a duplicate of the Great Pyramid to show building techniques, little valuable, applicable demonstrations have been offered. Often models or drawings are made to substantiate theories. Occasionally real stones are used in a demonstration, but they are ALWAYS of diminutive size. One-ton stones are moved in an attempt to show how two and one half ton stones or even sixteen ton stones are moved. The PRECISION of the original casing stones is never ever recreated or adequately addressed by Egyptologists or traditional experts. The results of the demonstrations are completely different from the original evidence the Great Pyramid provides. These "demonstrations" in both print and TV documentaries create results, which are only vaguely similar to and obviously quite primitive when compared to what has been demonstrated by the builders of the Great Pyramid.

These demonstrations offered by accredited authorities are lacking in authenticity and under intense scrutiny. Their results fail to lend credence to their suppositions. Invariably the results point to the opposite of the intent of the demonstration. In television documentaries we see people struggling to move one ton stones a distance of a few yards but off camera there are forklifts and trucks. We are told with confidence this is how fifteen-ton casing stones are moved. What is accomplished is not much more than a visual show. Compared to what the Original Builders demonstrated these television documentary demonstrations are reduced to surreal comic operas.

Egyptologists who profess to be scientists will gladly tell you how the Great Pyramid was constructed, but are extremely reluctant to engage in the scientific method to substantiate their stories with demonstrations.

Remember: when the Original Builders were assembling the Great Pyramid they were demonstrating how it was done. Every stone they moved and set in place was a demonstration of how it was done. The quarrying and finishing to perfection of every casing stone was a demonstration of how it was done. Regular working people were engaging in the scientific method every day by building the Great Pyramid. The Great Pyramid is the result of their demonstrations. Yet in our modern world Egyptologists will not and cannot recreate any of the pivotal demonstrations to scientifically substantiate their stories.

In the last two hundred years has it been demonstrated how a casing stone was quarried and cut to exacting precision with primitive tools by creating a full size casing stone in this manner? No. Has it been demonstrated how a sixteen ton casing stone was moved on and off a barge? No. Has it been demonstrated how a fifty ton block was dragged up a dirt ramp twenty stories high? No. Has it been demonstrated how 2½ ton stones were dragged around a corner of a spiral ramp? No. Has it been demonstrated how a regal funeral procession moved a mummy up and down the slippery step-less cramped passages of the Great Pyramid. No. The "science" of Egyptology has never substantiated their assertions or stories on these issues by subjecting them to the scientific method.

Proponents of new age ideas of the Great Pyramid are equally reluctant to offer any demonstration to substantiate their conjectures.

Has it been demonstrated how a fifty ton stone is moved using mind over matter, sonic waves, chanting, worshiping crystals or with the help of ancient astronauts? No. Has an operational model of the Great Pyramid as a vibrating power source been created to validate that assertion? No. In the last two hundred years very little if any of the important aspects of the construction of the Great Pyramid have been adequately demonstrated in any way by Egyptology or anyone else.

These construction processes and many other issues involving assembly have not been demonstrated. Even though conventional and unconventional theories abound it is evident many who make an excellent living in this arena of research have no intention of ever verifying their offered theories through demonstrating the pivotal construction procedures mentioned above.

An expert says: "The Great Pyramid was built using many workers and a big ramp."[8] Whoever the workers were is immaterial. Regular people who live in the real world, not in the world of ivory towered academic intelligencia reply: "Interesting, show us how by using a 50 ton block pulled up a dirt ramp 20 stories high." It is never demonstrated. Some other expert says: "The Great Pyramid is a tomb for a dead Pharaoh."[9] Regular people who live in the real world ask, "How do the strange and puzzling aspects of the interior of the Great Pyramid relate to a funeral or tomb?" The elaborate, convoluted and contrived explanations of several mid-construction design changes make little sense. The idea of multiple vents pointing to different stars for a single spirit's journey is equally nonsensical.

Another expert asserts: "The Great Pyramid was built using telepathy or levitation or even mind over matter."[10] Regular people reply, "That's nice, show us how by moving only one stone." It is never demonstrated. A researcher says: "The stones were levitated and moved using sonic waves."[11] Regular people respond with, "Show us the means the ancients used sonic waves to move a 2 ton stone so we can see." It is never demonstrated. Egyptologists say, "The casing stones were made by hand using primitive tools."[12] Regular people who have no vested interest in any particular theory say, "That's a nice story. Make a 16 ton casing stone accurate and square to 1/50th of an inch with primitive tools." It has never been demonstrated anywhere in the world. An author asserts, "The Great Pyramid is a power plant."[13] No attempt is made to demonstrate this hypothesis or to create such a power plant in a world which desperately needs cheap, clean energy.

Although much lip service is available, no expert offers an accurate demonstration of conventional or unconventional theories on how the Great Pyramid was built or why it was built. All of these conflicting experts are convinced their mutually exclusive assumptions are correct. But none will use the scientific method to show by demonstration the validity of their theories. The journalist Francois Gautier said it best. "Many live in the ivory tower called reality; they never venture on the open sea of thought." An open-minded researcher would not fear or avoid substantiation by demonstration. This type of substantiation is called the scientific method.

All of the experts have the same degree of conviction. The problem is determining which theory is consistent with the building process used by the Original Builders. How the Great Pyramid was built is *literally* set in stone. Only one theory can be consistent with the original building process. Theories, which represent a building process not used by the Original Builders, cannot be correct.

Theories are never proven or unproven. Evidence is sought and amassed which either supports or is inconsistent with the hypotheses suggested by a theory. Evidence is often supplied by valid demonstration. Theories stand only as long as there is overwhelming cumulative evidence supporting their basic tenets. When contrary evidence is amassed, the theory becomes untenable. It has to be modified in light of the new direct evidence or it is replaced.

This is what happened to the centuries old theory of the Great Pyramid as a granary. It was, at one time, accepted by many experts and layman alike as true, yet now it is not accepted as factual. (There are still those who feel that the pyramids are figurative granaries or symbolic storehouses of knowledge.)

In contemporary times there is another ongoing paradigm shift in understanding the purpose and construction methods of the Great Pyramid. This paradigm shift will be as vast as the previous one away from Biblical granary and massive mausoleum. It will more than likely take generations for this shift to become complete just as it has been for all other monumental understandings of the world around us. This paradigm shift is transcending the old notions asserting the Great Pyramid is a despot's tomb built using a ramp or that extreme precision was created with primitive tools by hand. This paradigm shift is moving away from the notions of the Great Pyramid being a holy place or built by the hand of God, or made with telepathy or any number of similar assertions.

We are in the midst of a paradigm shift towards the theories which embrace the following concepts. The Great Pyramid was built by mankind without the direct divine guidance of God or the assistance of outer-space aliens. Humans like us built it, except they were of a society possessing the genius, understanding, high technology, vision and courage to complete such a grand project. The Great Pyramid was built by a sophisticated civilization of humans, by themselves and for their own benefit and the benefit of their children. It was built not at great cost, but it represented an extremely wise investment. It was not built for the benefit of people four thousand years after its construction to tell us our own spiritual future or that the builders knew Pi. The Great Pyramid was not built as a static tomb but as an active device, not just a mountain of rocks but as a magnificent precisely built monumental machine. This structure was made not by a legion of slaves or willing volunteers or even taxpayers but by a highly skilled, *highly mechanized* and highly efficient workforce.

This workforce employed their unique forms of high technology and built on a very large scale. The Great Pyramid was not an example of the outlandish ego of a despotic Pharaoh. The intent of the Original Builders was not to serve the excesses of some brutal and bizarre burial cult but to serve their own needs, for the Great Pyramid was a tangible investment in the betterment of the lives of those who built this monument. The Great Pyramid was for the living, not for the dead! The creation of the Great Pyramid is not the result of multiple mid-construction design changes but it was built as originally designed.

It was a public works project fulfilling the wants, needs and desires of that distant long ago ancient advanced civilization which built it. The Great Pyramid is not symbolic; it is functional. These are the concepts, which are coming to the forefront and driving the creation of an emerging paradigm, which is a new and truer understanding of this magnificent structure.

Yet in modern times the Great Pyramid is both mystery and enigma. It is the result of building techniques, which have never been fully duplicated or completely demonstrated. Although all researchers have theorized as to the meaning and purpose of its marvelous passages and chambers, not one of the generally accepted theories seems to comply with logic. Why then is the study of this specific structure shrouded in the swirling sands of misunderstanding, wild speculation, and conflicting hypothesis? Why has this building, more than any other on earth, conjured up such fantastic notions instead of a logical, reasonable, understandable explanation?

Our culture in the last thousand years has produced uncounted minds directed towards unraveling the mysteries of the Great Pyramid and yet they have all (except one) fallen short of truly understanding how and why the Great Pyramid was built. Unquestionably any of the best of these conflicting experts knows far less in our age than any average person who witnessed the construction first hand. In this regard, knowledge and understanding has diminished instead of expanded.

The knowledge and understanding of the average individual of the time when this first wonder of the world was built was infinitely more accurate than any and all of the "experts" in the last three thousand years put together! These common individuals of long ago who experienced the construction and operation of the Great Pyramid had a much greater authority and more accurate understanding of this subject matter then all the experts living today combined. They had firsthand knowledge of the construction and purpose of this fantastic building. There was no Riddle of the Ages in their time.

In our time we do. For us the Riddle of the Ages would be answered by any common citizen who helped build the Great Pyramid or witnessed its construction. That reliable firsthand knowledge and understanding is unavailable to us. If they were here, these common workers could recreate the tasks they performed using the same tools to produce the same results as the original evidence. What wonderful and accurate demonstrations they could offer our modern world! These folks would be the ultimate scientists to answer the Riddle of the Ages for us. Yet their expertise, experiences, and eyewitness testimony is forever lost to modern mankind.

We in modern times can neither observe nor participate in the construction of the Great Pyramid. We cannot even get a firsthand account from someone who did experience or participate in the construction of the Great Pyramid. Therefore we have had to rely on a different way of knowing, which is second best. We have had to rely on experts to figure out the building method and purpose of the Great Pyramid by analyzing the remaining physical evidence and using the scientific method.

Unfortunately, the best efforts of so many of the best minds in modern times have failed dismally to unravel the Mystery of the Ages.

The reason for this is simple! Something went terribly wrong!

---

[1] Anne Wolff, How Many Miles to Babylon? Travels and Adventures to Egypt and Beyond, from 1300 to 1640 (Cato Institute 2003) 43.

[2] The World of Wonders: a Record of Things Wonderful in Nature, Science and Art (London 1883) 18.

[3] Helena Lehman, The Language of God in Prophecy (Pillar of Enoch Ministry Books 2006) 123.

[4] Brian M. Fagan Quest for the Past: Great Discoveries in Archaeology (Addison-Wesley Longman, Incorporated 1978) 3.

[5] John Anthony West, The Traveler's Key to Ancient Egypt: A Guide to the Sacred Places of Ancient Egypt (Quest Books 1995) 34.

6 William G. Scheller <u>Amazing Archaeologists and Their Finds</u> (The Oliver Press, Inc. 1994) 114.

7 John Anthony West, <u>Serpent in the Sky: The High Wisdom of Ancient Egypt </u>(Quest Books 1993) 11.

8 Craig B. Smith, <u>How the Great Pyramid Was Built</u> (HarperCollins 2006) 175.

9 Ibid. 86.

10 Shirley Andrews, <u>Lemuria and Atlantis: Studying the Past to Survive the Future</u> (Llewellyn Worldwide 2004) 149

11 Andrew Collins, <u>Gods of Eden: Egypt's lost legacy and the genesis of civilisation</u> (Headline, 1998) 35-36

12 Craig B. Smith, <u>How the Great Pyramid Was Built</u> (HarperCollins 2006) 90

13 Christopher Dunn, <u>The Giza Power Plant: Technologies of Ancient Egypt</u> (Bear & Co. 1998) 255.

Chapter 2
What Went Wrong?

The Great Pyramid is so fantastic that had it been somehow completely destroyed in antiquity references to it would be considered in our age purely myth. The idea of the Great Pyramid having a smooth surface was at one time considered an impossible fable by many experts. It was strongly debated for well over a century among most researchers and experts of the past whether the glass smooth casing stones ever existed.[1] Only until the rubble from the base was removed in relatively recent times and the few remaining casing stones revealed was this long and heated debate finally ended.[2] Had these last few casing stones been removed when the majority were taken the contemporary "expert's opinion" of the Great Pyramid would be quite different.

The Great Pyramid exists but how was it built and for what purpose? How did they build it and why? As eyes are lifted at this mountain of stone moved by man all researchers know these are the questions that must be answered. To know how and why is to know the answer to the Riddle of the Ages.

Long before the time of Herodotus, the 5th Century B.C. Greek historian, the Great Pyramid served the important purpose of tourist attraction. Tourists came from all over the known world to view and contemplate this mountain of mystery. Not unlike today, guides have made their living telling stories and tales about the Great Pyramid based *not* first and foremost on fact, but on a criterion of much higher priority to tour guides. That all important criterion is: whatever brings the best tip.

Stories of tombs and golden treasures or secret societies with forbidden rites and mystic rituals filled the ears of countless tourists throughout the ages both before and after Herodotus made his famous tourist stop. These fascinating narratives made for wonderful stories, captivating the hearts and minds of millennia of tourists and researchers alike.

In the eighteenth and nineteenth centuries efforts of systematic research, mainly in the form of accurate measurements were made and analyzed to a ridiculous degree. These researchers interpreted evidence, developed conjectures, extrapolated suppositions, made deductions, proposed meanings, formed hypotheses, presented elaborate convoluted explanations and offered solutions, all conflicting and all to no avail. After the collective research of all the great minds who have tackled this mystery of mysteries, their answers have all come up short. They have missed the mark. They have all failed in the same way.

No researcher until one man, discovered, understood, and accurately described the assembly process of the Great Pyramid. All other researchers, except for that lone researcher were unable to accurately ascertain what the construction method of the Great Pyramid was! This was because all other researchers misunderstood the Great Pyramid's function which was the faulty foundation that led to the rest of their assumptions and latticework of ideas to be marred by invalidity.

Of all great buildings or structures it is function which determines its form as well as its construction process.[3] Function is the governing parameter dictating all other features of a building. The shape of an aircraft carrier or submarine is dictated by the functions of these structures.

The shape, dimensions and building materials of a hydroelectric dam are determined by its function. Misinterpreting the function of any of these structures would be the faulty foundation leading to the misunderstanding of the features of the structure.

If a researcher thinks a hydroelectric dam is a religious temple then that researcher's interpretations of the features of that dam will be faulty. If a researcher thinks a submarine was built to be an elaborate tomb then that researcher's interpretations of the features of the submarine will be faulty. If an Egyptologist thinks the Great Pyramid was a tomb then the interpretation of the features of the Great Pyramid will be faulty.

What the Great Pyramid was built for was the principal deciding factor in every aspect of its design, construction and utilization. Misunderstanding the purpose of the Great Pyramid was the stumbling block for every historian and Egyptologist in the last 3,000 years.

Every expert justifies their interpretation of the Great Pyramid based on their understanding of the function of this building. The advocates of all conflicting theories justify their interpretations of the Great Pyramid by asserting the features and characteristics of the Great Pyramid promote the function they embrace. Although the function proposed by this theory is different from all other theories, the same features found in the direct evidence support the findings of this research.

Subordinate to function, there are other factors involved in how a building is constructed. Available materials, funding, available construction techniques and time constraints, are all important to how a building is constructed. All of these factors are subject to and subordinate to function. The purpose of a structure is the ultimate determining factor of how it is built and the nature of its materials. The characteristics of a building's structure are governed by what the building is made to accomplish. This is why submarines and tall skyscrapers are not made out of adobe. This material is not compatible with the function of these structures.

"Experts" and researchers of all eras have proposed so many functions for this building it has become ridiculous. During the middle ages expert opinion contended that the function of this building was a granary.[4] Now the most accepted opinion is the Great Pyramid, along with all Egyptian pyramids, were built to be tombs or at least funeral related.[5] Others feel the Great Pyramid is a power plant.[6] Still others embrace various esoteric functions to serve extra-terrestrial aliens or UFOs.[7] Some assert the function of the Great Pyramid was to be a celestial observatory.[8] While others have the belief the Great Pyramid was built with the intent of being an independent physical confirmation for Biblical prophecy.[9] Additional proposed purposes include performing secret rites for obscure mystery religions.[10] Some feel this building served many functions through the ages. Now the Great Pyramid is used as a machine (or attraction) to generate money through tourism. The purpose of this book is to explore the construction procedure the Original Builders used when they built this structure.

Is the original purpose of this building symbolic, cultural, ceremonial, or utilitarian? Was the function of the Great Pyramid, to serve ego, to serve a funeral, or to serve society as functional infrastructure? Was this building used as a storehouse for grain, a storehouse of esoteric knowledge, a storehouse for scientific knowledge, a storehouse for prophetic knowledge or a storehouse for a deceased Pharaoh's bodily remains? Is the purpose of this building scriptural or sepulcher? Was this building a temple, tomb or machine? Was this building's purpose all of these things or none of these things?

This book will offer an alternative to all mutually exclusive theories offered to the general public. I will try to show how a misinterpretation of an object's purpose or function will create a faulty foundation for the rest of the research of that object. The following short mental exercise is provided for illustration. Use your imagination to allow yourself to fully participate in this mental experiment and attempt to momentarily suspend judgment until the exercise is over.

G. K. Chesterton, the essayist and novelist wrote, "The function of the imagination is not to make strange things settled, so much as to make settled things strange." Many people and experts feel the Great Pyramid is a "settled thing." This book and the following mental experiment are about seeing the Great Pyramid with new eyes and to understand just how strange and marvelous this structure really is. Let your imagination transcend past the barriers of time, space and preconceived ideas and travel with me to the Giza Plateau in the year of 1843.

Fig 2.1 Four-Mummy Sarcophagus as it was being excavated from the sand at the base of the Great Pyramid.

Imagine it is the year 1843 and you are accompanying an archaeology dig on the Giza plateau. It is just past dawn and you stand watching the local hired Arabs excavate in a spot which seems a likely place to discover prized artifacts to take back to the museum, which has promised to buy the artifacts you remove from the dig. The early morning wind is a gentle breeze and the sun is warm but not yet uncomfortable and everything is going fine as you look up to ponder the Great Pyramid. A huge commotion erupts from the excavation.

Now imagine the diggers unexpectedly discovered and uncovered a 1957 Chevy. It is in good but not perfect condition. The tires are flat. The battery is discharged and there is no gasoline in the gas tank. Therefore the car will not start. If this astounding and seemingly out of place discovery happened, what would the archeologists and researchers of that long ago day do? They have never seen a car, an internal combustion engine, or even gasoline. The experts would study this artifact and announce their findings.

Front page headlines in newspaper across the entire world would proclaim,

First Four-Mummy Sarcophagus Found in Egypt!

The front-page story would read something like this:

> Last week on the Giza Plateau high-ranking Egyptologists discovered a four-mummy sarcophagus. Research indicates a little known Pharaoh and his family somehow perished at the same time and this huge multiple mummy sarcophagus was created for their use in the afterlife. No mummies were found undoubtedly because of the work of earlier tomb robbers.

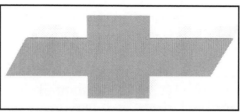

Fig. 2.2 Experts have concluded this hieroglyph found on the side of the Four Mummy Sarcophagus shows symbolically the entire spirit realm.

The article would include a picture of the Pharaoh's unique Cartouche embossed on the side of the equally unique four-mummy sarcophagus. The article would continue saying:

> Leading experts at the archeological site have determined the middle part of this cartouche to be the symbolic representation of the Nile and the upper part means sky or heaven. The lower part of this cartouche symbolizes the ancient Egyptian religious "underworld." Therefore experts agree based on the study of this hieroglyph, the Pharaoh's name means: "Ruler of the Royal Universe." After careful analysis it was determined the original Egyptian pronunciation for this ancient King's name is: Pharaoh Chev-RO-let.

The newspaper article would continue describing the exploits of those involved and what museum would get this new prize for display.

The purpose of this unusual artifact is misunderstood from the very beginning. The experts, however, "knew" the purpose of this object before it was even fully excavated. Therefore the study of this incredible find was hopelessly flawed from the very beginning. Never seeing an automobile or anything like it, study of this artifact would go something like this.

Researchers would marvel at the orientation of the sides of this sarcophagus, for coincidentally the sides aligned with the four cardinal directions. Obviously the culture, which created this unusual four-mummy sarcophagus, had surprisingly sophisticated knowledge of the earth. The researchers learned much of the religion and important symbolism of the ancient Egyptians from this four-mummy sarcophagus. Research indicated the four black things positioned at each corner (tires) symbolically represented the dark abyss of the afterlife. The steering column happened to point to the Orion constellation, indicating the culture, which made this artifact, worshipped this specific star group. (Or maybe even came from that star!) The clear spirit-world screens (windows) were used by the mummy's spirit-body to see their way through the infinity of the afterlife.

Once the four-mummy sarcophagus was removed from the excavation it was placed on blocks.

An entire discipline of research developed from the study of the dimensions of the artifact. This discipline became known as; Four Person Sarcophagus Sacred Geometry, (FPSSG). This unusual "sarcophagus" was measured to a ridiculous degree and those measurements were analyzed in every way possible. The four person sarcophagus was a convertible and therefore had no "lid." This lidless feature of the four person sarcophagus was considered to be very significant and profound in terms of ancient religious symbolism.

These researchers were astonished by the precision of the parts of the sarcophagus. The black round things on the corners of the four-mummy sarcophagus (tires) turned on their own axis, as did the afterworld worship ring. (What modern man would call a steering wheel.) The researchers deduced from this the ancients knew the earth turned on its own axis and they wanted to tell us in this symbolically profound way!

The height of this four-mummy sarcophagus is 1/500,000,000 of the distance from the earth to the moon. Therefore the ancients knew the distance from the Earth to the Moon and told us in this way!

It has been determined the mummy of the Pharaoh would be placed behind the large worship ring. Experts with the most accurate measuring instruments concluded the afterworld worship ring (steering wheel) is perfectly round! It is round! It is round!!! The ancients therefore knew the value of Pi and revealed this information to *us* in the most profound way. Experts would conclude that the value of Pi was integral in so many ways to the construction of this four-mummy sarcophagus. Such was the research of the devotees of FPSSG.

Other experts used a blending of religion and mathematics in their analysis of the four-mummy sarcophagus. They determined; if you take the number of mummies this sarcophagus holds, (4) and times that by the number of round things (four on each corner and the Pharaoh's steering wheel equals five) you get twenty. Times twenty by 3 (because of the Trinity) you get 60. Subtract the number of spirit-world screens (10 counting wind wings) and you get 50. Add the number of sides of the Great Pyramid (5 counting base) you get 55. Then add the number 2 for both the new and old Testaments giving the number 57. Subtract that number from 66 because that is how many books there are in the Bible. This leaves the number 9, which is considered very significant because it is the number of the trinity times itself! The number 9 is 3^2 telling us the Egyptians knew about exponents and wanted to tell us in this symbolic way. Add another 3 just for good luck giving us the holy number 12 found throughout the Bible. Then add 40 because this is the number of years the Jews spent in the wilderness to get the number 52. Use that number as an angle and plot a line from the base line of the two eastern black things (tires) and the line goes through Bethlehem. The four-mummy sarcophagus predicted the location of the birth of our Holy Redeemer, Jesus Christ, Son of the most awesome God! These righteous researchers would then proclaim the four-mummy sarcophagus was created with the inspiration of Almighty God! These devoted researchers would produce charts showing how features of the four person sarcophagus coincided with and proved Bible prophecy as a testament to modern mankind.

The construction of this relic is a showcase of workmanship. People would marvel as to how the ancient slaves, taxpayers or volunteers made such precision work with only primitive hand tools. In that it was the presupposition and unanimous professional opinion of all leading experts, the culture responsible for making the four-mummy sarcophagus were one step away from the Stone Age with only rudimentary and primitive hand tools. Therefore that is how the four-mummy sarcophagus was made. The assertion was given with confidence but actually making even one part of this artifact with only hand tools was never ever demonstrated. There was no need for any demonstrations because the experts already "knew" and were supported by the confirmation of: unanimity of expert opinion. The "proper context" of this very unusual artifact was conclusively established in this manner.

The conventional explanation provided by the learned experts of this unusual out of place artifact was that it fit exquisitely into the religious symbolism and societal parameters of the ancient Egyptians. The hood of the four person sarcophagus was deemed to be highly significant. When the hood of the four person sarcophagus was raised it was agreed that the massive artifact found beneath the lid was possibly the most symbolically significant aspect of the four person sarcophagus!

The V8 engine was interpreted to show the important religious duality of the physical world with the spiritual world. This separation of these two realms was symbolized by the two distinct rows of four cylinders pointing away from each other. The four cylinders of each row represented the four elements recognized in antiquity; fire, water, earth and air. This symbolic interpretation of the heavy artifact under the hood of the four person sarcophagus was verified to be true by the most stringent of all types of validation recognized by the experts. That validation process was the agreement of expert opinion, otherwise known as peer approval. It was established by these methods as fact that the four person sarcophagus fit into the religious symbolism, conformed to the cultural constraints, and was built by the ancient Egyptians. These finding were irrefutable.

Books were published, dissertations were written, and courses were taught. Careers and reputations were established on the research of the experts. Master's Degrees were based on this four-mummy sarcophagus. Experts studied its form but no one understood or even seemed to care what the real purpose of this artifact was. The experts already "knew" what it was even before it was completely exhumed from the archeological dig! Everyone was busy studying the dimensions of this relic to determine the unit of measure the ancients used. To know the unit of measure of the ancients would be somehow: "profound."

Researchers of many disciplines debated the various interpretations of the symbolism of this artifact in lectures, books and college classrooms. The relic itself was forgotten, unneeded, now that it was fully measured and "understood." It never really "fit" into the expert's conceptual constraints of the past anyway, so the four-mummy sarcophagus was finally relegated to the back of the museum's storage room. Displays of ancient golden jewelry, ornate gold inlayed sarcophagi and mummies stuffed with golden amulets and other golden burial accoutrements replaced it. These items were viewed as a more significant aspect of ancient Egyptian culture and religious practices. Also the gold seemed to bring in more paying wide-eyed patrons.

Time goes on. One hundred and twenty years pass and the year is 1963. The new curator of the same distinguished museum tells his building maintenance person, to clear out the old junk in the back of the warehouse. While removing the clutter, the maintenance man uncovers the dusty forgotten "four-mummy sarcophagus." Once again, this out of place artifact became a discarded relic. Once again it had been lost to the sands of time. Yet this time it has suffering the disgraceful burial in an impenetrable "tomb" of ignorance and misunderstanding.

The maintenance man, without a higher education and letters after his name, is able to achieve a true and accurate understanding of the ancient relic. This is because he understands its true purpose. He is unaware of the age and the unusual origin of this relic but he is able to understand its function and the intent of the Original Builders who made it.

He is able to discern its function and understand its intended operation. With a little work he gets it running and uses it as his own. He ponders why the museum had that old car, but he is grateful he now has transportation! This relic is now put to use and functions as it was originally intended.

Yes the above story is very farfetched but so is most of the study of the Great Pyramid. What hampered the highly trained and expert professional researchers, but not the maintenance man, in understanding the artifact is that the researchers misunderstood the purpose of this relic but the maintenance man was able to correctly recognize and understand the function for which this relic was made. The convoluted interpretation of the functions of the parts of the car didn't make sense just as the convoluted interpretation of the function of the parts of the Great Pyramid based on most prevailing theories do not make sense.

Both the car in the mental experiment and the Great Pyramid are out of place artifacts. Just as in the story, the world is faced with an out of place artifact, which does not readily fit the explanations of its existence. The Great Pyramid is an out of place artifact that does not fit the technology of the culture we are told created it. The Great Pyramid is an out of place artifact, which does not fit the prevailing worldview model of our historical origins.

Above all, the Great Pyramid is an out of place artifact, which does not fit any of the stories we are told about it by Egyptologists. In reality it is not the Great Pyramid which is out of place. It is the explanations of its existence which are out of place. The explanations we have been told cannot be substantiated by valid demonstration.

Imagine how different the prior mental experiment would have been had some researcher in the 1840's made the astounding assertion the four mummy sarcophagus was in reality a complex, highly sophisticated self-propelled enclosed horseless carriage with an internal combustion engine!! He would have immediately been branded crazy and ostracized by his collogues. The researcher who would have dared to offer such an explanation would have been dismissed as a charlatan and a lunatic by his peers. He would have been fired and never worked again. His manuscript would go unpublished, his findings unstudied. His peers would not speak of such absurdities as a self-propelled horseless carriage for fear of losing credulity with their colleagues or more importantly losing research funding. He would suffer character assassination at the hands of his peers and experts around the world.

Authors, college professors and museum administrators would hide behind an impenetrable wall of silence, not wanting to rewrite their books, alter their college courses or change museum displays. At best, the researcher who suggested the four-mummy sarcophagus was a self-propelled automobile, would have suffered lifelong ridicule, professional discrimination, humiliation, enforced obscurity, ostracism and poverty. Such is the fate of many brilliant visionaries and geniuses offering an understanding of the world, which is a paradigm shift from conventional thought.

In regards to the Great Pyramid there was such a visionary. He was a man with vision and understanding unclouded by preconceived notions. He dedicated his entire adult life in research on the Great Pyramid, developing an astounding and original theory as to its construction and purpose. His theory is consistent with and in context with the direct physical evidence. This man had the rarest of gifts. his gift was clarity of thought capable of unraveling a mystery indeterminable to all those who came before him and almost all after. He was a man whose life experience and education was grounded in the authenticity of the real world.

Although ignored and rejected to this very day by most of the "experts," this man developed the most plausible and reasonable explanation of the Great Pyramid's construction and purpose. This man's research married both the construction and function of the Great Pyramid into one consistent and convincing explanation. This man's research provided meaning, purpose and function to every major feature of the Great Pyramid. This man's research and findings are so fantastic many refuse to even read his book, *Pharaoh's Pump*, or dare touch it. They reject his book without becoming familiar with it. This man, currently unrecognized for his astounding genius was the independent researcher, lecturer, inventor, author, antiquities scholar and visionary, Edward J. Kunkel.

Kunkel's lifelong research led him to a discovery, which is being accepted and embraced by more people every day. Although when built it was common knowledge, Edward Kunkel *rediscovered* in our age the original building method and the original purpose of the Great Pyramid. He was the first man to unravel the Mystery of the Ages in modern times. Edward J. Kunkel discovered the Great Pyramid was designed and built to be a monumental and very sophisticated water pump![11]

The questions, which arise from that last sentence, are seemingly endless. What evidence, if any, is there supporting the Great Pyramid was a water pump? How did it pump water? In what way could the passages and chambers of the Great Pyramid pump water? What about the ramps to move the stones?   Where did it get the water to pump with no apparent water supply? Where did the pumped water go? How did water help construct the Great Pyramid? Are all the Egyptian pyramids water pumps? How can this fit in to the history of Egypt and the history of mankind? Why was such exacting precision required to make a water pump? Why is there no record of this in ancient times? What does this mean in today's world? How can this help us in our time? Has there been any experimentation or demonstrations to substantiate this theory? Why would the ancient Egyptians build a series of pyramid tombs for pharaohs then build a pyramid water pump, and then continue to build tombs for pharaohs?

These questions and many more are in the thoughts of those with an open questioning mind. By asking these questions, it implies an interest in the answers found in these pages. There is much material to discuss and much misunderstanding to overcome. This examination of what it took to build the Great Pyramid is not just a dusty, esoteric exercise in academic supposition. This research has direct application in the improvement of our quality of life, our environment, our health, our safety, our economy and the quality of life for our children.

The Great Pyramid we know today is only a wrecked remnant of its original grandeur. We are familiar with only the ravaged remains of this former shining glory, which once demonstrated the vision, genius and application of high technology used by the Original Builders.

It is my hope that we, like the Original Builders of the Great Pyramid, can muster courage, vision and understanding of the complexities and subtleties of the physical world around us to create a lasting legacy for countless generations to come. We too can and must utilize the high technology mankind mastered in antiquity to improve our daily lives and our troubled modern civilization.

But first, in preparation for the explanation of the Great Pyramid water pump's construction, the controversial issue of context must be addressed. In the minds of people who already have a strong predisposition concerning the Great Pyramid the issue of context seems to be the greatest obstacle in understanding the Great Pyramid as water pump. For these individuals who already embrace the current conventional explanation of the Great Pyramid, issues centering on context are a stumbling block larger than the Great Pyramid itself!

If your mind is already settled and your thoughts about the Great Pyramid are etched in stone the words in this book will not be able to budge you. For many it is easier to change the location of the Great Pyramid than for them to change their mind about the Great Pyramid. As the great Sphinx was covered for centuries by the shifting desert sand the Great Pyramid is swaddled in a cloak of contextual misunderstanding.

I hope your mind is *unsettled* about mankind's ancient past and realize there is so much yet to learn and discover. With an unsettled mind you have a good chance to transcend the current contextual constraints encapsulating the Great Pyramid.

---

[1] Charles Piazzi Smyth, <u>Life and work at the Great pyramid during the months of January, February, March, and April, A.D. 1865;: With a discussion of the facts ascertained</u> (Edmonston and Douglas 1867) 210.

[2] William Kingsland, The Great Pyramid in Fact & Theory (Kessinger Publishing 1996) 21.

[3] Hanno-Walter Kruft, A History of Architectural Theory: From Vitruvius to the Present (Princeton Architectural 1996) 357.

[4] Manly Palmer Hall, Secret Teachings of All Ages (Lulu.com 2005)92.

[5] Ernest Alfred Wallis, The Mummy. Chapters on Egyptian Funereal Archaeology (Budge Adamant Media Corporation 2001 edition) 343.

[6] Christopher Dunn, The Giza Power Plant: Technologies of Ancient Egypt (Bear & Co. 1998) 255.

[7] Joseph P. Farrell, The Giza Death Star (Adventures Unlimited 2002) 42.

[8] Wilbur Bradbury, Into the Unknown (reader's Digest Association 1981) 17.

[9] George R. Riffert, Great Pyramid Proof of God (Kessinger Publishing 2005) 123.

[10] H. Spencer Lewis, Rosicrucian Questions And Answers With Complete History Of The Rosicrucian Order (Kessinger Publishing 2004) 337.

[11] Edward J. Kunkel, Pharaoh's Pump (Warren, OH: Kunkel, 1977) 59.

Chapter 3
The Great Pyramid in Historical Context

The explanation of the construction techniques of the Great Pyramid offered in this book is a complete departure from current conventional understanding. Based on what most people have already been taught this book is "out of context." Because context is such an important issue in the minds of many it is important to address the issues of context which currently surround the first wonder of the ancient world.

Many will have no interest in issues of context at all. Their interest is in how the Great Pyramid was assembled, how as machine it operated and how to use this type of ancient yet high technology to improve our lives in a positive way. They know context is interpretation, which must be consistent with the physical evidence of the distant past. Yet there are others, who contend the issue of context is the pivotal aspect of any explanation regarding the greatest structure on the Giza Plateau.

In the book, *Giza: the Truth*, co-authors Ian Lawton and Chris Ogilvie-Herald analyzed various researchers' findings on the basis of context. In the minds of these authors, and most conventional researchers, authors, and professors, it is context which establishes the validity of invalidity of any researcher's findings, conclusions, or publications. These authors maintain all findings, interpretation of evidence, or explanations of the Great Pyramid which are "out of context" cannot be correct.[1] These authors are of the position that for any explanation of the Great Pyramid to be valid, the explanation must "fit in" to the widely accepted contextual explanation of Ancient Egypt.[2]

That sounds reasonable, but what actually is context and why is it a determining factor for validity in the minds of so many? How can a finding, discovery or explanation be in or out of context?

In studying the distant past in Ancient Egypt, Archeologists, Historians, Egyptologists and other experts gather evidence from a wide multitude of sources. These sources include hands-on research in archeological digs, the study of ancient architecture, language, writing, culture, religion, artifacts, ancient manuscripts, and the published works of other experts, just to name a few.

From these diverse sources study is conducted on both direct and indirect evidence. Direct evidence is comprised only of the actual ancient artifacts which remain in our age. Indirect evidence is comprised of the opinions and interpretations of direct evidence. Only the artifact is direct evidence, while the extrapolated purpose, meaning, and significance ascribed to that artifact is indirect evidence. It is the indirect evidence of expert opinion and interpretations of direct evidence which encompass the bulk of research into the distant past. From the synthesis of this varied research, experts develop a worldview of an ancient culture as it was in various stages of antiquity.

The process of gathering evidence and synthesizing interpretations of evidence from a wide variety of sources to create an overview of the characteristics of an ancient culture is referred to as the convergence of evidence.[3] Any worldview established from the convergence of evidence is a type of model representing the synthesis of "expert's" interpretation of the sequence of events, culture, technology, religion, architecture, and economy of the ancient culture under study. These historical worldviews of distant antiquity are often modified, based on new discoveries and occasionally entirely reconstructed to fit major new findings or to accommodate new research of direct evidence.

The contextual worldview is used as a tool to conceptualize of the ancient culture under study. Once a historical worldview of any ancient culture is established, additional findings are often either validated or deeded invalid based on whether or not the new research or findings complies or is in conflict with the contextual overview of the ancient culture. The contextual worldview becomes a benchmark or guide to judge additional ongoing research.

Unfortunately, these types of models or worldviews take on a life of their own and are seen as evidence in themselves, which they are not.

These historical worldviews, historical models or paradigms of the past can be as much a hindrance as help in understanding distant history. These worldviews are not a foolproof tool blessing any researcher or expert with the gift of infallibility. Rather, these models of ancient cultures are simply a latticework of ideas built upon interpretations of direct and indirect evidence.

In anthropology there is a worldview model of our species' ancient past, which includes the process of evolution. Anthropologists are presented with the evidence know as the Piltdown skull, which fit exquisitely into the latticework of extrapolations comprising the worldview of the experts in that field. The Piltdown skull was in context and was readily accepted by the expert community as valid. The Piltdown skull was evidence which converged with the ideas of anthropologists and with the interpretations of data they had amassed. The evidence of the Piltdown skull was consistent with the convergence of evidence and was enthusiastically embraced. The Piltdown skull was "in context." Unfortunately, it took this expert community over a generation to finally acknowledge the invalidity of this evidence for a missing link.

It is important to be mindful that for most researchers and experts, the need to be in context is a very powerful force, which has compelled some of the greatest minds to be not just wrong, but fundamentally flawed in their research. It was the compelling need to be in context with the accepted worldview, which kept the discipline of anthropology from seeing the file marks on the artifact called the Piltdown skull for over forty years! Similar *expert* acceptance happened surrounding the interpretation of the evidence of a pig's tooth, resulting in the "discovery" of the species know as Nebraska Man.

Many additional examples of interpretations of evidence, which have been in context with conceptualized worldviews, can be cited. There have been many other interpretations of direct evidence, which were considered in context by experts that have been subsequently recounted as erroneous. From our vantage point it is easy to look back and see that these interpretations of evidence were faulty. What is difficult for most is to look ahead to see what our civilization in the present accepts as true and factual because it is in context, yet is simply wrong. It takes a special mind to surmount that hurdle.

Context is just a blending of the interpretation of evidence, and the preconceived bias of the expert community, and nothing more. Context should be, and needs to be, subject to continuous scrutiny and evaluation. Context is not sacred nor set in stone; it is conditional to and *subordinate* to every aspect of the available original direct physical evidence.

In fact, the devotion to an outdated context over valid discoveries and research has been the greatest hindrance to the progress of improving our understanding of the world around us, as well as understanding our distant past. Researchers, historians, and Egyptologists often embrace these worldviews as a yardstick to determine which research is genuine and which is not. In reality it is evidence which determines the validity of a worldview, not the other way around. The revered worldview becomes a belief system. The adherence to it creates blind spots to phenomena which do not fit the current belief system.

I often encounter people who are skeptical of this understanding of the Great Pyramid. Open-minded skepticism is not feared but encouraged. Many who profess to be skeptics, you know are simply clinging to some beloved contextual understanding they hold near and dear to their hearts; to be truly skeptical, start on the ideas you accept as irrefutable.

But what *is* the currently accepted mainstream historical context of the Great Pyramid in the historical flow of mankind? We all know what traditional Egyptologists have maintained to be the context of this mighty and controversial structure. Egyptologists all over the world seemingly agree unanimously on the following. They believe the Great Pyramid was built in the fourth Dynasty by the Pharaoh called: Cheops (in Greek) also known by the Egyptian name Khufu.[4] Egyptologists tell us the Great Pyramid was built as a tomb and was preceded by mastabas and a number of pyramids of improving building techniques.[5] It is explained that the sequence of pyramid construction shows the steady improvement of the ancient Egyptians in the art of building pyramids.[6] The Great Pyramid was the pinnacle of the art of pyramid tomb construction followed by a decline in quality of workmanship.[7] Numerous pyramids were built after the Great Pyramid with a general decline in size and quality of construction.[8] Ultimately pyramids lost favor and were no longer built in the valley of the Nile by ancient Egyptians for a number of reasons including failure to be an effective protection to the Pharaoh's mummy and burial treasure from tomb robbers.[9]

We are further told building the Great Pyramid required a huge expenditure in human effort and resources. The method used to raise the stones according to Egyptologists was some sort of a ramp.[10] They tell us this ramp was either long, winding or of some other configuration and was used to move the stones to the necessary height.[11] Their story continues with explanations of stones pulled up the massive ramp by many workers be it slaves, peasants, volunteers, or taxpayers.[12]

Currently Egyptologists contend that the workers were not slaves.[13] They make a big deal about that. Yet, be it slaves, peasants, volunteers, or taxpayers what is important is how the workers accomplished the greatest construction project in antiquity and why they did it. To assert that the workers were not slaves does not help one iota in understanding what they did and why.

We are also told the puzzling interior of the passages and chambers of the Great Pyramid are the result of either symbolic, religious, and/or burial purposes.[14] Egyptologists also contend the interior chambers are the result of changing the design in mid-construction.[15] It is also explained that the casing stones were quarried to exacting precision by hand, using only primitive tools.[16] Such is the explanation, time frame, and methods used to build the Great Pyramid as unanimously told by all traditional Egyptologists throughout the world.

Traditional Egyptologists maintain the above is the contextual framework, consistent with their historical worldview, explaining every aspect of the Great Pyramid. It is their professional opinion any interpretation of evidence, or any observations, which deviates from this contextual framework is wrong. In the minds of traditional Egyptologists, their position in regards to context of the Great Pyramid is immutably etched in stone. These experts are as universally adamant about this contextual validity of their interpretation of the Great Pyramid as the experts were about the contextual validity of the Piltdown skull.

The above world view based on the convergence of the interpretation of evidence is what we are told to be true. But is it? Does the contextual framework established by the experts represent a description of the actual procedures used to build the Great Pyramid? If the conventional explanation of traditional Egyptologists is true, the entire account of the

Great Pyramid from this book is "out of context" and by *that* measure deemed to be erroneous. Current conventional explanations of the Great Pyramid are accepted as irrefutable fact beyond debate to most traditional experts. Yet, do the contemporary mainstream explanations we have all been told actually represent the events of what really happened so long ago on the Giza Plateau? Is the worldview currently held by highly educated and trained Egyptologists, who have established the contextual constraints of the Great Pyramid, actually correct? Are the stories Egyptologists tell about how the Great Pyramid was built and why actually true?

Many feel the questions of by whom, how and why the Great Pyramid was built has been answered irrefutably and even debating these issues is a sign of ignorance. The questions of who, when and why has been asked and answered to the unquestioning satisfaction of traditional Egyptologists around the world. Yet, it is the ongoing and building dissatisfaction with these very issues of context involving the Great Pyramid which is fueling the continuing raging debate by virtually all alternative researchers whose focus is the area known as the Giza Necropolis. We are currently in a reevaluation of these very contextual issues.

People who insist all understanding of the Great Pyramid must be "in context" with the current historical worldview ask questions like: Why would the ancient Egyptians build a series of pyramid tombs, then build a complex water pump in the shape of a pyramid that has no precedent, and then continue to built more pyramid shaped tombs? And why are there no references to the Great Pyramid being a water pump from any substantiated historical source? These questions are seemingly unanswerable to those who hold the criteria of current contextual constraints as the final determining factor for any research involving ancient Egypt. These questions presuppose that the conventional ideas of context are irrefutably valid. This book, in its entirety was written to address these very issues.

Is it really set in stone that the Great Pyramid was built in the fourth dynasty to serve as a Pharaoh's grave? Although the Great Pyramid is a very large construction project there is very little direct physical evidence as to who made this structure and when. There are mountains of interpretations of evidence but that is simply opinion.

As to the Great Pyramid, there is no surviving formal writing on any of its surfaces. There is no official decoration to indicate this structure's date of construction or even its purpose. No lavish and informative official funeral embellishments such as hieroglyphs found in many ancient Egyptian tombs were needed in the accessible chambers of the Great Pyramid. No Pyramid Texts or Book of the Dead was found in this structure. No pictographs or symbols which conform to any kind of ceremonial written language were ever in the interior of the Great Pyramid or were needed by the Original Builders. Apparently, the Original Builders did not need any type of formal writings, decorations, or paintings for the Great Pyramid to perform its original purpose.

A few crude quarry marks above the King's chamber in the so-called relieving chambers have been found. These markings were found by Colonel Howard Vyse in 1837.[17] There is still a raging debate as to the validity of these curious haphazard informal markings. It is beyond the scope of this book to continue the endless debate concerning the validity of these markings. Some say they are definitely forgeries made to promote funding for additional treasure seeking while others say with equal conviction that these markings are definitely genuine. Some say the majority of these markings were authentic but the *added* cartouche of a Pharaoh was a forgery. Traditional experts have not satisfactorily answered what these obviously slipshod and cryptic graffiti markings intended to communicate. Yet, in the book, Pharaoh's Pump, Edward Kunkel gives a fascinating hydraulic interpretation of these unusual so-called quarry marks.[18]

It is apparent some of these markings were created before the blocks were set in place. This is established as fact because some of the markings are in extremely awkward places between stones making it virtually impossible to create these writings after the stones were set in place. This has led many to feel the cartouche markings among these quarry marks are indisputably valid and proof positive the Great Pyramid was built by Pharaoh Khufu in the fourth Dynasty. The cartouche symbols found among these quarry marks are in accessible locations and could have easily been added by Howard Vyse.

In our age, most of us for various reasons revere the Great Pyramid and feel it is an awe inspiring or sacred place. We would never deface this structure by writing on it. Howard Vyse was from a different time and age. He had no reservations in defacing the Great Pyramid in this manner or any manner he chose. His use of dynamite was his tool of choice in treasure hunting by blasting his way into the relieving chambers.[19]

It is not known for certain if Howard Vyse did or did not forge the cartouche in the relieving chambers. However, it is known for certain that Howard Vyse gave these chambers names such as Lady Arbuthnot's chamber, Wellington's chamber as well as other names which served his purposes. By his direction these names were written in the relieving chambers. The evidence of those writings is still there defacing these chambers. So we know for certain that Howard Vyse had no qualms about writing on the walls or having someone write on the walls of the relieving chambers.

So did Howard Vyse or an assistant under his direction forge the cartouche markings in the relieving chambers? The jury is still out. It is not known for certain either way. Traditional Egyptologists cling to these crude and controversial markings as definitive proof establishing issues of who and when regarding the Great Pyramid. In a court of law the burden of proof must meet more stringent requirements. Based on the trail of evidence involving who found the cartouche markings and how, plus the potential and motive for forgery, this questionable evidence would be thrown out of a court of law.

The burden of proof required by traditional Egyptologists is evidently much less stringent especially when the debated "evidence" fits in with their presupposed contextual worldview. These cartouche markings are embraced as wholeheartedly as the Piltdown Skull was embraced by Anthropologists. To Egyptologists the cartouche markings are in context to their worldview, but that does not make them valid.

These controversial and inconclusive markings definitely do not establish conclusively a construction date or specific time frame for this building's creation. It has been said remarkable claims require remarkable evidence. To rely so heavily on such extremely controversial markings to be the definitive proof of so much, is at least wishful thinking, but for most it is an act of blind faith.

There have been a few reports of crude markings on some of the exterior blocks of the Great Pyramid which have been interpreted as being construction marks by gangs of workers involved in the task of moving stones. These marks could be graffiti from repair gangs or intrusive markings created after construction. There is also a pair of scored lines on the walls of the descending passage.[20] These scribe marks have acquired great significance to those who are faithful to a prophetic dating system based on the floor length and other features of the passages and chamber of the Great Pyramid.[21]

Before the smooth covering of casing stones was removed it was reported by Abd-al-Latif writing in the thirteenth century the outside of the Great Pyramid was covered with more writing than could ever be read.[22] It is unknown the content of that long ago writing, in what language it was written, and who wrote it. No examples remain to allow for examination. Many feel the writing was graffiti made by the multitude of tourists and curiosity seekers of distant antiquity. The exact origin, nature and purpose of this writing is unknown in our age.

Ancient manuscripts and books with descriptions of the Great Pyramid, which have survived intact from before the birth of Christ are almost nonexistent. Herodotus and even Strabo only speak briefly of the Great Pyramid and their writings conger up more questions than answers. The validity, accuracy and significance of what these early historians eye witnessed and wrote about is under constant debate. The significance of what these early writers saw was important. They saw the Great Pyramid and the Giza Plateau much closer to its original condition than any of us will ever see.

The origins of the Great Pyramid even in the time of Herodotus were extremely ancient. Much information was lost and unavailable even in his day because of the huge time span between his visit and the Great Pyramid's construction. Add to this the burning of great libraries of antiquity by religious zealots, conquering armies, and barbarians of all nations and ages, the available direct evidence to the Great Pyramid's origins has been reduced to what remains of the Great Pyramid itself! No one knows what wealth of information has been lost about the Great Pyramid and the history of mankind.

The slow and steady destruction of the Great Pyramid has been going on for thousands of years. The outer casing stones were torn from the monument so long ago.[23] The working moving interior parts described as doors on pivots were bashed to bits in hope of finding anything worth stealing. Treasure seekers and early researchers, no more than glorified grave robbers, flocked to the complex interior of the Great Pyramid. Many of them viewed it with as much disgust as awe because their preconceived notions dictated the Great Pyramid was built by "heathens."[24] The highly destructive nature of their research is infamous. Of the last two centuries the earliest "researchers" describe many important features to the Great Pyramid that are now missing. They studied and yet helped to destroy important evidence of how, why and who built the Great Pyramid. The Great Pyramid is a crime scene: the crime of destruction. With so much destruction endured by the Great Pyramid it is a difficult task to even imagine the Great Pyramid in its original condition, and understand how it was built and used. Although difficult, this task is the objective of this book.

Now, in this day and age, the Great Pyramid's primary purpose is to be a machine. This machine is a generator. The people who are in control of the Great Pyramid use it as a machine to generate revenue. If more money can be made by allowing research of the Great Pyramid that is what will happen. If more money can be generated by not allowing research then that is what will happen. Research and learning is subordinate to the generation of money. Research is primarily allowed as a method to generate funds, directly or indirectly. That is the purpose and function of the Great Pyramid for those who now control it.

There is a vast body of knowledge about the Great Pyramid. Of that knowledge much is misinterpretation of original evidence. There is a far greater amount of knowledge unknown in our age then when the Great Pyramid was built. Even though experts feel they are the definitive source of knowledge about a subject, not one expert today knows even a fraction of what was common knowledge of those who lived in the days when this structure was built. Although the experts profess to know volumes about this ancient wonder the current state of knowledge is that we are living in a dark age of misunderstanding concerning so many aspects relating to the Great Pyramid.

The experts know very little about this structure compared to any common person who was there when it was built. Archeologists, Historians and traditional Egyptologists are all trained to study the limited available direct evidence and develop an understanding of the past, which is consistent with their indoctrinated contextual constraints. Their understanding of the past is at best only *indirect* evidence based on their contextual interpretations of direct evidence. It is the rare member of these disciplines who look at an object and says, "I don't know." In fact, it seems the better the expert can take an object and force it to fit a particular scenario or historical contextual understanding the higher is his professional status.

There is very little evidence to determine the order of the construction of the pyramids in the Nile valley. There is scant direct evidence to indicate the way they were constructed. A few remaining chronologies and King's Lists were written well over a thousand years after the building of early pyramids.[25]

Some of these King's Lists and chronologies were written after intermediary periods about kings who reigned before such periods. Intermediary periods are sanitized expressions for times of chaotic anarchy. The chronologies are a form of history lesson for the time the King's Lists were written. I would say their accuracy is subordinate to the wishes of the Pharaoh who commissioned the lists.

The rein of the Pharaoh King Tutankhamen is missing from the King's Lists.[26] He as well as other kings were not listed for many reasons including political power struggles or religious strife. It is not known what other kings have been omitted or added to these lists. What is known is that the King's Lists do not represent an accurate chronology of the succession of Pharaoh's in the valley of the Nile.

The purposes of King's Lists were to validate the position of the reigning king instead of being faithful historical representations of what actually happened in the past. If a King's List did not validate a king's right to the throne then the King's List was modified until it suited the contemporary needs of the Pharaoh. History is always modified to suit the needs of those who write it. King's Lists have been viewed as a textbook of the chronology of leaders in the Nile valley. Textbooks are written not to serve historical accuracy but to best suit those who commission the textbook. That is one reason historical textbooks must always be rewritten. This is still true today.

Look at it this way. I don't mind giving Egyptologists all the credit they deserve. Even if Egyptologist's chronology and sequence of pyramid construction is 99 percent correct they could still be 100 percent wrong about the Great Pyramid. The Great Pyramid could have predated all the other pyramids in the Nile Valley. (This is elaborated on in later chapters.) An early and powerful king in the Nile valley revered as a man-god could have taken credit for the already existing Great Pyramid and professed this pyramid was his. He could have professed this in his formal writings and the preexisting Great Pyramid could have later been attributed to him by subsequent generations in King's Lists written a thousand years later. Khufu was Pharaoh and could have taken credit for the Great Pyramid had he built it or not.

The convergence of evidence used by archeologists and traditional Egyptologists have included the development of a scenario of the sequence of pyramid construction, which relies heavily on the relative quality of workmanship and construction methods of various pyramids. The basis of this understanding relies primarily on pyramids of relatively low quality of workmanship, built before pyramids exhibiting better construction methods and workmanship. We are told mastabas predated the step pyramid, then later came the bent pyramid, followed by the high quality Giza pyramids.

It is this idea of an improving state of the art of pyramid building, which is a major determining factor (among others) used by Egyptologists to "establish" the order in which these marvelous buildings were built. This sequence of the construction of the pyramids of Egypt is taught in schools and written in encyclopedias and textbooks.

The facts are the pyramids of Egypt were built with widely differing degrees of craftsmanship, greatly differing sizes of stones, differing precision of stone cutting, differing construction methods, and even differing materials. Some used sun-baked mud

Fig 3.1 Lap Joint

brick, some used limestone and granite and some incorporated wooden timbers. These are facts. The interpretation of those facts into a basis for the sequence of construction is only a theory which is in context with an agreed upon worldview. Again, traditional Egyptologists could be 99 percent correct about the sequence of the construction of the Nile valley pyramids and still be 100 percent wrong about the Great Pyramid.

Let's examine some other examples from the real world.

The current state of the art of most furniture manufacturing is to use very simple joinery. Dressers are an excellent example of this. Most new dressers are manufactured using a basic lap joint.

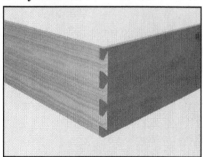

Fig. 3.2 Dovetail Joint

A hundred years ago fine joinery was used; most notably the complex and beautiful dovetail joint. After the passage of ten thousand years from now, and numerous intermediary periods (times of chaos) only a very few ancient dressers will remain to be studied. Based on the quality of workmanship and the quality of the materials used which dresser would be considered by the experts ten thousand years from now to be the oldest? Based on the same reasoning as Egyptologists, the newest one would be the oldest.

The historian in future times would write a book explaining the improvement of the state of the art of dresser making showing the simple lap joints in a dresser which predated the complex dovetail jointed dresser. He would assert the state of the art of dresser construction progressed as the joints became more complex. This is just one example of how determining the age of items based on their relative complexity can be faulty.

I discovered another example which illustrates this same concept when touring Hoover Dam located 30 miles from Las Vegas, Nevada. Built in the 1930's, it is constructed of poured concrete. As we went on the guided tour I was astounded at the exquisite workmanship of every aspect of this structure. It was like an industrial cathedral—built not to the power of gods but built to create power for its builders. On one part of the tour we entered a large access tunnel. After being in awe of the craftsmanship and quality of construction of the Hoover Dam, I was shocked at the obvious poor attention to detail and sloppy work of this large access tunnel.

I asked the guide about the poor workmanship. He said this particular tunnel was not built during the original construction. It was built much later. The tunnel was needed, and contracted out to the lowest bidder. The tunnel was completed and passed inspection. Ten thousand years from now all that will be left of the dam is a cement monolith with oddly shaped passages and chambers. The river will have changed course leaving the dam high and dry. All the innards will be looted by souvenir hunters and treasure seekers. Researchers from the very distant future will conclude the primitively constructed passage was made before the dam was constructed. The bases for their interpretation of evidence will be the different qualities of workmanship. It will be deemed by the experts the newer, poorly constructed passage was made before the older dam.

There are thousands of examples in the real world which demonstrate that quality of building techniques and craftsmanship are NOT always moving forward. If that is the presupposition one bases the chronology of the making of items (even pyramids) one can easily be led to the wrong conclusion.

During World War II, many of the isolated cultures of the Pacific islands were exposed for the first time to the machines of mechanized war. Seeing airplanes, jeeps and radios close up for the first time made a tremendous impression on such cultures.[27] The advanced culture with their high technology left after the war was over. After being exposed to this advanced technology, there were instances of the indigenous populations making from the materials at hand similar shaped objects. They would construct their own airplanes.[28] These airplanes would never fly, being made of sticks, shipping crates, branches, tree trunks and whatever else was readily available. These palm leaf airplanes were built to appease the gods of "Cargo Cults."[29]

It is easy for us to know and understand which type of airplane came first. Now imagine the passage of ten thousand years!! It is difficult to do but try. Those living ten thousand years from now will possess as little knowledge about us as we know of people who lived ten thousand years ago. Imagine distant future archaeologists digging in this remote island. Somehow they discover the airplane made by the locals as well as the remains of an airplane which had been shot down by warring nations.

If the archeologist used the crutch of assuming the general improving quality of workmanship and construction techniques his conclusions would be in error. Based on the same theory of relative state of the art of building practices used to determine the age and sequence of the Egyptian pyramids, the future archeologist would write a book explaining how the primitive plane was built first, while the advanced plane was built later. His career would be based on his interpretation of the evidence, which would be opposite to what really happened. He would conclude: the primitive airplane was constructed first. Then after the state of the art improved the sophisticated plane was made. No doubt his finding would be supported by the "evidence" of the unanimity of opinion by his peers. Evaluating quality of workmanship to understand a sequence of pyramid construction is far from foolproof.

There are other methods experts use to interpret the evidence of the Great Pyramid and its surroundings. Experts assert the graves around the Great Pyramid establish the historical context and date of construction of this mountain of stone. The great migration of the American continent occurred on the Oregon Trail. Tens of thousands made that long and arduous journey. For many it was the most awe inspiring and significant event of their entire lives. On that trail is a great landmark called Independence Rock. I have been there. This great monument was marked by the hand of thousands who passed this very special place. It was so special that many who traveled the Oregon Trail in their youth were buried at Independence Rock at the end of their long lives. Just as these people wanted to be buried by a significant mound of stone so did people in the ancient Nile valley. Because people are buried around a mountain of stone does not necessarily mean they were responsible for making the mountain of stone, nor does it determine the age of the mound of stone.

The experts may be right concerning the ages, construction sequence and Pharaohs attributed to 99 percent of the Egyptian pyramids. If they did, that would be something to be proud of. And even if they are, they could still be 100 percent wrong in their assessment of the Great Pyramid! Context is simply expert opinion and experts are people who know more and more about less and less. The intent of this chapter is to reemphasize that historical context is not established as fact and is currently under extreme scrutiny and reevaluation.

It is interesting to note of all the experts in whatever field of study, the expert opinion of each of our own personal doctors seems to matter most. The expert opinion of archeologists, historians, and especially Egyptologists pale by comparison. Doctor's opinions have a direct affect on our health and lives. When giving their diagnosis (opinion) they always suggest the importance of you, the patient, getting another opinion. Often, these opinions of highly educated doctors are mutually exclusive and contradictory, but it is up to the patient (you) to decide which diagnosis (opinion) best fits the circumstances (evidence). Even if the patient (you), does not have a relevant academic degree the patient (you) is the person who decides which diagnosis (opinion) is right! The doctor only supplies the opinion; the patient decides which opinion is correct.

The opinion of context is as much the source of controversy as anything about the Great Pyramid. I offer this book, which is an explanation of the Great Pyramid to you as a "second opinion."

Another issue creating controversy about the historical context of the Great Pyramid is the distinction between evidence and the interpretation of evidence. I do not want anyone to confuse direct evidence with either interpretation of evidence or context. Direct evidence in this case is the Great Pyramid itself. The physical material involved in the construction of the Great Pyramid is all the direct physical evidence remaining to us in our age. Interpretation of this direct evidence or any evidence in the valley of the Nile is simply a set of opinions. When any expert tells you why something is the way it is, or the purpose, or meaning of some artifact or structure, that expert is offering their opinion. Prevailing expert opinions change over time and are not evidence.

When any expert discusses context they are dealing with pre-established conceptualized models and that, too, is not evidence. Below are some examples, which differentiate between evidence, interpretation of evidence, and context.

There was a wall around the Great Pyramid. That is evidence. Traditional Egyptologists tell us the wall is to keep the unwashed masses away from the Great Pyramid for cultural, religious, and societal reasons.[30] That is interpretation of evidence. The casing stones were made with extreme precision. That is evidence. Traditional Egyptologists tell us this was accomplished by using primitive hand tools. That is unsubstantiated interpretation of evidence. The Pharaoh man-god has only one spirit and the Great Pyramid has four major chambers. That is evidence. Traditional Egyptologists tell us there are so many chambers resulting from changes of plans during construction.[31] That is simply an interpretation of evidence to make the evidence fit a conceptualized world view. The coffer is empty. That is evidence. Traditional Egyptologists tell us the mummy of the Pharaoh was either stolen in antiquity or buried in a secret place. That is interpretation of evidence. Very large monoliths were moved to enormous heights to build the Great Pyramid. That is evidence. Traditional Egyptologists tell us there must have been a very big ramp of some kind and multitudes of workers used to drag the stones up.[32] That is interpretation of evidence, never adequately substantiated by demonstration.

I could go on forever. The point is interpretation of evidence is not evidence; it is only an opinion. All opinions must be consistent with all the direct physical evidence. This book is a different opinion of the same direct physical evidence.

How fascinating it is, after a patient receives several opinions from doctors, the patient is the one who decides what the best treatment is. The experts give their opinion and the unlearned patient decides which is right. In the same way it is up to the reader and the general population to decide after thorough analysis what interpretation of evidence best fits the direct physical evidence.

It is equally fascinating that the United States judicial system works in the same manner. Highly trained lawyers present their case presided over by a distinguished experienced judge. In a jury trial it is the experts who are barred from deciding guilt or innocence. That most valued honor and solemn responsibility rests solely on the shoulders of the rank and file, off-the-street jury members. It is juries who are given the responsibility of deciding if a fellow human being will live or die. If regular people can decide for themselves' issues of that importance do not let anyone belittle you by telling you that you cannot decide for yourself how the Great Pyramid was built and why.

Other than a few open-minded researchers, I know very few have been swayed by controversial contextual issues presented in this chapter. It is only the special few who will genuinely undertake an examination of the validity of their own contextual mindset. Most skeptics never direct their skepticism to what is thought indisputable in their own minds. The establishment of "context," especially in regards to very ancient antiquity is as much an exercise in subjectivity as any endeavor can be.

Evidence interpreted through the veil of contemporary cultural biases and preconceived paradigms of the past must be eternally subject to ongoing scrutiny. The interpretations of evidence, offered without any substantiation using demonstrations by traditional Egyptologists, are ripe for reevaluation and replacement by more valid understandings. This ongoing reevaluation of traditional Egyptologist's assertions will be based on the technological requirements needed to actually duplicate the pivotal construction aspects, which are mute testimony of the Original Builder's advanced abilities and genius. The reevaluation of traditional Egyptologists interpretations will focus on technological issues and be accompanied by the utilization of the scientific method supported by valid demonstrations.

This book examines the construction process and purpose of a large scale construction project. I will leave the worry about how this research fits into some hallowed contextual constraints to others. Experts who worry about context over the pursuit of truth are people I do not worry about. As this book unfolds and provides a description of the construction and purpose of the Great Pyramid, allow yourself the luxury of transcending any and all constraints of interpretation of direct evidence known as context. Allow yourself the opportunity of open-minded inquiry into the ideas presented in this book. See for yourself if it is in context with the direct physical evidence and represents what happened when the Great Pyramid was built.

There has been an attempt by the expert community to answer the questions of who, how, when, and why the Great Pyramid was built. In doing so, they have succeeded in pigeonholing this structure into the contemporary traditional historical world view. By creating a historical model and cocooning the Great Pyramid into that model most experts have provided themselves with all the answers they need. Their expert interpretation of evidence, synthesized into a historical world view has, in their eyes, achieved an important goal. It has, for them, put the Great Pyramid "in context."

This is one way to do it; but there is a better way!

1 Ian Lawton, Chris Ogilvie-Herald <u>Giza: The Truth: The People, Politics and History Behind the World's Most Famous Archaeological Site</u> (Virgin 1999) 78.
2 Ibid.
3 Michael Shermer, <u>Why Darwin Matters: The Case Against Intelligent Design</u> (Times Books 2006) 12.
4 Craig B. Smith, <u>How the Great Pyramid Was Built</u> (HarperCollins 2006) 51.
5 Ibid. 44.
6 Somers Clarke, Reginald Engelbach, <u>Ancient Egyptian Construction and Architecture</u> (Courier Dover Publications 1990) 8.
7 E. A. Wallis Budge, <u>Egypt Under the Great Pyramid Builders</u> (Kessinger Publishing 2004) 148.
8 Ian Shaw, <u>The Oxford History of Ancient Egypt</u> (Oxford University Press 2003) 293.
9 Ann Rosalie David, <u>The Ancient Egyptians: Beliefs and Practices</u> (Sussex Academic Press 1998) 125.
10 Miroslav Verner, translated by Steven Rendall, <u>The Pyramids: The Mystery, Culture, and Science of Egypt's Great Monuments</u> (Grove Press 2002) 86.
11 Ibid.
12 Michael Haag, <u>Rough Guide History of Egypt</u> (Rough Guides 2003) 24.
13 Gerard C. A. Fonte, <u>Building the Great Pyramid in a Year: An Engineer's Report</u> (Algora Publishing 2007) 19.
14 James Bonwick, <u>The Great Pyramid of Giza: History and Speculation</u> (Courier DoverPublications 2003) 125.
15 Craig B. Smith, <u>How the Great Pyramid Was Built</u> (HarperCollins 2006) 194.
16 Zahi A Hawass, <u>Mountains of the Pharaohs</u> (American University in Cairo Press 2006) 61-65.
17 Mark Lehner, <u>The Complete Pyramids</u> (Thames and Hudson 1997) 53.
18 Edward J. Kunkel, <u>Pharaoh's Pump</u> (Warren, OH: Kunkel, 1977) 66-71.
19 Kevin Jackson, Jonathan Stamp, <u>Building the Great Pyramid</u> (Firefly Books2003) 142.
20 Peter Lemesurier <u>Decoding the Great Pyramid</u> (HarperCollins Publishers Limited1999) 42.
21 Ibid.
22 Kevin Jackson, Jonathan Stamp, <u>Building the Great Pyramid</u> (Firefly Books 2003) 119.

23 Gerard C. A. Fonte, <u>Building the Great Pyramid in a Year: An Engineer's Report</u> (Algora Publishing 2007) 112.
24 Richard Howard Vyse, <u>Operations Carried Out on the Pyramids of Gizeh, Vol. II</u>, Appendix, p. 335
25 Barry J. Kemp, <u>Ancient Egypt: Anatomy of a Civilization</u> (Routledge 1991) 21.
26 Christine El Mahdy, <u>Tutankhamen: The Life and Death of the Boy-King</u> (St. Martin's Press 2001) 40.
27 Peter Bernard Clarke, <u>New Religions in Global Perspective</u> (Routledge 2006) 138.
28 Edward Rice, <u>John Frum He Come: A Polemical Work about a Black Tragedy</u> (Doubleday 1974) xiv.
29 Ibid.
30 Rosalie David, <u>The Ancient Egyptians: Beliefs and Practices</u> (Sussex Academic Press 1998) 129.
31 I. E. S. Edwards <u>The Pyramids of Egypt</u> (Viking Press 1972) 86-67.
32 Zahi A Hawass, <u>Mountains of the Pharaohs</u> (American University in Cairo Press 2006) 62.

Chapter 4
The Great Pyramid in Technological Context

Alongside historical context created by historians there is another emerging method, or reference, used to understand the Great Pyramid which is of extreme importance. The Great Pyramid is not only a historical wonder it is also a technological wonder. The technology of the construction and purpose of this structure is being studied irrespective of any historical constraints imposed on the Great Pyramid. A number of researchers are focusing on the technological aspects of this structure and rightly so. The study of how it was constructed and the technology required to build it will provide new insight into the mysteries surrounding the Great Pyramid.

The proposed technology and method of the construction of the Great Pyramid must fit the direct physical evidence of this mighty marvel. Any context ascribed to the Great Pyramid must fit the technology required to create the Great Pyramid. Historical context must fit the direct physical evidence *and* the technology needed to create the direct physical evidence. In the minds of many this is the better way. This is the better way because it embraces the essence of the Scientific Method. Researchers who focus on the necessary technology required to create ancient artifacts seem to achieve a greater and more accurate understanding than those who simply offer up an edict from the confines of a lofty ivory tower.

The "science" of Egyptology does not seem to put much value in understanding the Great Pyramid in relation to the technology required to build it. When asked about how the Great Pyramid was built, Egyptologists instantly tell stories of a huge ramp, sweaty workers, ancient gods,

Pharaoh's hats, golden objects, and of course, mummies. Yet, Egyptologists abhor supporting their stories about how the Great Pyramid was built with any valid scientific demonstrations.

North of the Great Pyramid about 380 miles or so is the town of Damascus. This area is attributed as the historical source of the legendary and highly admired Damascus steel. In distant antiquity extremely high quality steel was produced in this area. This "high technology" steel was high in carbon and held a sharp edge but also was flexible instead of brittle. This beautiful metal's most fascinating and striking feature was fine lines indicating the alternating layers of high carbon and mild steel. Unfortunately, many of the processes used in antiquity to manufacture numerous types of this wonderfully advanced commodity were lost to the sands of time.[1] In our modern era, there was great debate as to the exact procedures to create various types of Damascus steel.

For many years a number of people tried their best to reproduce this unusual and sophisticated type of steel. They used varying ingredients and processes in their attempts to recreate this advanced technology of the ancients. It was not known exactly how certain ancient types of Damascus steel was produced. How then could one know if they rediscovered the same method used by the ancients who made the original Damascus steel? There were no original experts available to tell them if they were correct or not. There were no manuals or hieroglyphs surviving from ancient times describing in detail the highly technical process of creating Damascus steel.

It is important to note, traditional historical experts were of no help whatsoever. Their expertise concentrated on battles, ancient gods, political leaders, King's Lists, amulet scrounging, ancient religion, taking items from graves, and interpretation of pottery shards. Regardless of the education and qualifications of archeologists, historians and of course

Egyptologists all were ill-equipped in understanding or rediscovering the ancient technical process of making Damascus steel. In respect to understanding ancient technology, or recreating ancient technology the traditional experts were inadequately educated and untrained to make any meaningful contribution.

The only way to find out the ancient process of making Damascus steel was to try to recreate Damascus steel in modern times. Many different techniques and procedures were used in an attempt to recreate Damascus steel in our age. The method used to ascertain the validity of the various experimentations was to compare the results of the experimentation to the original artifacts made by the original ancient experts. When the results of the experiment were obviously different from the original artifacts it was easily understood that the process used in the experiment was different from how the original Damascus steel was made in antiquity. When the results of the experimentation were the same as the original examples of this ancient high technology it was determined the methods used to create these duplicates were the methods used to make the originals.

Only when the *results* of the demonstrations were the same as the original artifacts of ancient times was the process of making Damascus steel fully understood in modern times.

This procedure of creating repeatable experiments and analyzing the results is called the Scientific Method.

There is no massive ongoing controversy as to the context of the methods used in making Damascus steel even though there are no original eyewitnesses to confirm the validity of these demonstrations. There is no need for lettered experts well versed in mummy rapping, amulet polishing or King's Lists to "tell us a story" about how Damascus steel was made. This is because the end results of the demonstrations to make Damascus steel eventually matched the original artifacts in every important aspect. The results of these demonstrations are so much like the originals that questions of context and questions of how it was done are virtually nonexistent. There is no ongoing heated debate as to whom, how, or why Damascus steel was created. This is because the people who recreated Damascus steel used the Scientific Method as the preferred way of knowing.

Here is another example of a method used as a way of knowing. This example relies not on the Scientific Method, but rather on simply creating an interpretation of evidence made by an expert.

In the Walt Disney animated move called the Little Mermaid, the main character, Ariel, finds two artifacts created by humans. She knows nothing of humans or the artifacts they create so she takes these items to an expert called Scuttle. This highly esteemed expert examines the fork and tobacco pipe and interprets the meaning of these human artifacts.

He tells Ariel, "Human stuff, huh? Hey, lemme see." As he picks up the fork he continues, "Look at this. Wow — this is special — this is very, very unusual."

Ariel asks, "What is it?"

Scuttle responds, "It's a dinglehopper! Humans use these little babies . . . to straighten their hair out. See — just a little twirl here and a yank there and — voiolay! You got an aesthetically pleasing configuration of hair that humans go nuts over!"

Ariel: A dinglehopper!

Ariel's sidekick named Flounder asks the expert: "What about that one?"

Scuttle replies while holding the pipe, "Ah — this I haven't seen in years. This is wonderful! A banded, bulbous — snarfblat."

Ariel and Flounder both impressed reply: "Oohhh!"

Scuttle continues, "Now, the snarfblat dates back to prehistoric times, when humans used to sit around, and stare at each other all day. Got very boring. So, they invented the snarfblat to make fine music. Allow me." Scuttle then attempts to demonstrate his hypothesis by blowing into the pipe causing seaweed to pop out of the pipe and onto the expert.[2]

Those who saw the movie laughed because humor is always based on truth. If Scuttle were a human instead of an aquatic creature his profession would undoubtedly be an Egyptologist.

The two above examples show the difference between how true scientists seek truth and Egyptologists seek truth. Interpretation of artifacts seems to be the long suit of Egyptologists. Egyptologists are never without an interpretation of an artifact and they provide their interpretations with unwavering confidence. They validate their interpretations by consensus of opinion as well as by their "authority" instead of substantiation by demonstration.

As one can see, in establishing the historical context of the Great Pyramid experts rely on interpretation of evidence and expert opinions. It is difficult to effectively contradict these subjective validations other than to give an opposing opinion. When this happens the discussion devolves into comparing degrees of the differing experts to see which expert trumps the other. The expert whose degree and experience seems better is the one that has the highest "authority" which determines whose proclamations are accepted. To me that is such a terrible way to seek truth.

But when establishing a technological context concerning the Great Pyramid the requirements are much more stringent. Determining the technological requirements to build the Great Pyramid allows for and demands the extensive use of the Scientific Method. There is little wiggle room for an expert or Egyptologist to offer an unsupported explanation when focusing on the technical context of the Great Pyramid.

It is through a focus on the technical context of the Great Pyramid which will allow researchers to chip away at the stranglehold Egyptology has on this subject. Establishing the technical context of the Great Pyramid is the best way to expose the plethora of glaring errors Egyptology embraces as fact.

In terms of establishing the technological context of the Great Pyramid, the "science" of Egyptology has offered *nothing* to substantiate their assertions as to how the Great Pyramid was built. It has never been demonstrated how the ancient Egyptians accomplished the pivotal tasks needed with the level of technology they were reputed to possess. The technological context of how the Great Pyramid was built is not established at all. That is to say, not scientifically.

It is the unresolved issues involving the technological context of the Great Pyramid that have fueled the endless heated debate on virtually every aspect of this enigmatic pile of stones. We have all been told of the stories of ramps and tombs and how the Great Pyramid was built in very primitive ways but many do not accept these stories as factual. Any proofs, by convincing valid demonstrations, to validate traditional Egyptologist's assertions have not been performed.

Below is a very short list of things Egyptologists claim the builders of the Great Pyramid did. These are the very aspects Egyptologists endlessly assert as irrefutable truth but are unwilling or unable to show the world through demonstration. Egyptologist's position seems to be that ancient Egyptian working people could repeat all of these tasks on a large scale but Traditional Egyptology cannot demonstrate these tasks even one time.

- Have we been shown how the Ancient Egyptians quarried and cut even one full sized casing stone to exacting precision with primitive hand tools by a demonstration recreating what the ancient builders of the Great Pyramid demonstrated? No.

- Have we been shown how these massive limestone casing stones are moved on and off a barge with no handling scars by a demonstration recreating what the ancient builders of the Great Pyramid demonstrated? No.

- Have we been shown how a full size casing stone was moved to the site and set in place by a demonstration recreating what the ancient builders of the Great Pyramid demonstrated? No.

- Have we been shown how the Ancient Egyptians quarried a 70 ton granite stone to the same precision as the originals by a demonstration recreating what the ancient builders of the Great Pyramid demonstrated? No.

- Have we been shown how one 70 ton stone was pulled up a dirt ramp twenty stories high by a demonstration recreating what the ancient builders of the Great Pyramid demonstrated? No.

- Have we even been shown how to move a full sized casing stone around a corner of a spiral ramp by a demonstration recreating what the ancient builders of the Great Pyramid demonstrated? No.

These and many other unsubstantiated asserted "truths" are the tenets of the religion of Egyptology which are pivotal to their faith. The elitist high priesthood of Egyptology inflexibly recites this dogma to a world which is more and more unwilling to accept it. The pseudo-science of Egyptology is arguably the richest of all the sciences. With their priceless artifacts filling museums around the world generating ticket sales and endowments by wealthy benefactors, you would think some department of Egyptology somewhere would substantiate the stories they have told us. With an overabundance of highly paid professors and authors there is no reason why the pseudo-science of Egyptology cannot engage in the Scientific Method and show us how it was done by demonstrating the tasks listed above.

I call Egyptology a pseudo-science because that is what it is. A true science uses the Scientific Method which includes demonstrations. The common workers who built the Great Pyramid were better scientists than Egyptologists because the working people demonstrated each and every technological requirement necessary to build the Great Pyramid. Egyptologists do not, will not, and evidently cannot, recreate those same demonstrations accomplished by the workers who built the Great Pyramid.

Period authentic, valid demonstrations using stones the same scale as the originals which produce results equal to the original evidence and would lend credence to the assertions, proclamations and edicts handed down by traditional Egyptologists. Without valid demonstrations the unsubstantiated assertions made by traditional Egyptologists remain simply unsubstantiated guesses, nothing more.

The stories of massive ramps and exquisite precision created with only hand tools is only a story. It is an often repeated mantra, chanted only by a band of Ramp Cultists who represent a science as stagnant as Phrenology. Egyptology has fallen short and missed the mark in explaining anything of a technical matter relating to the construction of the Great Pyramid. Their explanations, without valid demonstrations have been given and found inadequate. Their elucidations of the technology and procedures used to build the Great Pyramid are slipping into the shadowy realm of witchdoctor mumbo-jumbo.

There is a better way to understand how and why the Great Pyramid was built than the methods employed by Egyptologists.

It is a fascinating endeavor to attempt to establish the context of the Great Pyramid on a purely technology focused perspective. There is very little need to provide or accept a subjective interpretation of artifacts. There is no need to give any artifact a religious, cultural or societal interpretation. There is little need for opinions of what the artifacts were for when the primary interest is in knowing how the artifacts were made. All religious artifacts were made. All social artifacts were made. All cultural artifacts were made. My interest and many people's interest lies in knowing how artifacts including the Great Pyramid were made. There is nothing wrong with that. To know how the Great Pyramid and its components were made is a foundation for understanding why it was made.

In fact, the focus on the ancient technology is more interesting to me and many other inquiring minds than King's Lists, the hat styles of Pharaohs, what amulet was shoved up which mummy, which gods were worshiped, and using Egyptian words in sentences as often as possible. None of these subjects has any bearing on the technology required to assemble the Great Pyramid.

Yet Egyptology has its own ways of doing things.

Instead of actually being a science, employing the Scientific Method, Egyptology has elected to use a different method. Egyptology will compare one piece of evidence anywhere in the Nile valley with some other piece of evidence and extrapolate an "expert opinion" from that comparison. Forgoing the Scientific Method in favor of just making extrapolations may be much easier and certainly cheaper but accuracy is sacrificed.

There is no need for extrapolations comparing how 100 pound sun baked mud bricks were moved to prove how the massive stones of the Great Pyramid were moved. There is no need for extrapolations comparing a 4 foot high inclined plain built somewhere in the Nile valley to prove a 45 story ramp was built to drag stones up to the top of the Great Pyramid. There is no need for extrapolations comparing rough hand cut surfaces or dolerite pounders in an attempt to prove that the same techniques were used to make surfaces true and flat to 1/100th of an inch. In determining the truth about the construction of the Great Pyramid these types of extrapolations of evidence are not needed because they are a detrimental unscientific method of "understanding" technical matters.

All of these extrapolations of direct evidence are provided with confidence by Egyptologists without any substantiation by demonstration. They must not need to engage in the Scientific Method by providing valid demonstrations, because they already "know." They maintain that their education and expertise in King's Lists and amulet extracting confirms they are correct in understanding how massive stones were quarried to precision and set in place. When addressing the questions of the strictly technological requirements necessary to build this building Egyptology has provided no demonstration to show how the ancient Egyptians built the Great Pyramid. Irrespective of the Great Pyramid's location, and its construction in distant antiquity, the technological requirements to build this building have not been *shown* to be in the possession of the ancient Egyptians.

It would definitely quench much of the controversy of who, how, when, and why the Great Pyramid was built if traditional Egyptologists would demonstrate what they profess to be fact. No, there is no need to recreate a full scale duplicate of the Great Pyramid. If they would demonstrate one or two of the pivotal aspects listed earlier it would help substantiate their assertions. If it could be demonstrated by the "science" of Egyptology how they profess ancient Egyptians did the important and necessary aspects of building the Great Pyramid, it would end the ongoing and intensifying controversy and rejection of traditional Egyptologist's interpretation of the building methods and purpose of the Great Pyramid. If traditional Egyptologists could show us by demonstration instead of just telling us a story it would prove their assertions and advance their "science." They seem unwilling and/or unable to (by valid demonstration) do anything to quench the fire of controversy and growing rejection of their own dogmatic "expert opinions."

The few demonstrations actually preformed under the approval and direction of highly regarded and esteemed traditional Egyptologists have been lacking in authenticity. We have all seen the TV documentaries. Always stones of a relatively small size are moved with great difficulty instead of showing how the largest stones are moved. Never are the precision casing stones or the massive granite stones recreated to the same accuracy as the originals. Often forklifts, flatbed trucks and steel cables are just off camera. The results of the demonstrations are always very primitive compared to the evidence provided by the Great Pyramid itself.

The results of these demonstrations are so different from the results of the Original Builder's demonstrations it is as if they are showing us how the Great Pyramid was *not* built.

There was much technology used in building the Great Pyramid. As with Damascus steel, how this technology was utilized can only be determined by demonstration. The result of any specific demonstration must be equal to the original evidence or the demonstration is flawed and/or inaccurate. The substantiation by demonstration is the cornerstone of any real science. To understand this is very important in knowing the validity of what you are told by any expert or author.

I would like to tell you a true story which illustrates the importance in understanding the result of a demonstration, and how it must resemble the original in every important aspect to be valid.

Tom, my child's ten year old friend came over to my family's home the other day. Tom had just returned from his summer vacation and had brought an old Indian arrowhead he had found in the dessert to show our family. He proudly showed me the arrowhead and asked how it was made. He had heard I make arrowheads. After I explained the reasons why I never remove arrowheads I find, I told him I would gladly show him how Native Americans made arrowheads. He is a pretty sharp young person and I wanted to use him in an experiment without his knowledge.

I said, "Sure Tom, I'll show you how Native American arrowheads are made."

I took him out to my workshop where I keep my extensive rock collection. He was impressed by my facility and reputation. I picked up a piece of soft soapstone and removed my pocket knife. As he watched, I proceeded to whittle the soapstone into the shape of a typical arrowhead. I handed my creation to the child and proudly proclaimed, "This is how Native Americans made arrowheads."

He looked at the arrowhead I made and the one he found and frowned. I asked him, "What is the matter Tom?"

He said, "The one you made looks kinda like an arrowhead and is shaped like an arrowhead but it doesn't feel like an arrowhead."

Keeping a straight face, I acted very confident and asserted, "It is an authentic arrowhead made in the same way Native Americans made arrowheads."

Tom hesitated then reemphasized, and said, "It is about the same shape and size as the arrowhead I found and it sort of looks like a real arrowhead but it doesn't feel the same as the one I found in the desert."

"How the arrowhead feels makes no difference." I said. "You know I make Indian arrowheads, and this is how they were originally made."

Tom said, "I can scratch a line on the one you made with my fingernail. On the real one I can't. The one I found is made out of rock that is much harder than the stone you made your arrowhead out of. The two are different."

I told him, "They are the same and now you know how arrowheads are made. Do you doubt my word or my authority in this subject?"

He examined the two arrowheads then said, "Your arrowhead is soft and mine is very hard. Your arrowhead is not sharp and mine is very sharp." He bent the soapstone arrowhead and it broke! "Your arrowhead is weak and mine is strong. They are different!"

I crossed my arms and acted perturbed telling him, "I am the expert and have the authority in this matter." In an accusing tone, I said, "That is how arrowheads are made. Even though there is some difference between the two arrowheads, it doesn't matter. I gave you a demonstration and that is how it was done. My demonstration is proof!"

He hesitated then said, "If the arrowheads were the same, not just close to the same maybe I would think you made arrowheads like real ones were made." With growing confidence he said, "I don't think Indians had pocket knives with steel blades either! The arrowhead you made is a lot different from mine. I think the real ones were made differently than how you made yours." Disappointed he handed me my broken soapstone arrowhead, and uttered a dejected thanks as he started to leave the workshop.

I stopped him and told him he was wise beyond his years saying, "You understood the result of the demonstration was fundamentally different from the original evidence of the arrowhead you found. You were also able to withstand the pressure from an authority figure."

I told Tom proudly, "Young man, you will go far in your understanding of the world. Now, do you really want to see how arrowheads are made?"

"Sure," he said.

I picked up a piece of obsidian and let Tom examine it. "Does your arrowhead look like it came from stone like this one?" I asked?

"It feels hard like my arrowhead, and the same color," he said.

I sat on my stool and showed him the piece of deer hide I use for napping. (Napping is the process of making arrowheads). The piece of leather is used to keep me from being cut by the sharp stone when shaping the arrowhead. "Did native Americans use deer leather?" I asked.

He nodded saying, "They make clothes and moccasins out of leather."

As I napped the obsidian into an arrowhead we discussed how well he was able to understand that my first demonstration was flawed because the results were different from the original artifact in many fundamental ways. He was fascinated with the demonstration and came to understand how Native Americans made arrowheads. When finished, I gave him the arrowhead I had napped. He examined them both and compared them with each other.

He said, "They feel the same and are made from the same kind of rock. They are both sharp! The one you made could have been made by Indians in the same way. Now I know how arrowheads were made." Taking both arrowheads he thanked me and went to tell his friends all about it.

In the mind of the astute young man the technical aspects of making the arrowhead was only established after a valid demonstration was preformed. Tom knew which of the two demonstrations were valid by comparing the results with the original artifact. The demonstration providing results like the original artifact was deemed valid. It was shown how the Native Americans used the resources of their environment and knowledge at their disposal to create the implements used in their civilization. The process of the demonstration created a result very similar to the original artifact. The demonstration lends substantial credence to the contention Native Americans made arrowheads and how they made them.

There was no interpretation of cultural, religious or social aspects of the artifact. We did not need to know the gods which were worshiped. We did not need to acquire an expertise in the interpretation of pictographs, petroglyphs or rock paintings. We did not have to be proficient in searching for and taking golden treasure from graves to put in museums. We did not need to know details of battles, be an authority in a "Chief's List" or be an expert in Native American language. None of that would help in understanding how the artifact was made. The only interpretation needed was the comparison of the new artifact with the original one.

Tom used the Scientific Method as his way of knowing. A proper demonstration provided a valid result which was the means for the child to learn and for science to advance. If a child can do it why can't traditional Egyptology!

You never hear anyone say, "American Indians could never break very hard stones and shape them into arrowheads and knives using their bare hands." If anyone would make such a statement someone would show how very hard stone was fashioned into useable tools by the process of napping. There is no question or controversy involved in the "technological context" of Native Americans making arrowheads. The materials and techniques were available to Native Americans. The modern day demonstrations of these techniques produce results which are the same as the original artifacts. The technological context of how and why the American Indians made arrowheads is confirmed by the valid results of appropriate demonstrations.

On the other hand, the realm of Egyptology has not been forthcoming or successful in their establishment of technical context of the Great Pyramid. Egyptology cannot produce a full sized casing stone. Egyptology cannot move a full sized casing stone around the corner of a spiral ramp. Egyptology cannot make a King's chamber ceiling stone or move this size of stone one inch. Evidently the high priests of the religion of Egyptology have interpreted the movement of full size stones to be displeasing to their gods.

Creating a full size casing stone using primitive methods is never ever attempted by Egyptologists. Yet regular working people produced well over a hundred thousand of them. A demonstration of creating and moving the largest sized stones is the definitive litmus test in how the Great Pyramid was built.[3] Egyptologist cannot demonstrate moving the largest stones but working people demonstrated it many times. These demonstrations are *required* by the Scientific Method to validate Egyptologist's explanations of the Great Pyramid. These demonstrations have never been performed and the controversy rages on. In reality, the burden of proof of Egyptologist's assertions by valid demonstration rests on their shoulders to scientifically substantiate what they maintain to be fact.

As far as I am concerned it is the Egyptologist's assertions which need to be put in context with the physical evidence of the Great Pyramid. It is asserted by all Egyptologists the huge casing stones were quarried with simple tools to the exacting precision shown by the originals. To put this assertion "in context" with the direct evidence of the Great Pyramid it would be nice if they would demonstrate to us how ancient Egyptians quarried, cut, moved and placed at least one casing stone like the ones still at the Great Pyramid. This would establish and verify their assertions and place their assertions in context.

Verification by demonstration is the foundation of the Scientific Method. For some reason the pseudo-science of Egyptology is not subject to the Scientific Method. Evidently Egyptologists feel to prove what they assert to be fact is unnecessary. They must think that their expert opinion is sufficient proof, or consensus of opinion is evidence. Apparent Egyptology is guided by consensus beliefs and majority rule, rather than by experimentation and demonstration.

For me, other researchers, and a growing vocal contingent of interested people, some sort of verifiable proofs in the form of demonstrations are required. It is this type of proof that will establish the context of who, how, when and why the Great Pyramid was built. With only the say so of Egyptologists the technological context as well as any context of the Great Pyramid is *not* established and definitely open to heated debate.

If it can be substantiated by demonstration that casing stones with the same size and precision as the originals of the Great Pyramid can be made by primitive tools and efficiently moved by dragging them up a ramp there is no need for the multitude of alternative ideas about this structure. If it cannot be demonstrated that casing stones were made using only primitive tools and systematically moved up ramps a viable alternative explanation of the building process is a *necessity*. It is as simple as that.

The nonprofit research foundation I established is doing something about this unanswered problem of establishing the technological context of the Great Pyramid. Our foundation is offering a $50,000 research scholarship. Basically, the requirements of this scholarship are to quarry and cut five casing stones to the size and precision of the originals. Then move and place these five casing stones in the manner Egyptologists claim it was done. Whoever accomplishes this seemingly simple exercise will receive the $50,000 scholarship. See the Appendix at the back of this book for the details of this research scholarship.

There is an old saying. Put your money where your mouth is. In effect, our nonprofit organization is putting our money where Egyptologist's mouths are. Hopefully this will help motivate someone (the scholarship is open to anyone) to demonstrate what Egyptologists have been asserting for generations. Our organization is contacting universities around the world to let them know about this funding opportunity. We are also contacting foundations, and benefactors who fund departments of Egyptology to let them know we are offering this scholarship. Maybe these providers of funding can all reduce their funding by $50,000 each. That's OK, because departments of Egyptology seem to be over-funded anyway. They do not seem to really need much money. They sure have saved a bunch of money by their ongoing lack of demonstrations to establish any technological context.

The only direct evidence we have to go on as to how the Great Pyramid was built is the Great Pyramid itself. There is no writing on the Great Pyramid explaining how it was built. There are no surviving ancient manuscripts, scrolls, golden fleeces or chicken entrails telling us how the Great Pyramid was built. All that really remains from the time of the construction of the Great Pyramid is the Great Pyramid itself and the remnants of a few sketchy legends and oral traditions which have been handed down through the ages.

Egyptologists use a very clever method of compensating for this. They often compare one aspect or feature of a building somewhere in the Nile valley and infer another building has this same feature. Mortar or plaster was identified to be used between some stones in pyramids that were built as much as 1,600 years after the Great Pyramid was built. Therefore the bonding agent between the casing stones of the Great Pyramid is asserted to be mortar. This is one way of "knowing" what the bonding agent is between the casing stones of the Great Pyramid.

There is a depiction in a tomb showing a statue of Djehutihotep on a sled being pulled by a number of people. Therefore it is asserted the stones used in the Great Pyramid were pulled to their final location in a similar manner. I ask

Egyptologists, "What part of the Great Pyramid is this statue?" I am told it is not part of the Great Pyramid but it shows how heavy loads were moved. I ask again, "Did the builders of the Great Pyramid create this scene in the tomb?" Egyptologists assure me that this depiction was made only a few centuries after the Great Pyramid and hence it is relevant. I ask, "How high is the statue being lifted as depicted in the hieroglyph—maybe 400 feet high?" I am told that the hieroglyph shows the statue being moved on a horizontal surface but I am assured this is how stones are moved up to great heights. I ask, "Does this depiction show how the statue was moved around the corner of a spiral ramp?" I am told no spiral ramp was involved in moving this statue and therefore no ramp is in the depiction." I ask, "How many statues are moved?" "Was one statue moved every two minutes or one every 2 hours or one every two days or one every two weeks or one every two months?" I am told this depiction shows only one statue being moved. Is this hieroglyph relevance in regards to the Great Pyramid? To Egyptologists yes, but no, it isn't.

Egyptologists even point out how liquid is poured out in front of the sled to make it move easier.[4] I always ask, "In building the Great Pyramid if water is poured on a ramp to make stone laden sleds pull easier, wouldn't that make it very slick for the workers pulling the next sled? Wouldn't that make it very slick for the workers to drag sleds every two minutes?" Because these are technical questions, Egyptologists have no congruent answers.

It is common practice for Egyptologists to compare some aspect of one building built in the Nile valley to the Great Pyramid, and then come up with some interpretation of it. Small one hundred pound limestone blocks may have been moved by hand. Does that necessarily mean 2 ½ ton or even 16 ton stones were moved the same way. No. Some rough stones on primitive pyramids appear to have been quarried and cut by hand. Does that mean the extreme precision seen in the Great Pyramid casing stones and other precision stone work was accomplished by hand? No. To compare one thing to another in this manner without substantiation by demonstration is both bad science and disingenuous.

This same technique of comparing one thing with another has been utilized by used car salesmen. They advertise a nice car at a good price but when you get to the used car lot they have other cars not as nice with a higher price. Egyptologists have chosen by their own volition not to show by demonstration, any aspect of how the Great Pyramid was built. Instead they have chosen to try and compare aspects of buildings all over the Nile valley which were built over a span of 3,000 years or even longer.

Fig. 4.1 © Copyright Dieter Arnold, Building in Egypt, p. 278. A drawing
like the one above was found in a tomb in Egypt.

Egyptologists show us a drawing that was found in a tomb with a sled hauling a square shape pulled by animals. Simply referring to that picture and then declaring that this is how the extremely massive stones of the Great Pyramid were moved is bad science. This technique is called bait-and-switch and is against the law with used car salesmen but standard operating procedure with Egyptologists.

This book's explanation of the Great Pyramid's construction and purpose does not use any fast shuffle or shell game tactics comparing aspects of pyramids or ancient building which do not relate to the Great Pyramid and assert that is how the Great Pyramid was made. This understanding of the Great Pyramid does not rely on dubious shucking and jiving with the sources of direct evidence by comparing very different construction techniques and simply professing they were done the same way. These and other false proofs used by Egyptologists are elaborated on in the book, *the Pyramids: an Enigma Solved*.[5] Although I do not support everything in that book, the descriptions of the six false proofs used by traditional Egyptologists is well worth reading.

If you take away only one thing from this entire book I hope it is this:

Context Must Be In Context With The Physical Evidence

Context is only what some people have agreed upon. That is all it is. Context is not evidence. It is only an agreement by some as to what they think the direct physical evidence is or means. In the San Marco church in Venice there is a mosaic showing the pyramids to be granaries.[6] Rest assured this picture was accepted by the experts to be in context when it was created. The leading experts of the world fully embraced the Piltdown skull and heralded it as a valid missing link because it fit exquisitely into their latticework of ideas, known as context. Anthropologists embraced the Piltdown skull for forty years and could not even see the visible file marks because this skull was contextually valid to them.

Context is simply interpretation. Context does not exist. You cannot point to it or touch it like you can physical evidence. Context only exists in the minds of those who create it. Contemporary real world experts who actually work in stone know the context Egyptologists have created to explain how the casing stones were cut is incorrect. Contemporary real world experts who move very heavy objects know the context Egyptologists have created to explain what is needed to move the heaviest stones is incorrect. Contemporary real world machinists and experts well versed in the requirements of creating precision fitting large scale projects know the context Egyptologists have created to explain what is needed to create the precision components of the Great Pyramid is incorrect.

Historical context as well as technical context of the Great Pyramid are not established at all. The context created in the minds of Egyptologists is only a house of cards. It *will* fall. All it will take is for enough people to reject their stories.

This book is an examination which focuses on the technology involved in creating the public works project we know as the Great Pyramid. This book concentrates on the technology involved in moving the stones and the technical purpose of this man-made structure. This book engages in the process of reverse engineering the construction process used to build the Great Pyramid by understanding the direct physical evidence of the Great Pyramid.

I read a book about the construction and operation of the Panama Canal. The book focused on technological matters. The book never did discuss the religious rituals of the builders or how the leaders of the builders were buried. If the book had talked about these things it would have been both distracting and insulting to the reader. I read a book about the construction and operation of the Grand Coulee Dam. The book focused on technological matters. The book never discussed the religion of the builders or how the leaders of the builders were buried. If the book talked about these things it would be both distracting and insulting to the reader.

On my way to Egypt I spent some time in Paris. While in Paris I went to the Notre Dame Cathedral specifically to see the flying buttresses. Notre Dame is a religious structure yet our very nice tour guide did not discuss the God worshipped by the people who built Notre Dame to explain the purpose of the flying buttresses. Our tour guide did not quote from the Holy Bible or describe the robes of the priest to explain the "symbolism" of the flying buttresses. Notre Dame is a technical masterpiece as much as a religious structure. Our tour guide discussed the technical reasons for the flying buttresses and that is how it should be. If our tour guide talked about religious matter to explain the flying buttresses it would have been both distracting and insulting to me.

In contrast, Egyptologists are more interested in studying ancient religious customs, Pharaoh's hats and the extraction of idols and amulets from mummies. (Euphemistically known as bobbing for amulets.) It is apparent that Egyptology is unable to produce meaningful scientific demonstrations of the technological requirements of building the Great Pyramid. Therefore their proclamations are unscientific. Egyptology has degraded into a bizarre mystery religion headed by an elitist priesthood glorifying ancient golden objects and ritually reciting the tenets of Ramp Dogma.

On the basis of the technology required to build the Great Pyramid and what was available to the Ancient Egyptians, the context of the Great Pyramid has not been established by demonstration. The context of the Great Pyramid is under very valid and justified dispute on many levels including the technology needed for this building's construction. What Egyptologists profess to be irrefutable facts concerning the construction of the Great Pyramid are simply unproven assertions, without any substantiation by demonstration. In any discipline of science other than Egyptology, these types of assertions without any valid demonstrations would be laughed off the face of the earth.

Yet, every aspect of the construction process to build the Great Pyramid has been demonstrated. It was demonstrated by the Original Builders. Egyptologists cannot or will not provide adequate demonstrations to substantiate their assertions. The reason for this is not a lack of time or money. It is because they are wrong! Their assertions cannot be demonstrated!

Consider this. Egyptology cannot even demonstrate the creation of one casing stone or even one surface of one casing stone. I submit to you the reason for their failure is that they are incorrect in their assessment on how it was done. The reason why they cannot create demonstrations for any of the pivotal tasks required to build the Great Pyramid is that the way Egyptologists say the Great Pyramid was built cannot be demonstrated! It is by focusing on the issues of technological context which will help people see the cracks in their stories and to see that much of their conjectures are unworkable in the real world.

Instead of rehashing the same old stories of religious interpretations of the Great Pyramid this book departs into a fresh direction of understanding. The Notre Dame Cathedral is a technological wonder and so is the Great Pyramid. This book talks about the construction and operation of the Great Pyramid focusing on the high technology relating to this structure.

---

[1] Manly P. Hall, Horizon the Magazine of Useful and Intelligent Living 1945 To 1946 (Kessinger Publishing 2005) 63.
[2] The Little Mermaid, dir. Ron Clements, perf. Rene Auberjonois, DVD, Disney, 1989.
[3] Edward J. Kunkel, Pharaoh's Pump (Warren, OH: Kunkel, 1977) 22.
[4] L. Sprague de Camp, Ancient Engineers (Barnes & Noble Publishing 1990) 39-40.
[5] Joseph Davidovits, Margie Morris The pyramids : an enigma solved (Dorset 1990) 53-64.
[6] Kevin Jackson, Jonathan Stamp, Building the Great Pyramid (Firefly Books 2003) 119.

Chapter 5
It's a Water Pump

As I mentioned in the first chapter, this book is about how we learn as much as it is about the Great Pyramid. The process of discovery, learning, unlearning and relearning new information is as interesting as any subject. These are very important issues when encountering the construction method described in this book. This chapter is intended to address these issues by relating to the reader an experience I had so many years ago.

In this experience, I had to go through the process of discovery, understanding and true learning. Those who accept the information in this book will travel a similar journey of understanding.

When I was in my late teens my family lived in southern California. We often went to the Mojave Desert to camp and relax away from the big city. My now departed father and I often hiked in this desolate area of the world, conversing on many subjects both trivial and profound. I was of the age when it was normal to have a rebellious attitude toward my father but I did not. Even then, I was in awe of him.

He had traveled the world and seen many things. He was accomplished at a wide variety of skills. He was resourceful and creative. He did not demand respect from anyone, but commanded respect and admiration from everyone he knew. He had achieved an unbelievable number of accomplishments and life experiences. Although he did not have letters after his name, he was a very remarkable and successful man. The experiences of his life were full and varied, and he seemingly drew knowledge and wisdom from everything he did.

One morning as my father and I hiked along a barely discernable trail we came across a hunk of metal partially buried in the desert sand. It was a piece of heavy cast iron about a foot across, flat on one side and bulged up on the other. Part of it was machined smooth but other areas were left rough. There were holes all around the perimeter and a hole in the center of the bulge. I stopped and poked at it with my walking stick. My father stopped alongside me to look at this piece of metal. After a moment of looking, I picked it up.

Fig. 5.1 My father and I looking at the object we found in the sand.

It was still early morning, before the heat would compel us to return to the shade of our camp. After pondering this unexpected relic I was at a loss to what it was or why it was located here. I turned to my father and simply asked, "What is this piece of junk?" Although I did not know the answer, I had no doubt he should know. For a man so mechanically inclined and well read and widely experienced, I thought the answer should be an easy one for him. I often relied on his help in this way; he was a great resource of both knowledge and wisdom. These were pre-internet days and he was my personal Wikipedia!

He took the cast iron piece and held it for quite a while. He didn't answer right away but seemed to be lost in thought. With this relic in hand, he looked at me and simply said, "It is a water pump."

My father and I shared a love for any kind of puzzle or riddle. To me, this seemingly cryptic reply was a signal this was some kind of puzzle to be solved. My father's answers to the questions I asked of him often created more questions than answers. Instead of just telling me a fact or information he often tried to draw the answer from inside me. Sometimes this was frustrating because it made me think of the answer instead of taking the easy way out and just being told the answer. He always felt that by using dialogue truth could emerge.

I rarely contradicted my imposing father but that morning I told him in a matter of fact manner, "It is not a water pump." He said nothing. After a moment I told him we are in the middle of a desert, with no water as far as the eye can see. I asked, "Doesn't a water pump need to have water to be a pump? No water, no pump!" My seemingly irrefutable answer seemed to comply with logic to me. Self-absorbed in my own confidence, I beamed with pride.

Still examining the piece of metal he said, "There is no water now, but it is a water pump for sure."

I told him, "Dad, there hasn't been water here for over a thousand years! This scrap iron is not that old. There has never been water here for ANY water pump!"

He said, "When this water pump was first here, there was water for it to pump. Now there is not."

I told him, "This is just a chunk of metal. This is not a pump because it can't pump water."

He replied, "The pump is not complete now as it was in the past. It is currently not in the same condition as it was when it was originally built. Parts are missing but it is a water pump."

I told him, "It is not a water pump because it is not finished."

"How do you know it is not finished?" My father asked.

"Look, in one area the metal is smooth being machined but most of this so called pump is very rough; therefore it is unfinished. The builders didn't finish this pump so it never pumped water." I told my father.

"The water pump is as finished as it needs to be," my father answered with a smile.

"There is no power source to power the pump. Pumps take energy to run so it can't be a water pump." I told my Dad.

To this he answered, "The power source is not readily apparent now, but the pump was powered." That didn't help me to understand so I said, "There is no farm here and never has been. There is no use for the water. There is nothing to pump the water to or from, so it has no purpose. There is no use for the water, so this piece of junk is not a water pump." I felt triumphant because I knew a water pump *must* have a purpose.

His reply was, "This water pump is a pump regardless of its purpose. If you or I cannot discern the purpose of this pump it has no effect on whether or not it was built to be a water pump. The original builders of this pump surely had a reason for building it. They were the ones who knew exactly why they built this water pump. What they knew is more important and significant than what we think we know about the purpose of this pump. It is evident, son; you are currently unaware of the purpose of this pump. Not knowing why this pump was built doesn't mean it is not a water pump. You, being unaware of this pump's purpose does not change the fact that this is a water pump. Your ignorance has no bearing on reality. Remember that!" The last part my dad said with emphasis.

Exasperated, and at wit's end, I asked, "What is the water of this so called water pump used for?"

He said, "If you do not think this thing is a water pump, then it doesn't make sense to ask what the pumped water was used for. If this is not a water pump to you, then to you there was no pumped water to use. Agreeing with or disagreeing with the purpose or use of the pumped water has no influence on if it is a pump or not. You cannot confirm it is a water pump or rule it out by understanding what the water was used for. These are two separate issues." Calmly he continued, "Asking about a use for the water assumes this is a pump."

"What was the water used for?!" I demanded.

He thought about that question for a long time. He knew I was leaning towards the idea this was somehow a pump. His strong hands held this artifact with the same gentle manner as an archeologist would hold the Holy Grail. His usual friendly manner was now gone; replaced with as serious an expression I had ever seen. He looked me in the eye, man to man, and told me, "Water has many uses, and it depends on how you want to look at it. This pump was built and water was pumped right here in the desert to keep you from speaking a foreign language as your native tongue. That, my son, was the purpose of this water pump."

Dumbfounded, I didn't know what to think or even how to reply to what my father said. I did not know what he meant. I knew he was now very serious and appeared to know what he was talking about, but it didn't make any sense to me. How did this hunk of iron pump water? Where did it pump water from or to? Why was it here and why was this location chosen? Who made the pump and what was its power source? I knew Native Americans lived here but surely they didn't make it. I knew that would be out of "context." Most of all, how could a nonfunctioning water pump in the desert determine what language I spoke? All I knew was this was no game and it was very important to my father for me to understand, but I was stumped. At a loss for words, all I could say is, "I don't understand."

My father sensed that at my tender age, I did not have the experience or understanding it took inside me to draw out the answer so told me. He said, "Son, this *is* a water pump. It is from the engine of one of General George Patton's tanks. He was on training maneuvers in this area before World War II. This trail we are walking on is actually the path one of his tanks took while he was training his troops (the trails left by these military tanks are still visible today). Evidently, one of the tanks had water pump problems and the pump was replaced near where we stand. In a very real way those men were training to keep their unborn children from speaking the native tongue of their enemy. To accomplish that goal they needed water pumps like these to keep their tank engines at the right temperature."

He went on to tell me how the water pump mounts on the engine and showed me were the water comes in and out. He explained how the missing impeller shaft turned and how it was powered. He told me why the very smooth surface was machined. This precision was required to provide a flat surface for a watertight gasket. The relatively rough casting was smooth enough to house the pump impeller. The different degrees of precision served to support the function of this machine.

He carefully set the cast iron piece down leaving it as we found it. Heading back silently to camp, we were both lost in thought. Father's mind lingered on memories of his experiences in World War II and their implications. My thoughts were on the unbelievably broad effects seemingly unrelated things can have on one another and how everything in the world is inexorably interrelated. Neither of us spoke on our walk back to camp.

When we got back to camp, I was the first to speak. I turned to the man who raised me and said: "Father, it is a water pump."

This book is about a different water pump, built in a different age, and in a different desert then the one my father and I encountered back when I was in my youth. But the thought processes as well as the mental obstacles to understand both water pumps are still the same. As my father tried to help me understand one water pump, this book is to help others understand the Great Pyramid water pump.

The Great Pyramid is a water pump. It was built by the Original Builders and completed as originally planned: to be a water pump. It is a water pump unlike any known by our culture. It is a water pump unrecognizable to most experts in the fields of water pump design, Engineering, Physics, Archeology and of course, Egyptology. It is a water pump built with technology unknown by the civilization we are told built the Great Pyramid, and high technologies very different from our own. It is a water pump who's purpose, placement, extreme precision, and design do not fit the model of the current accepted historical world view. It is a water pump seemingly out of "context." Irrespective of all these issues, the Great Pyramid is a water pump.

Besides objecting to issues of context, people feel the Great Pyramid is too important, too significant, too symbolic or too "profound" to be simply built as a water pump. In the year 1947 what was the largest structure ever built by the hands of man? The largest structure on earth at that time over shadows the Great Pyramid in size. It too is a massive structure, with no ornamentation, containing oddly shaped passages and chambers, constructed in the middle of a dry valley which has a huge river flowing through it. This biggest structure ever built (at the time of its completion) was created by its Original Builders as a water pump. This building is known to us as the Grand Coulee Dam in central Washington State. This dam is a self-powered, self contained water pumping system capable of continuously irrigating over 1/2 million acres of dry desert land! Although the Grand Coulee Dam and the Great Pyramid operate in *completely different ways* they both were designed and built to pump water.

In our present time what is the largest structure ever built in the Nile valley? This building, many times the volume of the Great Pyramid sits in the middle of a dry desert valley. This structure without ornamentation, with oddly shaped passages and chambers is the Aswan High Dam. This structure is the keystone to an irrigation system that has changed the valley from desert to garden. The Nile valley irrigation system involves massive water pumps throughout the area permanently tethered to the Aswan High Dam by delicate wires. These wires convey the power created by the Aswan High Dam to the irrigation pumps. The pumps convey the water to where it is needed. Without the electrical power generated by the Aswan High Dam, the extensive Nile valley irrigation system would instantly cease to function.

No, the Great Pyramid water pump is not a hydroelectric dam. It operates nothing like a hydroelectric dam, however, it is still a water pump. Modern mankind uses hydroelectric dams to power an extensive water pumping system in the Nile valley. Ancient mankind in the Nile valley pumped water too. They also used a very large structure, with oddly shaped passages and chambers, but it functioned much differently from the water pumping systems created by modern mankind.

Do not let anyone tell you being a water pump is not a significant enough purpose to justify a structure as big and magnificent as the Great Pyramid. The technical expertise and precision of construction to create this building has been interpreted to have religious, cultural, funeral or any number of convoluted hocus-pocus purposes. This book's understanding of the Great Pyramid transcends all these outdated concepts and gives a functional purpose to the otherwise baffling features of this magnificent machine.

I want you to join me in the adventure of understanding how the Great Pyramid was built. This is a journey of inquiry to understand the high technology used to build a technological wonder. Our journey has the purpose of reverse engineering the Great Pyramid, by correctly understanding the direct physical evidence which has survived to modern times. As we travel together on this journey to understand the technical processes involved I want you to make this journey in a very special way.

I do not want you to embark on this adventure as a historian because that will not help you! A historical perspective is not needed and will be detrimental. To know of clothing, battles, makeup and social customs of ancient cultures will not help you understand the technology and building procedures necessary to create the Great Pyramid. You do not need to know the gods worshiped by the Original Builders in understanding how this structure was built. No matter what gods the Original Builders worshiped, it was the Original Builders who had to move the stones. Do not allow your vision or understanding to be tainted by any historical interpretations or opinions.

I do not want you to embark on this adventure as an Egyptologist because that will not help you. The perspective of an Egyptologist is not needed and will be detrimental. Mummies, amulets and burial treasure have absolutely nothing to do with the movement of massive stones. To know if your Ben-Ben has adequate Ka will not help you to know how the stones were moved. Using the word Imhotep and Ma'at in sentence after sentence will not help you or anyone else know the highly technical aspects relating to the Great Pyramid. To study gods, religion, golden amulets and the type of hat Pharaohs wore will not help you understand how the stones were cut to precision, moved and set in place. We, in our adventure of understanding, want to use the direct evidence instead of bits of papyrus and "inventories" written at least 1000 years after the Great Pyramid was built.

No Egyptologist has ever made a precise sixteen ton casing stone or even authentically moved a stone of this weight the distance of one foot. In the history of the entire "science" of Egyptology it has never been shown how a single casing stone surface was finished to perfection, let alone an entire casing stone. To look to Egyptologists to understand the technology involved in building the Great Pyramid will guarantee failure. Their back muscle mantras and ramp chants have been found much too unacceptable to believe and impossible to demonstrate. If you want to know how to unwrap a mummy to get at the golden amulets I refer you to an Egyptologist. If you want to understand the building procedure of the Great Pyramid, Egyptologists are a hindrance and a stumbling block instead of a help.

You do not even need to know the language spoken or written by the Original Builders. This book is about what they did, not what they said. Experts are astounded by this statement because they have devoted their lives to interpretation of hieroglyphs and potshards. To make my point I ask you the reader, do you understand how the High Aswan Dam in the valley of the Nile was built and why? Did you have to learn to speak, read and write Russian fluently to understand the technology of the High Aswan Dam which was financed, designed and built by the former Soviet Union? Probably not. Do you need to know a "Leader's List" of the USSR or read the writings of Karl Marks and Vladimir Lenin to understand the technology of how the High Aswan Dam was built and how it was used? Of course not! The building process is expressed through the building. We want to use direct physical evidence instead of interpretations of potshards, reciting the Book of the Dead or analyzing headwear styles of man-god Pharaohs.

   Walt Disney was responsible for the creation of Disneyland. With the passage of ten thousand years and several chaotic "intermediate periods" Disneyland will be gone; only a few cement foundations will remain. Imagine if a "Californiaologist" from the distant future digs up a body thinking it is Walt Disney. Then the Californiaologist checks the body's clothing for valuables, does a body cavity search for golden objects and puts this withered body on display in a museum. Will that help anyone understand how the rides in Disneyland were designed, built, and operated? No, it would not. Similarly, if an Egyptologist digs up someone in the Nile valley does it make him an expert on the technical aspects of monolithic stone construction? No, it does not.

   Even though the Great Pyramid is a huge pile of rocks, this ancient man made mountain has been put in a box. Historians and Egyptologists have encapsulated this structure into a box of misconception, misinterpretation and misunderstanding. Experts have a misconception of the Great Pyramid's purpose. Experts have a misinterpretation of the Great Pyramid's construction procedure. Experts have a misunderstanding of the Great Pyramid's huge potential to help us live freer, cleaner and safer lives. To understand this book and the Great Pyramid you must break free from the constraints experts have for the Great Pyramid and think outside of that box!

   This is how I want you to embark on this adventure. This is how I want you to direct your efforts in understanding the Great Pyramid. I want you to look at this structure not as a historian or Egyptologist because if you do you will become entrapped by their preconceived errors taught as facts. Strip away all preconceived ideas and start afresh using new eyes. Conduct this search for truth from the eyes of the Original Builders. To understand the building procedures I implore you to simply put yourself in the position of the Original Builders. This is a simple but profoundly elegant way of knowing the building procedure.

Putting yourself in the place of the ancient engineers will greatly enhance your ability to reverse engineer the Great Pyramid. Allow yourself to be faced with the same challenges as the Original Builders faced but do not allow yourself to be ensnared in the limited view historians and Egyptologists have for the Original Builders. Unfortunately, because of the mountain of misinterpretation which encapsulates the Great Pyramid you will have ideas and preconceived notions which will hinder your understanding of the explanation provided in this book. You, too, will have to struggle with the same kinds of questions I did when I was in the desert with my father. I know you too can overcome these obstacles.

An ancient civilization constructed a massive structure with no ornamentation, no formal writing, containing oddly shaped passages and chambers in a valley of a large river to improve their culture, and our culture does much the same thing. Our modern civilization has built massive structures in river valleys throughout the world. The construction techniques and the nature of operation of these massive structures of our civilization differ greatly with the construction techniques and the nature of operation of the Great Pyramid.

This book describes how a gigantic structure was constructed in antiquity without unneeded formal ornamentation inside or out. This book is a narrative of how that structure, with incongruously shaped passages and chambers was built. This narrative describes the deep understanding of physics the Original Builders had as well as the application of this understanding to create high technology now tragically lost to the sands of time. It is this same ancient lost high technology which our modern world desperately needs.

This technological wonder, the glory of the ancient civilization who built it, pumped water. With the purpose of pumping water, we will begin our exploration of how the

Great Pyramid was built and why. I welcome you on this journey.

Chapter 6
Introduction to the Assembly Process

There seems to be as many theories of how and why the Great Pyramid was constructed as there are people who offer such theories. No theory of construction, including assertions of massive ramps *accompanied* with adequate demonstrations has ever been presented to the general public in the last 1,000 years.

It is interesting to note the 5th century B.C. historian Herodotus wrote of the building of a ramp but it is considered to be the causeway leading to the Great Pyramid.[1] The causeway "ramp" would have only elevated stones up to the base of the Great Pyramid. Most traditional Egyptologists as well as alternative researchers agree the causeway was not used for the transport of stones to the building site.[2] Yet to use a ramp the Original Builders would have needed to still raise stones to the height of the top of the Great Pyramid.

In contrast, the Original Builders demonstrated every aspect of the construction methods they used. The result of these demonstrations, preformed thousands of times, is the Great Pyramid itself. In modern times, the many proposals and few demonstrations for the Great Pyramid's construction or purpose are inconsistent with the direct physical evidence of this magnificent structure.

No other theory but the one offered in this book unifies the purpose of the Great Pyramid with its construction techniques and design. For the first time, an explanation of the purpose of the Great Pyramid will be congruent with the explanation of the construction of the Great Pyramid. The features of the interior of the Great Pyramid exquisitely interface with the unique construction procedure used to build this mighty structure. Its function is consistent with its form!

The construction procedure presented in this book is radically different from any commonly known by the general public. The process of building the Great Pyramid found in these pages is contradictory to and a departure from all other theories transcending any contextual constraints. Yet this understanding of the construction procedure is consistent with the direct physical evidence. Egyptologists, archeologists and other researchers who have misunderstood the function and purpose of the Great Pyramid have misunderstood the construction procedure as well.

Their best offer seems to be stories of some kind of monstrous ramp and multitudes of slaves. (Lately, instead of slaves, it is now asserted the workers were either paying taxes or volunteers proud to sweat for the Pharaoh.) Be it slave, taxpayer or volunteer, the workers are characterized in stories as being harnessed like animals to pull an almost endless number of massive stones up a gargantuan mega-ramp.

None of the critical aspects of the slave-ramp construction method have been demonstrated in the entire history of the "science" of Egyptology. The ramp-cultists chant their manta with religious devotion but that is all they offer. Has a 70 ton stone been pulled up a ramp to the height of 200 feet? No. Has a granite block been quarried and finished to the same size and precision as those in the Great Pyramid? No. Has a 16 ton casing stone been moved on and off a barge? No. Has a 2½ ton stone been dragged around a corner of a winding ramp? No. Has even one casing stone like those that remain at the Great Pyramid been created in the manner described by traditional Egyptologists? No! These construction activities and many other pivotal aspects of using primitive tools or monstrous ramps, although universally asserted by traditional Egyptologists, have never been demonstrated.

The ramp-slave theory attempt at explaining the Great Pyramid is nothing more than an unproven, undemonstrated piece of speculation. It is simply a story that has been told. The ramp-slave concept is the most labor intensive, brutish and beastly portrayal of ancient mankind ever concocted. This ghastly opinion of ancient mankind is diametrically opposed to the magnificence and wonder of ancient mankind's greatest achievement. It is in the belief system of many Egyptologists that the Great Pyramid was built using this hellish (and unproven) method of construction.[3]

Egyptologists currently emphasize that it was not slaves who built the Great Pyramid. Now we are told it was farmers "paying taxes" by working in the flood season who performed the majority of the stone moving. Yet, it matters little if the bulk of the workers were slaves or taxpayers. Be it slave or taxpayer, Egyptologists are unwilling or unable to provide demonstrations to support their stories as to what these workers did and how they did it.

Less main stream thoughts on the construction of the Great Pyramid have not made any progress in being accepted by the minds of the general public in the last 75 years. This stagnation of acceptance of the plethora of New Age theories being asserted is because they too are presented without any adequate demonstrations.

Offering ideas asserting the stones were moved by priests who concentrated on sacred crystals or played musical instruments is fine if the proponents of that theory can show how it is done. If sonic waves were used to move the stones, why can't that method be used to show us today? People are people, now as in the distant past. The immutable laws of physics are the same now as in the distant past. Whatever theory is embraced by inquisitive minds on this subject must be possible now as in the distant past.

This includes the notion of a big ramp. Although the conceptualization of a ramp being used to drag stones up to the needed height is currently the most accepted method, it too is offered without validation by adequate demonstration.

Fig. 6.1 The site where the Great Pyramid will be constructed had an outcropping of rock and was near a big river shown in the foreground. In terms of constructing a building, there is nothing magical or mystical about the rock or the river. Yet that mound of limestone was the location of a construction site which will be the most ambitious project and famous structure built by ancient mankind.

The entire science of Egyptology has never dragged a fifteen ton casing stone around a corner of a spiral ramp. Egyptology makes the assertion that the precision cut casing stones were made by hand using bronze chisels yet this "science" cannot even duplicate one surface of one casing stone in this manner. Although the notions of Egyptologists are currently the most accepted, they are no more proven than any other theory that has ever been suggested.

Along with the lack of verifying demonstrations there is yet another issue that has caused rejection of many theories about the Great Pyramid. This issue is that the purpose of the Great Pyramid must be consistent with the design of this building. The design must actually support the function of this structure.

This is one of the major reasons the tomb theory has been rejected by so many. A Pharaoh has only one body but the Great Pyramid has many rooms in which to put that single body. A Pharaoh has only one spirit but there are four "vents" for his soul to be transported to one of four different stars. The Great Pyramid was designed and built to have long open passages with doors on pivots as well as sliding portcullis stones. Yet how these features somehow keep a pharaoh's carcass and golden treasure safe is not adequately explained by the "science" of Egyptology.

In effect, Egyptologists admit the Great Pyramid does not fit the tomb theory because they have to contend that the structure went through several supposed design changes. They offer a bizarrely convoluted elucidation of the complex interior of the Great Pyramid to somehow give a tomb interpretation some validity. In grandiose style they rely on the ever present crutch of giving the design cultural, religious and societal interpretations of the highly intricate design of this structure.

Yet things are different in the real world. In the real world the design of a structure actually fits the function of the structure.

The design, construction procedures, location, materials, and purpose of any building are interrelated to each other. Even the varying degree of precision of each component has a justification. Each of the aspects of a building has a relationship to every other aspect of that same building. Purpose dictates location as in the Panama Canal. Available building materials dictate construction procedures as in the use of adobe in the southwestern United States. Purpose dictates design as in a factory building or aircraft carrier. Where, how and why a building is constructed, are all inexorably interwoven. But it is the purpose of the building which is the most important determiner of what a building is made of, how the available technology to build it is utilized and the structure's design.

This alternative view I offer you is a description of the Great Pyramid's construction which gives glory to the genius of the ancients. This theory describes some of the high technology possessed by the people of distant antiquity. This explanation ties together the function of the Great Pyramid with the form of the Great Pyramid. This theory is consistent with the direct evidence of the Great Pyramid. Also much of the most pivotal aspects of this theory have been thoroughly demonstrated.

What follows is a description of the activities involved concerning the Great Pyramid's construction. A broad overview is presented to help become familiar with the unusual procedures used in building this structure. More detailed explanations of various aspects of the construction process will be offered throughout the book.

Nothing of this theory defies any laws of physics or requires a leap of religious faith. This theory explains the assembly of the multitude of massive blocks at the building site and why the effort was expended for this accomplishment. The greatest hurdle to understanding this theory is to be able to transcend the misinformation all of us have been exposed to for our entire lives. If one can overcome that formidable obstacle one is well on their way to acquiring the knowledge to answer the Riddle of the Ages.

Preliminary Construction Work

The Great Pyramid now stands in silent testimony of its builder's ingenuity and determination. This site was once devoid of any structure. Some say the construction took place before the Biblical Flood.[4] Most say the Great Pyramid was built in the Fourth Dynasty.[5] There is enormous contention whether or not this area was a barren desert as it is today or a lush savanna during the time of the Great Pyramid's construction. Certainly, there is great debate as to the age of this structure.[6] The Great Pyramid is not the only structure on the Giza plateau whose date of construction is under question.

At one time, it was considered an indisputable fact that the three major pyramids, as well as the Sphinx on the Giza plateau were built within just a few generations of one another.[7] To many, this "fact" is now under review to say the least. There is even debate as to what culture built the Great Pyramid. The above issues although very interesting and important, would each require many books to adequately explore. I will let others debate the issues concerning who and when that surrounds the Great Pyramid.

On the Giza Plateau and surrounding area there are a number of rock outcroppings or escarpments. The head of the sphinx is carved from a natural escarpment.[8] The site chosen for the Great Pyramid contained a huge rock outcropping. [9] The exact size and shape of this outcropping before the Great Pyramid was constructed is, in our age, undeterminable. Although the location of the Great Pyramid needed to be in the Giza Plateau area, it is this huge outcropping, more than any other reason, which determined the exact location chosen by the Original Builders for this structure.

It has been estimated this outcropping to be possibly 32 feet higher than the base of the Great Pyramid. Yet this outcropping of living rock, now covered by the Great

Pyramid, could have been much larger.[10] Although little is now known of this outcropping of rock, its volume and height could have exceeded all contemporary speculations. It could have filled a large portion of the lower half of the Great Pyramid. This outcropping could have accounted for filling the area that would otherwise require upwards to 500,000 to 750,000 blocks or more. The purpose of this outcropping will be explained in later chapters. This outcropping of living rock still exists inside the Great Pyramid.

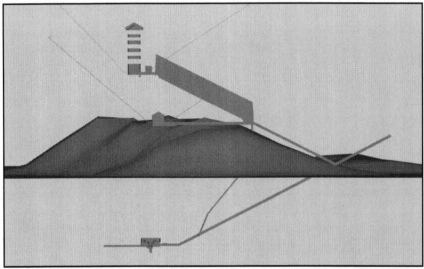

Fig. 6.2 The mound on which the Great Pyramid was built could have been much larger than traditionally thought. This image shows the possible relative height of the mound in relation to the future location of the internal chambers. The rock outcropping could have been even higher then depicted in this image. The exact original size, height and shape of this outcropping is now unknowable.

When people tell you how many blocks were used to create the Great Pyramid they are at the very least, deluding themselves. A relatively close estimate, even with a huge tolerance of twenty percent is undeterminable. Many who are inexcusably unaware of the existence of this large outcropping of indeterminable size and shape presuppose the Great Pyramid to have an almost flat foundation. Estimates range from anywhere between 2.5 to 4 million blocks were used to build the Great Pyramid. But without evidence as to the exact size of this outcropping the number of blocks or even the volume of material moved is unknown.

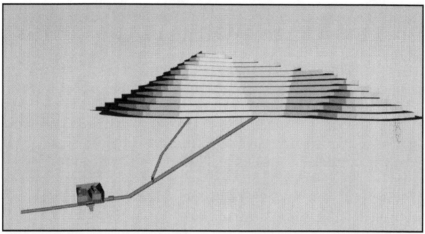

Fig. 6.3 The outcropping has been shaped into steps to receive the layers of rough cut interior stones. In addition, the subterranean cuttings have been created during these early stages of construction.

What is known is that the larger the outcropping the less material moved. One of the purposes of this mound was to reduce the amount of material required to build the Great Pyramid. The other purpose will be discussed in detail in a subsequent book. To look at it another way, because of this outcropping of living rock high in the inside of the structure, in a very real sense the Great Pyramid does NOT have a bottom side. Edward Kunkel, in his book Pharaoh's Pump, estimated the height of portions of this outcropping to be possibly well above the height of the Grotto.[11]

Sophisticated and exacting surveying operations were conducted to determine the level of the base perimeter of the Great Pyramid. The exact methods and tools available and used by the Original Builders to perform the surveying are up for conjecture. What is known by all is the surveying methods produced astounding accuracy. The degree of accuracy is chronicled in most other books on the Great Pyramid and therefore will not be repeated again here.

Logic and evidence dictates the base of the Great Pyramid was cut and leveled only up to the huge outcropping.[12] Then the outer portion of this outcropping was cut into steps to receive the 2 1/2 ton interior building blocks.

Only the perimeter of the base was made level and flat with exacting precision, not the entire bottom of the Great Pyramid.[13] This perimeter area will soon be covered with paving stones upon which the first level of casing stones will be placed. This high degree of precision is required to construct a very tall structure in the sophisticated manner used by the Original Builders. Included in the process of preparing the perimeter is the creation of the four corner sockets in the bedrock. As all books on the Great Pyramid attest, this perimeter was surveyed with utmost accuracy and leveled with astounding skill.[14] The purpose of this preparation is to place the paving stones which will provide an extremely accurate base for the first layer of casing stones.

While the necessary tasks are preformed on the bedrock surface of the construction site the subterranean cuttings are made. These excavations include the descending passage and the passage leading down through the escarpment to the descending passage. These two passages are designed to meet deep below the Great Pyramid construction site. Also the excavation of the Subterranean chamber located 100 feet below the bedrock is preformed. Great care is made in the construction of these cuttings. The subterranean cuttings were made with utmost precision and completed as planned. The basic functions of these cuttings are detailed later in this book.

Included in this excavation work was the preparation of the small chamber called the Grotto. Workers excavated down through the rock escarpment to prepare the Grotto. This small chamber is located at the lower portion of the escarpment and was constructed at about the same elevation as the base of the Great Pyramid. This small chamber was prepared to serve a functional purpose.

The Original Builders also constructed a substantial wall around the construction site. Little of this wall has survived from the time of its construction to our modern age. William Flinders Petrie as well as other early researchers often called these structures, "peribolus walls."[15] In this book the term enclosure wall will be used because it best describes the function of the wall. The enclosure wall, approximately 26 feet high, was built about 33 feet from where the first casing stones will be placed.[16] These walls formed an enclosure of about 14 acres encompassing the entire building site. The important purpose of this wall in the construction process will be explained later.

A causeway was constructed between the catch basin in the Nile up to the building site. This structure is essentially like an inclined plane. Herodotus saw this causeway and wrote of it.[17] Books written by Egyptologists tell us that this inclined roadway is to provide access to the Great Pyramid.[18] That is their interpretation. How this structure was really used during construction will be discussed later.

Another important preliminary task in the construction of the Great Pyramid was to build a series of water locks from the catch basin at the Nile River up to the building site. Although no known masonry of these water locks remains, there is evidence of their existence.[19] There is a stair-stepped cutting from the northwest of the Great Pyramid leading down to the catch basin by the Nile. That is evidence. Traditional Egyptologists interpret these cuttings as quarrying for building blocks used in the construction of the Great Pyramid.[20] Some of the stones removed from these cuttings were probably used for that purpose, but the cuttings themselves served a completely different purpose.

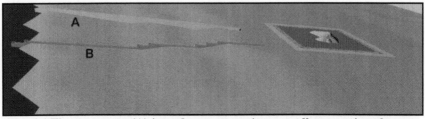

Fig. 6.4 The causeway (A) is under construction as well as a series of water locks (B) from the building site on the right to the Nile River on the left. The mound is faceted into steps to receive the successive levels of rough cut interior stones. The bedrock is prepared to exacting precision particularly where the perimeter of the Great Pyramid will be. The subterranean cuttings are completed.

Researcher Edward Kunkel never for a moment thought these cuttings were simply a quarrying operation.[21] He understood these cuttings were too regular and too precise to be merely a quarry site for building blocks.[22] The primary purpose of these cuttings is to accommodate water locks. These step-like cuttings have been filled in to make a modern asphalt roadway and parking lot.

These cuttings, like giant steps, start from the Nile River and proceed up to the building site. The exact size and number of treads and risers of these "steps" is unknown. Because no real importance to these cuttings was identified by traditional Egyptologists, exact information on these now covered cuttings is very scarce. Surely additional information about these cuttings is somewhere and the publication of this book may help to make it available.

If there was ever to be an excavation of the area between the Nile and the building site, *to look for* the vestiges of water locks the evidence would include parallel pairs of foundations for walls, and possibly the round holes used to house the bottom pivot for the lock gates. This type of direct physical evidence could and would be interpreted in many ways by different experts.

Egyptologists are of the opinion there are no mummies or golden treasure to take from graves in this region so I doubt if there will ever be excavations in this area. Water locks in this vicinity cannot be adequately confirmed to the satisfaction of all skeptics with overwhelming undisputable direct physical evidence. Yet the construction of water locks in this area cannot be ruled out based on the physical evidence either! There has been so much masonry removed from the Giza plateau since ancient times. Most of the structures known as funeral temples have been removed as well as almost all the casing stones.

Traditional Egyptologists scoff at the idea of mankind in antiquity having the brain power to understand and use the simple yet elegant concept of water locks. Yet it is traditional Egyptologists who cannot demonstrate how even one casing stone was quarried and moved. Herodotus did write that the canal which supplied water to the ancient Lake Moeris was dug by King Min.[23] Herodotus described this canal in such a way that his description indicates the use of water locks.[24] The ancient writer Strabo maintained this canal and lake were equipped with locks.[25]

The independent researcher and Hungarian surveyor István Sörös, author of the book, *Pyramids on Water, Floating Stones*, has determined there is a great deal of evidence supporting the opinion of water locks at one time existing between the Great Pyramid and the Nile.[26] His book details information of water locks and canals in this area and at other pyramids in the Nile valley. His research concentrates on the use of water to assemble ancient pyramids and temples. This book is a worthwhile read.

Unfortunately, the Giza plateau is now controlled by those who have not demonstrated a genuine open minded pursuit of truth, wherever it leads. Additional evidence of water locks now lies buried and is inaccessible. It is trapped by both the mounds of shifting sand and the unwillingness of the controllers of the Giza Plateau to allow this area to be examined and analyzed with the objective of finding direct evidence of water locks.

These water locks and associated masonry could have been removed right after construction was finished. This is because as soon as the Great Pyramid was completed the water locks were no longer needed. Or the precision cut stones of these water locks were removed in distant antiquity by vandals, scavengers, destroyers and thieves as was most of the precision stone work of the Giza plateau.

Egyptologists say entire temples were destroyed, being disassembled and carted off by scavengers.[27] More than likely the water locks in this area suffered that same fate. When and who performed the removal of the masonry, gates and other accoutrements of the water locks is unknown.

Yet many feel there is not enough conclusive evidence to convince them the geniuses who built the Great Pyramid could understand and use water locks. This certainly does not prove water locks were not used. Imagine if all of the casing stones of the Great Pyramid were removed a thousand years ago instead of 99 percent. There would be people today who would maintain there is no substantial evidence of their existence, "proving" there never were any!

In fact, a casing stone controversy raged on in the 18th and 19th centuries. Many scoffed at the idea the Great Pyramid was covered with a smooth layer of exquisitely cut stones. With sand and debris covering the few remaining casing stones there was ongoing debate as to the existence of the smooth casing stones that once covered the Great Pyramid. This debate ended in 1837 with Howard Vyse uncovering some of the few remaining casing stones still at the Great Pyramid.[28] The water lock debate will rage on until overwhelming, indisputable physical evidence is made available. Only then will the skeptics and scoffers catch up with the Original Builders.

For water locks to work, water has to be available above the highest water lock.[29] Without a supply of water at this height water locks cannot function. There is no water at the Giza Plateau necessary for the operation of water locks. This seems like a problem and it would be for modern mankind but we are dealing with the genius of the ancient mind. They were innovative problem solvers and used efficient methods to achieve their goals.

There are a number of strong possibilities as to how the Original Builders brought water to the building site. Herodotus mentioned numerous fascinating tidbits of water related information on and near the Giza Plateau. He wrote that there was an artificial conduit from the Nile River to the Great Pyramid.[30] He also wrote that the Pyramid attributed to Chephren (more commonly known as Khafre) did not have an artificial conduit from the Nile River as did the Great Pyramid.[31]

How an artificial conduit could bring water which was down at the Nile River up to the Great Pyramid was not made clear by Herodotus. Most have interpreted his writings to mean that some water entered deep below the Great Pyramid and into the Subterranean chamber to have the Pharaoh's sarcophagus somehow encircled by water. There is no subterranean conduit between the Nile River and the Great Pyramid to give credence to this interpretation to the writings of Herodotus.

Herodotus described what he saw. Peering up at the Great Pyramid he writes that the sepulchral chambers were like an island. He also writes of an artificial duct to deliver water the source of which he indicates is the Nile.[32] Most historians and Egyptologists have interpreted what he wrote to mean that only the sarcophagus was surrounded by water. It is more likely that these so-called "sepulchral chambers" in their *entirety* were as an island, which included the entire

Great Pyramid structure, surrounded by water. This square lake was impounded by the enclosure wall around the Great Pyramid.

Herodotus seems to be describing features that he was an eyewitness to. Wading through the translations and interpretations of what he wrote, and knowing he did not enter the structure, it seems that he saw the Great Pyramid surrounded by water.

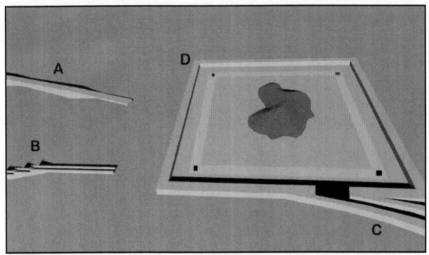

Fig. 6.5 All the preliminary preparations are nearing completion. The causeway (A) and water locks (B) will connect to the building site. The four sockets have been cut into the bedrock and the artificial duct (C) is completed. The enclosure wall (D) surrounds the construction site.

How interesting it is that Herodotus saw an entire temple which was surrounded by water brought by canal from the Nile. Another reference from Herodotus describes the temple of Budastis nearly surrounded by water from two separate canals from the Nile.[33]

Although the temple mentioned above was described as being surrounded by water, the question still remains how the water was brought to the building site of the Great Pyramid. Even though there is no deep subterranean passage from the Nile River to the subterranean cuttings below the Great Pyramid, Herodotus felt it was important to mention an artificial conduit used to bring water from the Nile. Even if there was a cutting deep below ground from the Nile River to the Subterranean chamber this would still not provide the needed water at the base of the Great Pyramid. There is no such underground passage to bring water to the passages under the Great Pyramid.

Herodotus never entered the Great Pyramid yet he wrote of an artificial conduit used to supply water giving the impression that at least part of this conduit was visible above ground.

There is scholarly debate as to the exact path and method water was conveyed to the Giza Plateau. It is speculated that the large and deep cutting in front of the Great Pyramid called the Charm possibly was part of the system used to convey water to the Great Pyramid. This substantial cutting could have had the purpose of being connected to the artificial duct from the ancient Lake Moeris. Further investigation of this important cutting is now impossible because this cutting in the bedrock has been sealed off.

Lake Moeris was much larger in antiquity then it is now. The elevation of this lake varied greatly in distant antiquity.[34] This lake was described as occupying almost the entire basin of the Fayum.[35] Herodotus again gives tantalizing clues to an artificial duct when he was at Lake Moeris. He wrote: "The natives of the place moreover said that this lake had an outlet underground to the Syrtis which is in Libya, turning towards the interior of the continent upon the Western side and running along by the mountain which is above Memphis."[36]

The exact location of the water system used to bring water to the Great Pyramid has been lost to the sands of time. This canal or artificial duct originated either from the ancient Lake Moeris or directly from the Nile River providing water to the Giza Plateau. Needless to say every aspect of this water delivery system is not known in modern times. Egyptology is no help because they do not research this type of information.

Herodotus was an eye witness of an artificial duct which connected the Great Pyramid to a water source.[37] Portions of the delivery means of this artificial duct could be by surface canal and also by underground passages or tunnels. The genius of the Original Builders met the goal of providing water to the building site of their most ambitious construction project. Although the exact nature and path of this artificial conduit remains hotly debated, this book concentrates on how the Original Builders put to use that water to build their greatest achievement.

In review: the preliminary work in building the Great Pyramid consisted of:
- Preparing the limestone bedrock at the building site
- Excavating the subterranean passages and chamber
- Construction of the enclosure wall
- Building a causeway from the Nile to the building site
- Building water locks from the Nile to the building site
- Building an artificial water duct to supply water to the building site

The description of each activity in this chapter has been merely a very simple overview of preparing the site. The purpose for each of these preliminary tasks will be examined in greater detail in following chapters. The preliminary activities required much work to be completed. With the above activities accomplished the building site of the Great Pyramid is prepared and ready for the actual construction process to start. The stage is set for the commencement of one of the largest and most significant construction projects attempted by the human species.

The preparation is complete. Water was available at the Giza plateau construction site brought from either the ancient Lake Moeris through an artificial duct or directly from the Nile River. An enclosure wall has been constructed around the building site. The bedrock supporting the perimeter of the Great Pyramid is leveled to exacting precision. The four corner sockets are cut into the bedrock. Water locks and a causeway have been built from the Nile River up to the building site. The subterranean cuttings were made and completed as planned.

So far no massive stones were moved. So much effort and activity yet there seems to be little progress towards the construction of a massive pyramid.

All this work was necessary before real progress could take place. Just as in the construction of modern high-rise buildings today, much time and effort are expended on the excavation and foundation of the structure. After that work is completed, the structure rises efficiently and quickly. This is true for the ancient high-rise building we call the Great Pyramid.

The site is ready and the preparations are complete for the actual assembly to begin.

---

[1] David Hatcher Childress, Technology of the Gods: The Incredible Sciences of the Ancients (Adventures Unlimited Press 2000) 261.
[2] Ibid.
[3] Kevin Jackson, Jonathan Stamp, Building the Great Pyramid (Firefly Books 2003) 65.
[4] Robert J. Boerman, Crop Circles, Gods and Their Secrets: History of Mankind, Written in the Grain (Adventures Unlimited Press 2004) 89-93.
[5] Roger Herz- Fischler, The Shape of the Great Pyramid (Wilfrid Laurier University Press 2000) 9.
[6] Ian Lawton, Chris Ogilvie-Herald Giza: The Truth: The People, Politics and History Behind the World's Most Famous Archaeological Site (Virgin 1999) 77.
[7] I. E. S. Edwards The Pyramids of Egypt (Viking Press 1972) 98.
[8] Ibid.

9 Zahi A. Hawass, Mountains of the Pharaohs: The Untold Story of the Pyramid Builders (Doubleday 2006) 61.
10 Edward J. Kunkel, Pharaoh's Pump (Warren, OH: Kunkel, 1977) 13.
11 Ibid.
12 Kevin Jackson, Jonathan Stamp, Building the Great Pyramid (Firefly Books2003) 27.
13 Mark Lehner, The Complete Pyramids (Thames and Hudson 1997) 109.
14 Ibid. 212-214.
15 William Matthew Flinders Petrie, The Pyramids and Temples of Gizeh (Field & Tuer 1883) 100.
16 Mark Lehner, The Complete Pyramids (Thames and Hudson 1997) 109
17 Herodotus, The Histories. (5th century B.C.) Translated by Aubrey de Selincourt (Penguin Classics, 1972) Book 2, Chapter 124.
18 Mark Lehner, The Complete Pyramids (Thames and Hudson 1997) 109.
19 Edward J. Kunkel, Pharaoh's Pump (Warren, OH: Kunkel, 1977) 15.
20 Kevin Jackson, Jonathan Stamp, Building the Great Pyramid (Firefly Books 2003) 50-51.
21 Edward J. Kunkel, Pharaoh's Pump (Warren, OH: Kunkel, 1977) 16.
22 Ibid.
23 Herodotus, The Histories (5th century B.C.) Translated by Aubrey de Selincourt (Penguin Classics, 1972) Book 2, Chapter 101.
24 Herodotus, The Histories (5th century B.C.) Translated by Aubrey de Selincourt (Penguin Classics, 1972) Book 2, Chapter 149.
25 Strabo, The Geography English translation: Horace Leonard Jones (Harvard Univ., Press 1944) Book 17 Chapter 1 Section 37.
26 István Sörös, Pyramids on Water, Floating Stones (Mandorfi 2001) 68-69.
27 Margaret A. Murray, Egyptian Temples (Courier Dover Publications 2002) 14.
28 William Kingsland, The Great Pyramid in Fact & Theory (Kessinger Publishing 1996) 21.
29 David McCullough, The Path Between the Seas: The Creation of the Panama Canal, 1870-1914 (Simon and Schuster 1977) 595.
30 Herodotus, The Histories (5th century B.C.) Translated by Henry Cary (G. Bell 1885) Book 2, Chapter 127 page 132.
31 Ibid.
32 Herodotus, The Histories (5th century B.C.) Translated by Henry Cary (G. Bell 1885) Book 2, Chapter 124 page 132.
33 Herodotus, The Histories (5th century B.C.) Translated by Henry Cary (G. Bell 1885) Book 2, Chapter 138 page 135.
34 David George Hogarth, Joseph Grafton Milne, Bernard Pyne Grenfell, Arthur Surridge Hunt, Fayûm Towns and Their Papyri (Offices of the Egypt exploration fund 1900) 15.

[35] Karl Baedeker (Firm), <u>Egypt: Handbook for Travellers</u> (C. Scribner's sons 1902) 175.

[36] Herodotus, <u>The Histories</u> (5th century B.C.) Translated by Henry Cary (G. Bell 1885) Book 2, Chapter 150 page 140.

[37] Ibid. Book 2, Chapter 127 page 132

Chapter 7
Construction Begins

The Great Pyramid's unusual building process involves techniques that are unique to the Great Pyramid. These unusual building processes (to us) were not universally used in all pyramid constructions but were used to build the Great Pyramid.

This information is new material to most and deals with a quantum leap of understanding away from what has been taught both in the past and in the present day. There are processes involved, when first explained, create more questions than answers but all aspects of this sophisticated construction process cannot be explained at once. This book is about what happened on the Giza plateau so long ago. What follows is a preliminary narrative providing an overview of *what* happened. Detailed explanations as to *how* each step was accomplished will be provided throughout the book.

When the preparation activities described in the previous chapter were completed, even though not a single stone of the Great Pyramid had been moved to the building site, more than likely work came to a complete stop. Although there are no newspaper accounts or video of the event, I imagine there was a pause for celebration. The leader of that great long ago high culture stood with his delegation on a stage or platform constructed for this ceremony so he could be seen by the excited crowd assembled on this ancient historic day. There was no pyramid on the Giza plateau but all knew that would soon change. Speeches by dignitaries were made and high priests preformed the appropriate rituals and prayers.

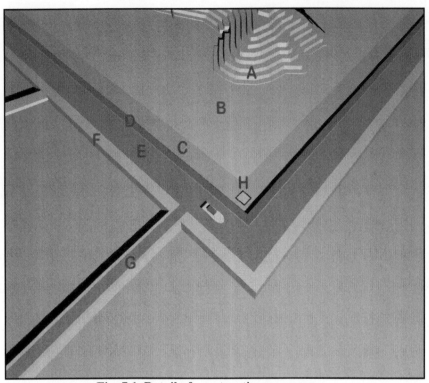

Fig. 7.1 Detail of construction processes
A. Central mound has been cut into steps. The bedrock has been leveled to receive the first layer of rough cut interior stones.
B. Bedrock
C. This area is prepared to receive the paving stones which will support the first layer of casing stones. In each corner there is a socket cut into the bedrock.
D. A small temporary wall which impounds the canal around the building site has been built. This wall keeps the area prepared to receive the paving stones dry.
E. The canal impounded by the enclosure wall allowing stones on barges to be brought up the water locks to the building site.
F. The enclosure wall impounds the canal around the building site.
G. The canal and water locks leading up from the Nile River are used to bring stones on barges to the building site.
H. The socket cut into the bedrock will receive the corner paving stone.

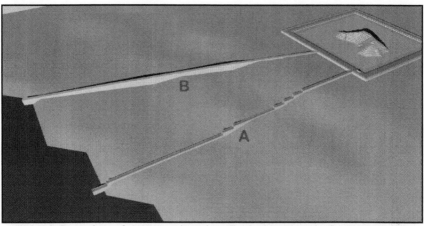

Fig. 7.2 Overview of construction site. Both the water locks (A) and the causeway (B) connect the building site with the Nile River. Water has been introduced into the building site from the artificial duct. This created a "moat" around the building site which is impounded by the enclosure wall and the little wall. Water is also available to supply the water locks.

All was ready! The building site was supplied with water from a number of possible sources. One of these possibilities was water brought to the building site from the ancient Lake Moeris incorporating the cutting known as the charm in front of the Great Pyramid. Another possibility was to bring water to the building site directly from the Nile River through the artificial duct described by Herodotus.[1] The exact method that would be accomplished is under debate.

Most books dealing with the subject of the ancient Lake Moeris indicate the elevation of this lake has varied greatly throughout ancient times. These same books indicate that the elevation of the ancient Lake Moeris was generally below the elevation of the base of the Great Pyramid. Certainly the base of the Great Pyramid is well above the elevation of the Nile River. Therefore, supplying water to the base of the Great Pyramid required water to be moved up to the building site.

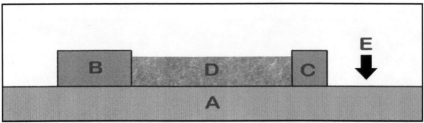

Fig. 7.3 Cross section of the construction process.
A. Bedrock
B. Enclosure wall
C. Small temporary wall
D. Canal or moat which surrounds the building site
E. Location where the paving stones will be placed to support the first layer of casing stones.

The exact location of the artificial duct and the exact method of supplying water to the base of the Great Pyramid is under ongoing research. The encroachment of the city of Cairo has covered up a treasure trove of archeological evidence of the activities conducted by the Original Builders. This evidence will probably never become available for modern independent researchers to analyze.

Yet much has been discovered in analyzing what evidence and information is currently available. Since this book focuses on the assembly process and original purpose of the Great Pyramid, an exhaustive disclosure of the research conducted about how the water was delivered to the construction site will not be included. That information will be addressed in depth in a subsequent book.

The water supplied to the building site formed a square canal which surrounded the building site. The canal was impounded by the enclosure wall and the small temporary wall. This small temporary wall was built between the enclosure wall and where the perimeter paving stones will be placed. There is a row of holes in the bedrock in just this area.[2] The purpose of these holes could have been to anchor the small temporary wall to the bedrock.

Fig. 7.4 Barge with paving stone entering the series of water locks from the Nile River. This barge with stone will travel up the water locks then enter the canal or moat impounded by the enclosure wall. Then the stone and barge will be moved to a location right next to where the paving stone will be placed! How the paving stone is moved from the barge, over the small wall and to its final resting place is detailed later.

The canal surrounding the building site contained enough water to allow a barge to float yet the paving stones were set and cemented onto dry bedrock. This was necessary to allow the bonding agent to cure. The Original Builders created a square canal which encircled the entire building site yet the center of the building site was still dry. The central dry building site was surrounded by water like an island.

The water from the pool had entered and filled the series of water locks through the valves and gates manned by loyal skilled workers. Barges loaded with large paving stones already cut to the required size and shape floated on barges in the catch basin down at the Nile.

The leader of this proud, intelligent and resourceful civilization, who gave his commitment to this great project, stepped forward as the crowd hushed. All eyes were on their wise and benevolent leader dressed in his most regal garments. After a long dramatic pause the mighty and revered king gave the signal to the designer of this soon to be Great Pyramid. The designer motioned to the chief engineer who instantly commanded his capable supervisor to start. The supervisor signaled to his most experienced foreman who gave the command to the trusted workers to begin the largest construction project ever attempted by our species at that time.

The first barge loaded with a precision cut paving stone was moved from the catch basin of the Nile into the bottom water lock. The gate was closed behind it and water came in through a valve from the immediate lock above. The crowd was silent as the barge with precision crafted paving stone rose in the water lock. Once this lock was full, the gate which links the first water lock to the next was opened by that water lock's gate tender. With effortless ease, the barge was moved to the next water lock. The lock gate was closed and the second lock was filled with water from the adjacent water lock above it and the stone laden barge was raised to the top of the second lock.

The king watched in silence, understanding the implications of this event to his society. The crowd watched in silence, understanding the implications to their own lives. The workers too understood their toil is not as beasts of burden because the work is performed by the devices they are operating. Workers and technicians with their families watched knowing the result of their skills, training and efforts will be a soon to be prosperity for themselves and their loved ones.

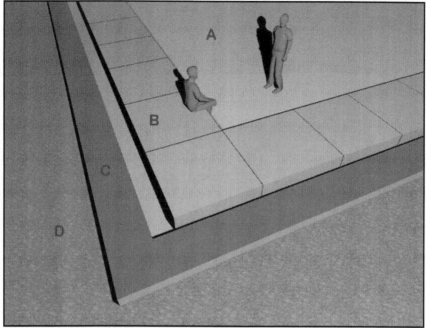

Fig. 7.5 Construction progress to the point where the paving stones which support the first layer of casing stones are set in place. The socket in the bedrock is below the corner paving stone.

A. Bedrock
B. Paving stones which will support the first layer of casing stones
C. Small temporary wall
D. Moat or canal surrounding the construction site

All watched the fascinating process as the first barge with paving stone is levitated silently and effortlessly by the principle of buoyancy from the surface of the Nile to the shimmering square canal high up on the Giza plateau. As this barge with precious cargo is raised in the last lock, then moved into the sparkling pool high on the Giza plateau the crowd remained silent no longer. Screams of joy, cheers and applause were heard throughout the valley they call home. The people were exuberant for the success of their work so far, and had confidence in completing the work to come.

After the ceremony was completed the construction continued at a steady pace. It is unknown in this day (but well known in the time of the Great Pyramid's construction) which paving stone was placed first. This information would be of great significance and "profound" to some researchers fascinated by esoteric information but not in this description of the construction process. More than likely the first paving stone was a corner paving stone.

The corner paving stones each had a protrusion on the underside which fit into the four corner sockets cut into the bedrock. The structural purpose of this socket and protrusion arrangement is not for added strength. The sockets are very shallow and would not serve to provide structural integrity. The sockets in the bedrock were for alignment purposes and assisted in placing the corner paving stones exactly as required. Some assert the bonding agent between stones was stronger than the stone itself, so a socket would not have added additional strength.[3]

At this early stage of construction the paving stones being set in place were the ones which will soon support the casing stones. These first paving stones, when placed, will surround the construction site like a square "road." But this was not a road; it was the exquisitely precise foundation for the first layer of casing stones.

The purpose of the paving stones was to create a very exact surface for the first layer of casing stones. The paving stones served as an interface between the bedrock and the casing stones. The bedrock was prepared with great precision to receive the paving stones. The paving stones provided a surface of even greater precision which was a foundation for the casing stones. This extreme precision was necessary and justified. The paving stones were the foundation for a structure to be built approximately 45 stories high.

The paving stones were cemented in place, with a bonding agent, and formed the foundation for the most sophisticated public works project ever completed by ancient mankind. Although the words cement and bonding agent are used to describe the material applied between the casing stones and other precision stonework in the Great Pyramid, the exact composition of this ultra-strong bonding material is unknown. The material between the joints of the casing stones is certainly not plaster. Plaster is relatively weak but the bonding agent used in the Great Pyramid is legendary for its extreme strength![4]

Flinders Petrie was astonished about the cement used between the casing stones and how it was applied between the 16 ton behemoths. He wrote:

"How, in the casing of the Great Pyramid, they could fill with cement a vertical joint 5 x 7 feet in area, and only averaging 1/50 inch thick is a mystery; more especially as the joint could not be thinned by rubbing, owing to its being a vertical joint, and the block weighing about 16 tons. Yet this was the usual work over 13 acres of surface, with tens of thousands of casing stones, none the less than a ton in weight."[5]

This mystery of the Great Pyramid which confounded Petrie over a hundred years ago has never been adequately addressed by Egyptology. Petrie, as the father of Egyptology, was acutely aware of this technological feat. Yet how the working people who built the Great Pyramid accomplished this task was a mystery. This mystery is addressed later in this book.

At this stage of construction only the paving stones which will support the first layer of casings stones were set in place. The next step was to place the first layer of casing stones on these paving stones.

It is assumed the first of the casing stones set in place was a corner stone. In our day and age it is not known if the top of the corner paving stones had a socket to receive a protrusion from the corner casing stone. If the corner paving stone did have a socket, there would have been a corresponding protrusion on the bottom of the corner casing stone. However, none of these corner casing or paving stones has survived from antiquity. We only have evidence of sockets cut into the bedrock to receive the corner paving stones. There is no direct evidence to indicate whether any other sockets or protrusions were or were not used in the four corner casing stones. I feel if it were the case it would be for alignment purposes and not for strength.

The perimeter paving stones are now set in place. These stones have been set on dry bedrock prepared for them. They have been cemented in place and the extremely strong bonding agent has cured. The purpose of these paving stones is to provide an extremely precise foundation for the first layer of casing stones. Now that this foundation is in place the next step of the construction process will begin.

The first precision cut corner casing stone rests on a barge in the catch basin at the Nile River. This corner casing stone on a barge makes its effortless journey up through the water locks into the enclosure pond. Still on the barge, this huge yet flawlessly faceted stone is moved right next to its final resting place. The movement of this massive stone to the building site was easy, fast and efficient. It was then moved from the barge and cemented on the precision cut paving stones. How this massive sixteen ton payload was moved from the barge to its final resting place is described in detail later. After so much work, time and effort the first casing stone has been quarried, barged to the catch basin in the Nile, moved up the water locks into the enclosure pond and set in its chosen destination.

The first stone of the Great Pyramid is now in its final resting place! That is, until centuries later, when it was stolen by scavengers and robbers! After so much planning, preparation and expense this is the moment the Great Pyramid starts the process of taking shape. This moment is the genesis of the actual realization of the greatest feat of ancient mankind.

At this early stage of construction, there exists on the Giza plateau a large square canal of water impounded by the enclosure wall surrounding the building site and the small temporary wall. This canal is kept full by a source of water provided by the Original Builders. This water source was through the artificial duct which Herodotus saw and wrote about. The particulars of this source water have no bearing on the assembly process. The perimeter of paving stones, which will support the first layer of casing stones, is set in place. Also, one corner casing stone has been set in place and the requisite ceremonies have been performed.

In the center of the building site, the huge outcropping of limestone protrudes up, towering over the workers. It stands like a misshapen, distorted, surrealistic obelisk guarding and overseeing the process going on around it. Although merely a huge inanimate protrusion of rock, how wonderful it would be if it could only talk and tell us the story of what happened so long ago. What an interesting description of the Great Pyramid's construction that would be. This sentinel of towering rock witnessed the process of its own entombment.

As in all public works projects of great magnitude, efficiency is crucial. Efficiency in labor, materials, transportation and time are all of tremendous importance. All these areas of efficiency are interrelated and rely on one another. This sentinel of "living rock" in the midst of construction witnessed the busy efficient systematic operation of this monument's building process. Do not let Egyptologists tell you that the Great Pyramid was built by squandering time or by using inefficient construction methods.

The Original Builder's exceptional efficiency of manpower is manifest in stone. The direct physical evidence is a testimony to the Original Builder's productivity. Yet it took much more than efficiency to build the Great Pyramid. Efficiency in manpower, in and of itself, is not responsible for the creation of the Great Pyramid. Egyptologists are efficient but they cannot demonstrate or recreate virtually all the specific tasks that the Original Builders accomplished while building the Great Pyramid. This is because Egyptologists assessments of how these tasks were accomplished are wrong. If "efficient" Egyptologists were responsible for the construction of the Great Pyramid, it would have never been started let alone finished.

Fig. 7.6 The first corner casing stone has been set in place on top of the paving stones. The water in the moat is held back by the small wall.

Virtually nothing is known about the barges used to move the casing stones. There are no surviving barges or remains of barges used in building the Great Pyramid. There are no drawings of any barge or historical reference to the design of the barges used in moving the monolithic stones of the Great Pyramid. Even without any surviving direct physical evidence of barges, it is acknowledged the ancients used barges to move stones.[6] The use of barges in conjunction with water locks to move heavy payloads is an extremely efficient system. This is in contrast to the widely accepted assumption of virtually unlimited brute manpower squandered by a vacillating, design changing, man-god Pharaoh.

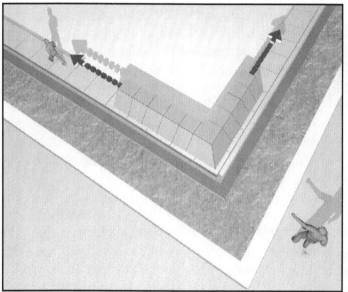

Fig. 7.7 Casing stone placement begins with the four corner casing stones. Then the two casing stones adjacent to each of the corner casing stones are set in place. The casing stones placement starts from each of the four corner casing stones and progresses towards the middle of each side. This allows workers to be engaged in the process of placing eight casing stones at the same time.

At this stage of construction the only paving stones set in place are the ones on which the first layer of casing stones will be placed. Also one corner casing stone has been set in place. On barges, the three remaining corner casing stones were quickly brought up the series of water locks and into the square canal and then set in place.

Each corner casing stone may or may not have a protrusion on its bottom side which would have been placed into the possible corresponding socket set in the paving stones. There is no evidence to support or refute any additional use of sockets. These four corner stones were cemented in place with an extremely strong bonding agent. The small temporary wall kept water in the moat from interfering with the curing of the bonding agent.

After all corner casing stones were set in place the casing stones which abut the corner casing stones are set in place. Teams assembled the first layer of casing stones in eight areas of operation. From each corner casing stone, two crews worked, moving casing stones from barges to the prepared paving stones. These eight crews moved precision cut casing stones from the barges to their final resting place. The specialized procedures used to move these stones off the barges and to cement these magnificent stones in place will be detailed later.

The casing stones were placed successively from the corners to the midpoint of each side. These stones were cemented on the exquisitely finished surface of the paving stones. The casing stones were cemented using an extremely strong bonding agent applied to the bottom of the paving stones and to the vertical sides of the adjacent casing stones. Finally, the four casing stones which are located in the midpoint of each side are set and cemented into place creating a wall of casing stones around the large outcropping of stone.

These massive casing stones were placed so exactly their faces are almost perfectly aligned. They were also placed within 1/50th of an inch to the adjoining casing stone and these stones show no handling scars. I would like to see Egyptologists demonstrate that same task the way they say it was done. The reality is that Egyptologists are unable to give credence to their stories with valid demonstrations.

Fig. 7.8 Detail of the water lock system incorporated into the casing stones. The canal in the foreground leads up from the Nile allowing barges to traverse those water locks to reach the building site. The water lock shown is built into the first layer of casing stones. The water lock gates are "doors on pivots" made of short wooden planks. This water lock will allow stones on barges to travel from the canal surrounding the building site up to the pond impounded by the first layer of casing stones. Filling that pond is the next step in the construction process.

The first layer of casing stones are cut with extreme precision and cemented in place with an extremely strong bonding agent. The reason the Original Builders used extreme precision and bonded the casing stones together was to create a watertight wall. The precisely cut and cemented together casing stones will be used to impound a pond. This pond, when filled, will be at a higher level than the square canal around the building site.

The first layer of casing stones is almost complete. To finish the first layer of casing stones a water lock was built in the wall of casing stones. This water lock was an integral part of the wall of casing stones and was created to receive barges from the enclosure pond and raise these barges to the level of the pond impounded by the first layer of casing stones.

After the first layer of casing stones with water lock were completed the temporary wall was not needed. It served its purpose and allowed the paving stones to be set in place and cemented to dry bedrock. The temporary wall was removed at this stage of construction. This allowed the square canal to be impounded by the first layer of casing stones instead of the small temporary wall.

Even at this early stage of construction the separation of labor was obvious. Barge handlers, valve tenders, water lock operators and stone setting teams all performed their assigned tasks. Each group worked under watchful supervision. The movement of stones was systematic, fast and efficient. Barges with stones filled the flight of water locks from the catch basin in the Nile up to the building site. The lifting medium of water was efficiently used over and over and over again in each successive lock. The same water used to raise stones in the uppermost lock leading up to the building site was used again to raise the barges in each successive lock below it.

The system worked well so far. What was the next step? Water, in the Nile River, provided the massive lifting force to move these stones on barges from the quarries to the catch basin. Again water, channeled through the artificial duct observed by Herodotus, from either the large ancient Lake Moeris or directly from the Nile itself using a system still under research, supplied the voracious appetite of the series of water locks moving stone laden barges up into the canal surrounding the building site. But the building process requires barges to be moved to even greater heights.

The next step in this building process is for water to fill the area impounded by the first level of casing stones. When this pond, impounded by the casing stones is filled, barges with interior stones can then be moved up through the water lock in the wall created by the first layer of casing stones. Passing through this water lock, the interior stones on barges will be used to fill the interior of the first layer of the Great Pyramid.

Without water higher than the highest lock the system can no longer function. There is no water on the Giza Plateau at this height to supply a water lock higher than the water brought into the base of the building site and continue the process. For this system to continue to work, a tremendous volume of water must be moved to a level higher than the water in the pond impounded by the enclosure wall. Water must be somehow moved up into the area impounded by the first level of casing stones creating a new higher pond. This higher pond will be the source of water for the water lock built into the first layer of casing stones.

At this stage of construction a water pump was needed. The Original Builders used a huge water pump to raise water up from the level of the pond created by the enclosure wall at the base of the building, up into the pond impounded by the first level of casing stones. This water pump kept the pond, impounded by the first level of casing stones, filled with water. This water pump supplied water to the water lock which communicated between the canal surrounding the building site and the pond above it. This would allow the easy movement of interior stones on barges to be moved into the pond created by the first level of casing stones.

This pump is not an artifact lost to the sands of time, existing only in the shadow realm of mythology. This water pump is not a hopeful dream to support an eccentric theory. This water pump is not a device to make the Great Pyramid vibrate. This water pump is not a contextual conceptualization without physical evidence to support its existence. There is much evidence remaining of this gargantuan ancient water pump. It is still with us today. The only thing lost is the realization of its existence and the understanding of its operation.

This water pump is an example of a lost technology of the Great Pyramid.

This water pump provided the lifting force to move millions of tons of rock. This water pump is the embodiment of an ancient civilization's sophisticated knowledge of their physical world expressed through high technology. This ancient lost high technology is neither understood nor utilized in our age. This water pump embodies technology capable of making *our* lives better, freer, cleaner, safer and more prosperous.

This massive water pump, radically different from any known today, which is now part of a tourist attraction, is none other than the Subterranean chamber and passages cut into the solid rock!

---

1 Herodotus, The Histories. (5th century B.C.) Translated by Henry Cary (G. Bell 1885) Book 2, Chapter 127 page 132.
2 Mark Lehner, The Complete Pyramids (Thames and Hudson 1997) 218.
3 Tom Valentine, The Great Pyramid: Man's Monument to Man (Pinnacle Books 1976) 13.
4 John Edgar, Great Pyramid Passages And Chambers Vol. 1 (Kessinger Publishing 2006) 53.
5 William Matthew Flinders Petrie, The Pyramids and Temples of Gizeh (Field & Tuer 1883) 171.
6 William Stevenson Smith, The Art and Architecture of Ancient Egypt (Yale University Press 1999) 54.

Chapter 8
Completing the First Three Levels

We have all been repeatedly exposed and indoctrinated with the Egyptologist's best guess fairy-tale of some sort of massive ramp populated with thousands of human beasts of burden dragging stones. We have all watched numerous documentaries on television showing Egyptologists overseeing the movement of relatively diminutive stones in an attempt to show us how the Great Pyramid was built. We are all familiar with the often told stories of the volunteers, who are taxpaying worker-slaves marching up a mega-ramp to construct a bizarrely designed, monstrous, manmade gigantic anthill to put a dead guy in.

This book is a departure from all of those notions. Using the same direct physical evidence everyone else has it offers a completely different description of the construction process. It was not a mega-ramp which was used to lift the stones to the needed height. In constructing the Great Pyramid there was no ramp used. Rather, it was water, with the power to lift battleships which was used to raise the stones to the needed height. The principle of buoyancy was used by the Original Builders to assemble the Great Pyramid. This water was made available by the subterranean cuttings in the bedrock which were designed and completed to be a water pump. This pump was used during the construction of the Great Pyramid and is referred to as the construction pump.

This construction pump will not be described in great detail now but for the moment just a few basic aspects will be discussed. The water source for the construction pump is the water impounded by the canal around the Great Pyramid. Water was already at the building site so there was no need to somehow draw water directly up from the Nile for the construction pump. The input of the construction pump is the upper end of the descending passage.

During this early stage of construction there was a temporary airtight conduit between the upper end of the descending passage and the water impounded by the enclosure wall. This conduit served as a temporary water source for the construction pump. The output for the water pump was the passage leading up through the Grotto and out the escarpment in the center of the building site.

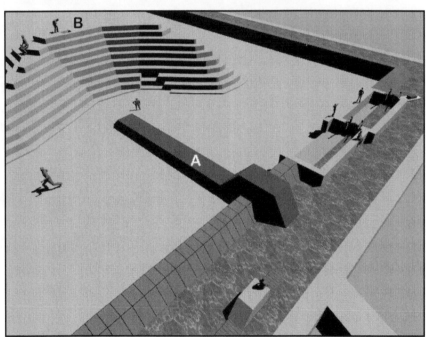

Fig. 8.1 Water is supplied to the construction pump from the canal which surrounds the construction site. The temporary watertight duct (A) allows water to move over the wall of casing stones and into the upper end of the descending passage. Water exits the construction pump out of the passage (B) cut into the top of the central mound of rock.

The fascinating construction process is consistent with the direct physical evidence and is straightforward yet sophisticated and elegant. This process is the epitome of efficiency in both time and labor! It is this description of the assembly process which acknowledges the true genius of the Original Builders and verifies their advanced knowledge of physics which they have demonstrated by their application of high technology.

What follows is a description of what actually happened during construction of the Great Pyramid so long ago on the Giza plateau.

We left the end of the last chapter at the stage in which the first level of casing stones were set in place, creating a square watertight wall. On the north side of this wall is a water lock which will allow stone laden barges to move from the canal around the building site into the pond impounded by the first level of casing stones. The canal around the building site has water in it but there is no water available at the needed height to fill the area impounded by the first level of casing stones.

Finally the time is ready to use the construction pump! Planned from the beginning, the Original Builders designed and built this functional and unique water pump to be operated at this stage of construction. The construction pump is started and the water shoots out of the central mound as a pulsating geyser. Like a massive heart beating, the construction pump supplies the needed fluid to bring the Great Pyramid into existence. The construction pump fills the void created by the first level of casing stones.

Now at the building site there is a glistening thirteen acre square pond whose height nears the top of the first level of casing stones. This new pond is higher than the water of the enclosure pond, yet these two ponds are connected by a water lock. Even though this newly created pond is filled, the construction pump does not cease. There is much more water needed. The heartbeat of the construction pump continues.

With the introduction of water into this pond, stones on barges easily move up from the enclosure pond into the higher newly formed pond. Stones are brought from the catch basin in the Nile, up to the building site and finally into the enclosure pond through a series of water locks. From the enclosure pond, the stones on barges continue up into the higher pond impounded by the first level of casing stones. The continuous operation of the construction pump keeps this pond full as well as supplying water for the water locks.

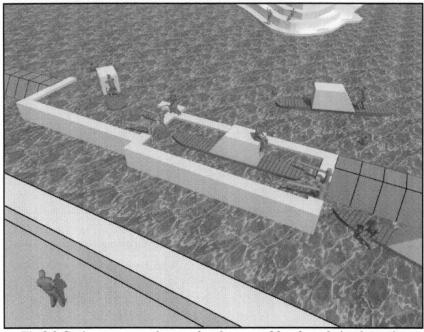

Fig 8.2 Casing stones on barges for the second level are being brought through the water lock into the pond impounded by the first layer of casing stones. The barge is raised in the water lock. Then the barge travels from the filled water lock into the construction pond impounded by the first layer of casing stones. This pond is waist deep.

The process continues efficiently and quickly. Stone after stone on barges are brought up to this newly formed pond. The work of lifting the stones is accomplished by use of the principle of buoyancy and the water locks. The workers simply operated the locks and valves and effortlessly moved the stones on barges up into the pond impounded by the first level of casing stones.

As odd as it may seem at first glance, the next important step is to set in place the second level of casing stones before the first level of interior stones are set in place. This is necessary because if the first level of interior stones were set in place, the upper pond would be filled with stone. This would prevent barges from entering this upper pond to place the second level of casing stones. Therefore the next stage of construction is to place the second level of casing stones onto the first level of casing stones.

The tops of the first level of casing stones are prepared with the bonding agent before the second level is set in place. This bonding process occurs above the level of the pond and the water does not interfere with the bonding agent as it cures. The vertical joints between the casing stones are bonded together as well.

Only after the second level of casing stones are set in place and bonded together are the interior stones for the first level brought onto this pond. The interior stones are brought on barges into this upper pond, easily moved to their final destination, and then set in place. The interior stones are placed first near the south side of the pond farthest away from the water lock. Interior stones continue to be placed systematically from the south to the north end of this pond. The last interior stones for this level are placed near the water lock on the north side of the pond.

When these last interior stones for this level are placed it signifies that a very momentous event has occurred. This event, eyewitnessesed by the people who were responsible for it, is not generally understood by modern experts. Filling this pond with stones signified the completion of the first level of the Great Pyramid of Giza!

With the constant supply of water from the construction pump and the precision cut casing stones bonded together to make a watertight wall, a pond, with an area almost the size of the base of the Great Pyramid, was formed on the Giza Plateau. Water and water locks did the lifting work of moving stones on barges to this pond. The filling of the pond with interior stones meant the first level of the greatest technological achievement of ancient mankind was completed.

Fig. 8.3 Egyptologists contend a pyramid shaped structure like that on the left was built and then covered by a layer of casing stones. That is wrong. The Great Pyramid was built level by level as depicted on the right.

With the second level of casing stones set in place a second water lock was built in the north face in the second level of casing stones.   These two water locks are configured so that the upper end of the first water lock is connected to the lower end of the second water lock. When water locks are connected in series they are called a flight of water locks just as stairs configured in a similar manner are called a flight of stairs.[1] The construction process is ready to continue.

With the assembly procedure described in these pages being so contrary to the current unproven orthodox ramp paradigm, it takes a little time to describe every aspect of the unusual construction process used to build the Great

Pyramid. It also takes time and reflection by people interested in this research to contemplate how this construction process is consistent with the direct physical evidence.

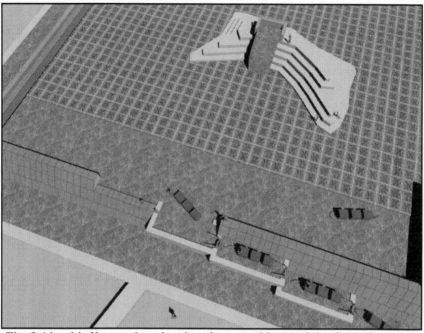

Fig. 8.4 is a bird's eye view showing the second layer of the Great Pyramid nearing completion. At the top of the image, water is exiting the construction pump. The water migrates through the cracks in the rough cut interior stones and keeps the construction pond full and supplies water for the water locks. The second water lock allows stones on barges to enter the construction pond. The pond is being filled in with the second layer of rough cut interior stones. The third layer of casing stones has been set in place and the bonding agent between these stones is curing. The construction pond is only waist deep.

To help make the explanation of the construction process much easier a few terms need to be clarified. Also, a systematic arrangement of nomenclature is needed to designate each successive water lock and pond making the description much clearer.

Generally in the books and literature written describing the Great Pyramid the word *course* is used to describe each level of the Great Pyramid. The word course is generally used to describe levels of structures made of bricks.[2] For example, a brick wall may be ten courses high. However, I have chosen to use the terms *level* instead of course in describing the horizontal levels of the Great Pyramid for several important reasons.

One reason is that the Great Pyramid was built in a much different way than brick structures are built. Even though the components are very large they are not simply big "bricks." So, to differentiate between ideas of manually moving stones and the system of using water to move stones the term level will be used.

The other reason is unlike all other proposed methods of stone moving, water is a significant part of the construction process. Therefore, each successive "course" of casing stones and interior stones are described using the word level. Common construction levels use a clear tube of water with a bubble to determine level. "Water seeks its own level" is another saying which associates the words water and level. Water locks are also built in a series of levels not courses.

Most, but not all, Egyptologists assert the Great Pyramid's casing stones were added after the rough cut interior stones were assembled![3] In contrast, this construction process describes each successive level being completed *including casing stones* before the next successive level is completed. The Great Pyramid was finished level by level. So level is the term I have chosen to describe each successive "course" of stones.

In this description, each level of casing stones will have a number designation. The first level of casing stones is level one. The casing stones that were set on top of the first level of casing stones is level two. This systematic numbering system continues up the Great Pyramid. As you have probably assumed each successive level of casing stones will impound its own pond. Each pond is named after the level of casing stones which impounds it. The first level of casing stones impound pond one. The second level of casing stones impound pond two and so on.

Just as the ponds are numbered corresponding to the level of casing stones, the water locks are numbered by the level of casing stones they are built into. The first level of casing stones contains water lock one built into this level. The second level of casing stones has water lock two and so on.

The wall around the building site is called the enclosure wall. It impounds the canal which surrounds the building site. The construction activity is focused on the construction pond. This pond is not one specific pond at a specific level, but it rises as each level is completed. The construction pond is the ever rising uppermost pond, moving up as construction progresses.

The purpose of this numbering system for casing stones, water locks and construction ponds is simply to help convey the basic concept of the construction process. After the basic construction process is described, additional details concerning the water locks and this construction procedure will be provided in subsequent chapters.

Water has already been used to place the casing stones of level one. Water lock one was used to bring the casing stones for level two from the enclosure pond into pond one. After the casing stones for level two were set in place the interior stones of level one were set in place, and level one of the Great Pyramid is complete.

The stage is set for the assembly process to proceed to the next step. Have you guessed what the next step is? No, it is not filling pond two with water.

Before pond two is filled with water two specific tasks must be completed. First, there must be a water lock constructed in the north face. This water lock receives stones on barges from the lock below it and brings these barges up to the level of pond two.

The second task which is completed is the extension of the airtight artificial duct bringing water from the enclosure pond to the upper end of the descending passage. This must be extended over the ever increasing wall of casing stones. This artificial duct is essential in carrying water to the input of the construction pump and must be moved higher over the wall created by the second level of casing stones. This process of raising the artificial duct for each level is only required for the first few levels of casing stones. When the artificial duct meets the descending passage this process does not need to be carried out any more. The reason for this procedure will be explained later.

It is now time for the next step in the construction process. I am sure you know what it is. But those with a hellish and brutish view of the nature of ancient mankind and a blunted understanding of the brilliance and genius demonstrated by the achievements of the Original Builders would have a different idea. They would say, "Just use a massive bucket brigade to bring the water to the needed height." They would probably suggest building a huge ramp covered with countless slaves (or volunteers or taxpayers) carrying buckets in hand marching back and forth like mindless ants bringing water to fill pond two and supply the water locks. There would be no need to worry about the loss of water in the buckets by constant spillage or even evaporation caused by the hot blazing sun. That loss of water would be replaced by the sweat pouring off the "volunteers." This perspiration would keep the buckets full. Others would probably suggest using huge containers filled with tons of water pulled up massive ramps by multitudes of luckless humans reduced to the role of beasts of burden pulling their guts out.

There are people who would advocate rounding up 100,000 workers and letting them have at it so they can, in some way, pay a tax. If somehow Edward Kunkel (God rest his soul) could respond to such insanity he would stop the madness and yell, "Hey, don't conceptualize a mega-ramp, just turn the construction pump on instead!!"

No, there was no bucket brigade. There was no ramp to transport water. There was no ramp used or needed to build the Great Pyramid! Even the "priest" whom Herodotus talked to in the 5th Century B.C. knew that. The next step was easy and simple. The next step was to fill pond two with water using the construction pump. Water was allowed to enter the upper end of the descending passage through the temporary watertight duct from the enclosure pond to the upper end of the descending passage. Water exited the construction pump through the passage in the rock escarpment filling pond two. This kept pond two full as well as supplying water to the flight of water locks consisting of water lock one and water lock two.

At this stage of the construction process there is a strikingly beautiful square canal in the Plateau called Giza on the west bank of the mighty Nile River. This square canal is impounded by the enclosure wall. In the midst of that square canal there is a square pond impounded by four bent-in walls consisting of the first two levels of casing stones. This pond is only waist deep because the bottom of the pond is comprised of the interior stones of the first level of the Great Pyramid. It looks like a precision built man made square flat topped mountain with a beautiful lake encompassing its entire top. Up from the center of this square lake is a rocky escarpment protruding towards the sky. With a hole in the top of this escarpment, it is similar to a volcano which flows not hot lava, but cool clear water. Oh what a magnificent sight that must have been. I wish I could have been there to see the brilliance of the Original Builders first hand!

At this stage of the assembly process, the first stones which are brought up are the casing stones for level three.

These casing stones are brought up through the water locks into pond two and bonded in place on top of the second level of casing stones. This process continues until the entire third level of casing stones are in place creating a watertight wall—except for where the next water lock will be built. Casing stones for the next higher level are always set in place first before the interior stones for that level are set in place.

While the bonding agent in the joints of the third level of casing stones is allowed to cure, the interior stones are brought up the water locks into construction pond two filling in the pond with interior stones. These interior stones are placed starting at the southern wall of the construction pond and progressing towards the north wall. The last interior stones of level two are placed by the water lock just as in level one. When the interior stones of level two are all set in their final resting place, level two of the Great Pyramid is completed in the same manner as level one. Again, once the second level of interior stones is set in place the second level of the Great Pyramid is completed including casing stones!

This systematic, efficient process continues.

The artificial duct for the input of the construction pump is moved up. As before, a water lock is built in the third level of casing stones. This water lock receives stones on barges from the water lock in the level below it. This water lock raises stones on barges up from the flight of water locks to the level of pond three. When the artificial duct is raised and water lock three is completed the next step is begun.

The construction pump is used to pump water from the canal around the building site into pond three which is impounded by the third level of casing stones. Using water lock three for pond three, casing stones for the forth level are brought in and cemented in place with a bonding agent. As these cemented joints cure the interior stones for level three are set in place completing level three of the Great Pyramid.

Each level has its own water lock which is used to lift stones on barges to that level. Once that level is completed, each lock is used to bring stones on barges to the lock above it.

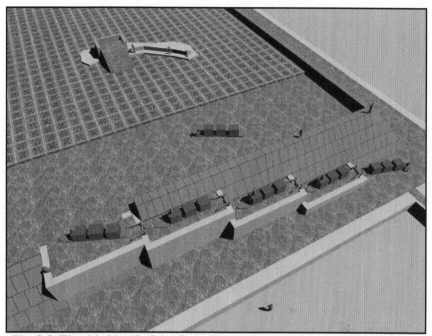

Fig. 8.5 The third level of the Great Pyramid will be completed as soon as the remainder of the rough cut interior stones are set in place. There are three water locks which bring barges up to the construction pond which is at the third layer. What looks like a fourth water lock is simply an enclosure which receives the barges from the third water lock. As the construction process continues this enclosure will become the fourth water lock. The construction pond is only waist deep. The fourth layer of casing stones has already been set in place. As soon as the third level is completed, the fourth water lock will be built and the process will continue.

Just as with all large public works projects, the assembly process continued day and night 24 hours a day, 7 day a week, year after year. Canals and water locks all over the world have always operated around the clock. The exacting placement of the casing stones would surely be done in daylight but the interior stones could easily be moved up the locks and then to their final resting place with the light from the moon or torches. Water is used efficiently and repeatedly because the water is reused in each successive water lock.

This brief overview gives the basic idea of the systematic procedure of construction used by the Original Builders to create the Great Pyramid. The intricacies of this construction method are elegant and efficient.

As the Great Pyramid is a wonder, so is the method used to build it. Describing this wonderful method of construction in ever greater detail is the subject of the following chapters.

---

[1] Leveson Francis Vernon-Harcourt, Civil Engineering as Applied in Construction (Longman's 1910) 393-394.
[2] Allen B. Schlesinger, Explaining Life (McGraw-Hill 1994)108.
[3] I. E. S. Edwards, The Pyramids of Egypt (The Viking Press 1972) 207.

Chapter 9
Let's Take a Ride!

All of the thousands who worked on the Great
Pyramid had a story to tell. Their oral accounts would be
absolutely fascinating and a resource of greater value than
most of the books written about the Great Pyramid. These
lost oral histories would have had their origins from the
actual events which took place on the Giza Plateau.
These firsthand accounts would have been told to friends,
relatives and neighbors and would have been passed down
through the generations. It is tragic that not a single detailed
firsthand account from any of the thousands of workers who
participated in this building project has survived to the
present era.

The multitude of oral histories now lost in the sands
of time would have related how these original workers came
to work on this project, what type of work they did or the
interesting people they worked with. These stories would
have been as varied as those who worked on this project.
One worker's story may be an overview of the whole project;
another person's story may be about a single memorable
event which vividly and indelibly stuck in his mind. If only
the collective body of the worker's stories and verbal
accounts could have stood the test of time as well as the
wonder of the world which was a product of their own
efforts! Had these stories survived intact I suspect our
understanding of the Great Pyramid would be much more
true and accurate than what is generally accepted today.

With this tragic loss of all the firsthand accounts of
the experiences of those workers, I have chosen to describe
the water locks, movement of stones on barges and the
assembly process, in story form. I feel that it will make the
description more personal, engaging and hopefully more
interesting than simply a stale, dry, explanation of these

processes. The names of the characters have been made up but the motivations, observations, opinions and comments of the characters of the story below are as genuine as can be imagined and appropriate for the situation. By introducing some human emotion and characteristics to the people in this story I have intended to bring to life the individual human beings who are now forever lost to us in obscurity. In this way I want to honor those fortunate souls who had the privilege of fully understanding what is now, to us, the Riddle of the Ages.

Below is one man's account as I have imagined it. This is his story, as he would have told his grandchildren.

Gonna-no's Story.
My First Day at Work!

It was a long arduous trip to arrive at my destination. Starting from my small village far upriver on the Nile, I traveled further than I had ever been from home. I left all that I knew and all my family and friends, traveling this great distance for one reason. I was looking for employment. Even as far away as my home village, there was constant talk of much work available on the Giza Plateau. The possibility of good steady employment was the driving motivation for my journey.

My village had suffered from a long drought. I left during the third year without water. My father's farm had suffered from the drought and consequently our family suffered too. Farming was never in my blood as it was with my good father. Working with my hands as a carpenter had been my passion. Entering my 19th summer I had much experience in constructing buildings, boats and all aspects of working with wood back in the village where I was raised. I heard the rumors and stories of a grand building project being built near the bank of the Nile on a plateau called Giza. Never traveling so far from home, I could only imagine the grandeur and enormity of this project I had heard so much about. My home village was far upriver and I made my journey to this place in a little raft I built myself.

Fig. 9.1 When Gonna-no first saw the Great Pyramid under construction he was in awe. From his vantage point down at the river all he could see was the massive structure in the distance. The only feature on the building he could see was what looked like massive steps zigzagging up the side. Around the structure was a relatively small wall.

After traveling for many days I finally reached my destination. Looking up from the small boat in the harbor on the Nile adjacent to this project was when I first saw it. Even from this distance I knew it was the largest manmade thing I had ever seen or would ever see. It was surely the biggest thing ever built by man that I knew of. Head tilted up in awe, as I sat in my small boat, I saw an incredibly huge, windowless, glistening white structure, like a box tilted in on all four sides. It was longer than it was tall, with a flat top.

Now came the hard part. I knew this was a structure made of stone and I was a worker of wood but I thought in a project this large, wood was somehow used in some aspect of this construction project. I was pleased and relieved to see a seemingly endless procession of barges loaded with stones on the river, either leaving the harbor empty or arriving loaded. I smiled because I knew I could repair or even build barges such as these.

Stepping off the little raft onto the dock by the river, I stopped a passing workman and asked, "Where's the boss?"

The worker paused for a moment, sizing me up and replied, "Do you want to talk to the big boss? He is up there." He pointed to the huge oddly shaped building on the plateau. Then he added with a knowing smile, "Or do you want the boss who does the hiring?"

I replied showing my appreciation, "The boss who does the hiring will be fine. Where is he?"

"He'll be in the office building for a while. Good luck!" the worker said as he pointed to the building near the harbor on the Nile.

The office building was made of stone and very impressive. Anywhere else a building like this would be considered a temple, but this one was obviously used to house the administration of this operation.

Entering the building I was impressed with the opulence surrounding me. The large room was filled with workers busy compiling figures, writing in ledgers and discussing issues which seemed important to them. I gave thanks to the god of my home village for letting me get this far and this close to the job I wanted and needed. As I looked around the room I saw partitions along both side walls which seemed to lead to smaller rooms with similar workers in them. Finally, I saw someone motioning to me to come over and talk. This person evidently was the one who received visitors.

"What is the purpose of your visit?" was the immediate and piercing question asked. This person was both insistent and in an obvious hurry.

"I am a boat builder and accomplished carpenter and I wanted to talk to the person in charge of hiring." I said with all the confidence I could muster.

"Do you have an appointment?" was the immediate response.

"No, but I am a good worker and traveled from far away looking for..."

Interrupting, the receptionist said as if reciting from memory, "Without an appointment you cannot speak to anyone. If you have no further official business, please leave the office building and construction site now. Thank you and good-bye." Looking into a room to the side with open door I saw an older man motioning for me to come to him.

The receptionist said, "Well, evidently you're in luck young man. He will see you now, even without an appointment!" Then the receptionist briskly walked off.

Entering the older man's office I saw the workplace of an orderly man. Everything was organized throughout the office. Behind the man was a large window providing a grand view of the entire construction project, from the large structure up on the plateau as well as the catch basin in the Nile River.

The man was deeply tanned, which was a telling sign he did not spend all of his time in an office. With graying hair, stocky build, and hands showing signs of serious work, I knew I was finally with someone knowledgeable and in authority.

"Are you in charge of hiring?" I simply asked.
He said, "My name is Hon-cho. I'm not the Big Boss. He, the engineers, and their staff are in their own office building up at the construction site. They like to be close to the project. You won't be talking to them. I am in charge of the movement of materials here at the building site. I am also the superintendent of barge maintenance. I overheard your conversation with the receptionist. From your clothing and

speech I can tell you are from upriver quite a distance.
Where are you from young man?"

"I am from a small village in the land called Nubia. I
am a carpenter and boat builder by trade and my reason for
being here is that I am looking for work," I told him.

Hon-cho replied, "As you can see, this is a building of
stone, not wood."

I answered, "You have many barges which require
maintenance. I have seen several the short time I have been
here which could use repairing."

"You have a sharp eye Gonna-no." Hon-cho said with
a smile. "This project is ahead of schedule and the barges
have been subject to wear from the heavy loads and constant
use. In a staff meeting earlier today we decided to add
additional barge maintenance crews to the operation."

"Keeping boats in good condition is what I do best!" I
proclaimed to Hon-cho.

"You look like a good worker and have traveled a long
way to be part of this project. I think you'll do fine." He told
me.

"Don't you want to see my wood working skills?" I
asked.
"The final decision is up to your foreman. If he is satisfied
with your work you'll be here as long as you want. If your
work is unsatisfactory you're gone. When this project first
started I was in the quarries operating machinery, now I'm
here. It is a good place to work." Pointing out the window in
his office he continued, "Your foreman is on the harbor dock
now. He will show you around and then put you to work."

Filled with confidence by the kind words and
encouragement from a man whose position required him to
be a good judge of character, I had renewed strength. My
long journey to this wonderful place was well worth it. I
thanked Hon-cho and went out to the dock to meet the
foreman.

Even though the foreman was busy with other tasks at hand he saw me coming and knew why I was approaching him. Hon-cho had motioned through his office window that I was his new workman. I introduced myself to my new boss and told him my skills, experience and where I was from. Although smiling, this foreman was a tough man, interested in getting things accomplished. This man also seemed fair and honest, only wanting good workmen to do what needed done.

"I'm the barge maintenance foreman and there is much to do. You see that big white building up on the plateau?" he asked me. "The construction phase of this pyramid has been going on everyday nonstop 24 hours a day for five years and we are well over half done. Things are going very smoothly and it is my job to keep it that way. This is a good place to work but it is different than anything you have ever seen. You just keep the barges in good shape and you won't have any problems."

"The building has a big flat top; it doesn't look near half done." I commented.

"Don't contradict me!" The foreman bellowed. Then he calmed down realizing he was talking with a new man. Patiently he said, "It's a pyramid! Most of the bulk of the structure is in the lower part. The higher up we go the smaller each level is. You'll learn it all real quick and soon you'll be a real pro like the rest of the guys working here." He laughed a big laugh and slapped me on the back.

This mighty construction site all seemed so strange to me. The foreman was right, I had seen nothing like it ever before or since. I did not want to admit I did not know what the building was for or why it was being built. The workers all seemed to be in good spirits and well fed. I knew I wanted to be a part of this project.

I asked, "Where do you want me to work on the barges, down here on the Nile?" I thought that was a logical assumption but I was wrong again.

"Of course not! There is no time or facilities here to work on barges." was the foreman's reply. "We do our maintenance up at the construction site. We work up there." He said while pointing to the large white flat topped building. "There is a staging area where the barges are waiting to go up or down the locks."

Being my first day, I did not know what the foremen meant by locking the barges up. Maybe there were thieves in the area. I did not know why barges would be worked on up on a plateau instead of at the river. I was new and did not want to look dumb. I asked my foreman, "Do you want me to go up there and start work?"

"That's what you're here for isn't it?

"Yes!" I told him enthusiastically as I gathered my belongings and started walking up to the building. It was hot and the walk in the soft sand to the construction site carrying my tools and belongings was to be a daunting task.

"What are you doing?" my foreman asked in disbelief.

"I'm going to work, sir." I said trying to show my eagerness.

My boss told me, "That's a hard day's work just walking up there in this hot weather. We don't work hard around here, we work smart. Remember that! If you find yourself working hard you're doing something wrong. Everything at this construction site is setup to be efficient including you! I have to go up there now anyway, so I'll show you around. Hop on a barge."

He continued saying, "Come on Gonna-no, let's take a ride!"

He and I stepped on a barge in the harbor just entering a canal. Its cargo was a beautiful large white stone shaped with sharp corners and odd angles. The stone was like a gigantic faceted jewel. Already on the barge was one man, named Bud-De. He was the barge tender. The foreman introduced me to Bud-De and they spoke as the barge glided along the canal. This canal started out as being dug in the ground but as we traveled just a short way the canal was made of stone. Very fine masonry lined both sides of this canal with the joints between the stones almost imperceptible. Ahead were a few workmen high up on finely made stone walls. The canal was blocked by what looked like barricades made of short wooden planks. With the canal blocked this would be a short trip I thought.

Motions were made between the workers and then something happened I did not expect. The barricade was in reality massive wooden doors on pivots. These doors swung away from us towards the sides of the canal and we passed these doors only to be met by other doors. The doors behind us were swung shut and we were trapped in a very deep canal with high masonry walls on both sides and wooded doors on pivots in front and behind us. I tried not to panic but the foreman said, "It looks like you have never seen a water lock before."

"It looks like we are the ones locked in here." I said with apprehension.

The foreman told me, "Don't worry young man, at this job you will see a lot of things you have never seen before. By the way, you will be keeping these water locks in good operating order as well. Are you up to it?"

I nodded, not knowing if I was. The water lock doors seemed fairly simple but made very well. I could do that. A few words were exchanged by the workers at the doors on pivots, a hand signal was given and the workers moved a lever and I heard rushing water below me. The still water of the canal showed some movement and suddenly I felt the boat with massive stone start to rise straight up. I have never moved **up** in a boat, before that day. We moved up until we were eye level with the workers manning the doors on pivots made of short wooden planks.

Not seeing me before the workers asked the foreman my name and where I was from. The foreman introduced me as Gonna-no from Nubia. One gate tender said with mock emphasis, "Oh, he's a newbie!" Everyone laughed but this kidding didn't bother me. I was in awe of the marvelous thing I had just witnessed: a loaded barge moving straight up!

The doors on pivots in front of the barge swung open and the barge was easily moved into the next water lock. The doors behind us swung closed and the same process started all over again. For the barge and stone to be lifted only took a few moments. Workmen were stationed at each lock gate.

"How does it work?" I asked my new foreman.

"Very well." he assured me. After a pause he continued, "This canal is built watertight. It is built in steps one higher than the next, like stair steps. Each section is divided by these large doors. When closed the doors form a watertight seal. When the doors are closed the water lock is like a box that is filled with water. The doors have valves under the water level which are controlled by the workers who open and close the gates. The valves are used to raise and lower the water. There is nothing magical about the process. It is very simple and straightforward, but very ingenious. That is how everything is done around here."

"I have never seen giant stones on barges lifted, using short wooden planks before" I said in amazement.
The foreman reassured me with his hand on my shoulder saying, "Kid, you haven't seen anything yet."

We rode in silence as we progressed up the water locks. I watched the workmen all doing their separate individual tasks, yet everything worked together. Ahead of us were stone laden barges in the water locks. I looked behind me and I could see barges with stones progressing up the water locks. As we came closer to the base of the gleaming white structure I realized I traveled faster by barge up the water locks then I would have made the walk up the hill!

When we reached the base of this gleaming white flat-topped mountain I could see it had a wall all the way around the structure. The wall was used to impound water. This massive structure was like an island surrounded by water, as if it had a canal or moat around it. The building was like a square island in a square lake. The windowless building stood like a gigantic gleaming crystal. It was so perfect it was as if it had never been touched by human hands.

I noticed a series of water locks built into the side of the building. It was the only feature I saw on the sloping sides of this structure. The barges ahead of us entered the series of water locks leading up the side of the structure and we followed right behind them. As we were about half way up the side of the construction project I asked, "Where did all this water come from and how did it get up here on the plateau?" I asked.

"Everyone asks that question including new workers as well as traveling tourists." Pointing down towards the wall which encircles the building site he said, "You see that artificial duct where water is coming in? That is the source of water. It keeps the pond around the pyramid full and supplies the needed water for the water locks which come up from the Nile."

"Tourists come all the time and inquire about the water. Then they write down their thoughts in their journals. One of the first things we did was build that artificial duct to supply water to the building site. We needed the water to lift the stones on barges from the Nile to the construction site. "You don't think we are going to drag all these stones uphill?" The workers within earshot had a big laugh over something so absurd. "The canal around the building site is called the enclosure pond. That is where you will maintain the barges. But first, let me finish showing you around."

I agreed with my boss, which is almost always a wise thing to do.

Still riding on the barge as we traveled higher up the flight of water locks I could see the canal around the building. The water was clear and cool, nothing like the muddy Nile. I could see in the distance buildings where the men were fed and slept. I could also see the wonderful temple-like office building used by the chief engineer and his staff. In the water locks traveling up the side of the huge structure I was so close to the building I reached out and touched it!

The white stones were as smooth as river rocks but were as flat as the surface of calm water. The stones were very large yet fitted together with utmost care. I was close enough to touch it yet I could hardly see the joints. I was glad I am a carpenter instead of a stone mover. I thought the work involved to move just one stone must be unbearable! I found out the truth in just a little while.

Fig. 9.2 As the barge they are riding nears the top of the structure Gonna-no's foreman continues the orientation of his new employee.

"We're going to the top to see how things are done up there," the foreman told me. The barge with stone easily moved up the water locks built into the sloping wall of this marvelous building. We rose up the side of this white flat-toped mountain step by step. Occasionally the foreman spoke to workers, giving orders or just making small talk. Everyone seemed to know what they were doing. It was odd to me that I had yet to see anyone doing anything I would call "real work." There were no windows, balconies, columns, stairs or any feature on the side of this building except for the water locks. There was not even a path to get to the top. There were only smooth sides and a series of water locks up to the top.

As we neared the top I looked over the landscape. I could see all the way down the water locks to the canal around the building. I could also see the water locks leading down to the harbor at the Nile. I could see the progression of barges each with their precious stone cargo. From this vantage point I tried to get an idea of the number of people working here. I saw far fewer than I thought I would.

Only being here for such a short time I could tell everyone had a specific job. There were supervisors, barge handlers, valve-tenders, and maintenance people. There were plenty of assistants and helpers where needed but no one appeared to be unnecessary. No one was really working hard. Everyone was just operating devices. It was strange and wonderful. It was a well run operation.

As we progressed up the side of this man made mountain my mind was filled with so many thoughts and questions. Was magic used to build this building? What was the building for? Was it a platform for a large statue to appease a very powerful god? Were they trying to build a tower to heaven itself? Water flowed down the water locks from the top of the building. Was there a river up at the top of the building? The tension and apprehension built inside me as we neared the top.

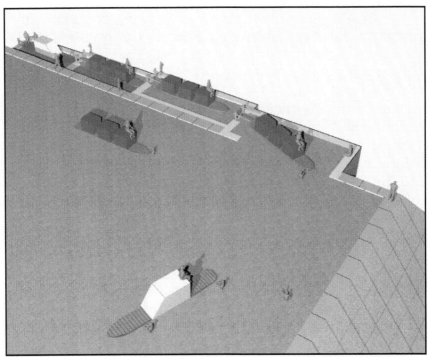

Fig. 9.3 Arriving at the construction pond at the top of the massive construction project. As always the construction pond is only waist deep. Workers are standing on the rough cut interior stones wading in water as they perform their duties.

I did not know what was up there or what to prepare for. It even crossed my mind that I was being tricked into being brought to the top of this white square flat-topped mountain to be sacrificed to some unknown god. I sat there on the rising barge trying not to let my apprehension and fear show.

When we arrived at the top the boss said, "Thanks, men." I was not prepared for what I saw. I did not have much time to think about it. I thought there would be teams of many workers straining to move the massive stones into place but I would have never dreamed I would see what I saw. There before me was a beautiful square lake encompassing the entire top of the building!

Gonna-no's story is not finished. His account of his first day on the job continues in the next chapter. Yet, I want to pause for a moment and take the time to ponder the absolute wonder of the construction process used to build the Great Pyramid. Can you imagine what it must have been like for people seeing this construction process for the very first time? What wonder would have filled their being as they saw the first wonder of the world as it was being built? Maybe it was a story like Gonna-no's which was repeated and handed down that is the seed for the legends which speak of the stones being moved effortlessly to build this structure. Maybe it was firsthand eyewitness stories which were like Gonna-no's story, flowing through the passing of eons, intertwined into mythology of the stones being somehow effortlessly "floated" into place.

Yet, in our age, we are separated by time from the actual events of the construction process. We focus on stones and design features and have lost a real sense of the emotions and feelings of the people who actually moved and set the stones in place. Their thoughts, impressions, and experiences would have filled volumes and probably did. Unfortunately for us none of those volumes and none of the accounts of the original worker's experiences have survived for our enjoyment and enlightenment.

But to get a feel of what these now lost stories were like, we will find out what Gonna-no experienced at the construction pond at the top of the unfinished structure.

Chapter 10
The Ride Continues

In your mind's eye, imagine if you will an old man who in the days of his youth was a worker that helped build the Great Pyramid. Bent and crippled from years of daily exhaustion, he looks twice as old as he really is. He appears as if he had suffered a brutal beating every day for decades. Now weak, infirm and debilitated by endless excruciating work all he can do is reminisce about days gone by. He is unable to care for himself and lives with his daughter's family.

It is his 47th birthday (probably his last) and as he sits in his chair his grandkids circle around him. The youngest one, with innocent concern asks timidly, "Grandpa, what happened to you? How come you ended up like this?"

With the attention of his grandchildren the old man perks up and smiles saying with raspy voice, "Well now, do you want to hear a story?"

The solemn children nod but with apprehension.

The old man says with pride, "I helped build the Great Pyramid!"

Children, always being hard to impress, simply stare at the old man.

"What did you do?" one child asks.

The old man replies, "Many things. When a stone was put on a sled I was one of the workers who helped drag the stone up the big ramp!"

The children never change expression.

The old man continues, "Yes, we dragged the stones up the big ramp. We did that all day long."

Another child asks, "Grandpa what did you do the next day?"

The old man laughs and coughs letting out a big wheeze. Regaining his breath he says, "We did the same thing the next day too. I helped with the dragging every day, all day long, for over 20 years."

Thinking the grandkids would be impressed the old man saw instead these youngsters becoming restless so he added, "Oh, I did other stuff too."

"Like what?" another child asked.

"Well, every time we finished a layer we had to rebuild the ramp. I worked rebuilding the ramp. You should have seen it. It was so big and I dragged stones on it in the hot sun for over twenty years."

The oldest grandchild named Noti almost in his teen years asked, "Why did you do that grandpa?"

The old man acts insulted. "Don't you kids know?" he asked in astonishment. "I did it for Pharaoh! To build the Pyramid is to maintain the natural order of the universe and ensure the safety and power of his Ka!"

"Why did you decide to work on the Great Pyramid?" another child asks trying to find out why her grandfather ended up this way.

"Dear child I was paying my tax to Pharaoh. Working on his final resting place for his mummy and treasures for his afterlife was a way to give back to Pharaoh. I was paying taxes and I was also a volunteer, happy and proud to serve my glorious divine leader!" he said with solemn pride.

Noti raised his hand. The old man acknowledged him and said, "Yes what is your question my firstborn grandson."

"It seems to me my dear grandfather that Pharaoh has charged you a very high tax. It is my intent not to pay that same tax and I certainly will not volunteer to serve Pharaoh in that manner."

The gathering of grandchildren nodded their heads in agreement.

Slumped in his chair the old man had not the energy to respond and one by one the uneasy grandchildren left their decrepit grandfather, meeting in the yard to play a game.

If the Ramp Cultists were correct in their unproven hypothesis of how the Great Pyramid was built, the above story would be true ten thousand times over. But that is not how the Great Pyramid was built and the story of the old man is like everything associated with the Ramp Dogma; it is simply a fabrication. Just as a huge ramp did not exist, neither do stories such as the one above.

In the previous chapter, Gonna-no's story was used to bring a human element to the building process. The story of his account is used to describe the events and process of constructing the Great Pyramid as seen by someone who was there at the time. This same literary device is used to describe Gonna-no's eyewitness account of what he saw on his first day at work on the construction pond as the Great Pyramid was being built. Let's continue with Gonna-no's story. In the last chapter we left off with Gonna-no emerging from the top water lock and entering the construction pond for the very first time.

Seeing the pond up at the top of this mountain of stone I tell my foreman, "Now I know what is going on. This whole structure is filled with water."

"Actually the structure is filled with stone." The foreman replied. "Look into the pond encompassing the entire top of the structure. This pond is called the construction pond. It is only about waist deep. Below that is a level of interior stones. Stones fill the entire building layer by layer. It is a solid structure except for a few pressure chambers and water passages."

Gonna-no was astonished! He said, "Look, there are cracks in-between the stones in the bottom of this pond! What magic keeps the water from leaking out?"

The foreman responds, "Think kid! Use your brain. There are cracks in-between the interior stones but the water does not leak out because there is nowhere for it to go. The sides of this entire structure are watertight all the way down to the bedrock! The watertight walls of casing stones keep the water from leaking out of the building. Each wall of casing stones is like a dam, impounding the water. There are cracks between the interior stones all the way down to bedrock but the casing stones hold the water in!"

Fig. 10.1 The depth of the pond is only about waist deep. The floor of the construction pond consists of the interior stones of the previous level.

"Why don't you use tar to seal each level? Wouldn't that be better?" Gonna-no asked sheepishly.

The foreman shook his head and said, "As you can see, that is unnecessary. Kid, you'll get it figured out soon enough, but not all at once. There is a lot to take in and a lot you have never seen or thought of before. Don't get discouraged."

I looked across the lake at the top of the structure and it was filled with activity. There were barges with stones, barges without stones, oddly shaped barges, boats too large to fit in the water locks, stone platforms which held stones and even stone islands in the lake at the top of the mountain of stone. I was most amazed at what I didn't see. There were no gangs of men straining to move even one stone anywhere.

Still sitting on the barge I was dumbfounded. I asked, "What's going on?"

The foreman cryptically replied, "Many things, all at once." After a pause he continued, "Everything is being done in a systematic manner. This stone here on the barge we rode up on is called a casing stone and it fits on the outside of this building. It will be set in place in a just a few minutes. Let's get out of the way and watch what happens." We stepped onto the wall of casing stones at the edge of the pond out of the way of ongoing work.

Fig. 10.2 (A) The barge with casing stone is moved between two stone supports. (B) Then water is allowed to enter the barge which lowers it. This causes the casing stone to come to rest on the two support stones. The barge is still floating but it is riding very low in the water. That is why it is hard to see. (C) Then the partially flooded barge is moved from between the two supports. After that the barge will be moved to the edge of the construction pond.

The pond was shallow enough to wade in yet deep enough to allow the barge to float. Workmen wading in the water helped move and guide the barge to wherever they wanted it to go. That seemed like a nice cool job! The barge we rode up on with the casing stone was easily moved between stone platforms. This barge was narrow and the casing stone was wider than the barge and over hung on both sides. Immediately this barge started to sink! Not knowing why the barge was sinking, I excitedly told the foreman of this problem. One thing I did know is a sinking barge was not good.

The foreman acted calm and said, "It is supposed to do that. The barge isn't sinking, it is lowering. That worker is letting in water so that the barge will move down vertically between these two stone supports. Watch how the casing stone is now resting on the supports instead of the barge. That was easy wasn't it?"

Fig. 10.3 Water is removed from the barge by siphoning it out over the edge of the construction pond. The siphon hose is full of water and the upper end is inserted into the barge. The lower end of the siphon hose has a valve which is operated using linkage. When the valve is opened water is quickly and easily removed from the barge.

I agreed replying, "It only took a few minutes and looked very easy indeed." But as a carpenter I was still worried about the barge half floundering in the water. This

can't be good I thought to myself. This barge was still
buoyant and not completely sunk to the bottom of the waist
deep pond. It was quickly moved from between the supports
and towards the edge of the pond. A different set of workers
attended this half sunk barge and I could not see exactly
what they did but the barge was quickly and effortlessly
emptied of water and it was as good as new. This took no
more than a few minutes. Everyone knew what they were
doing and there was no wasted time or movements.

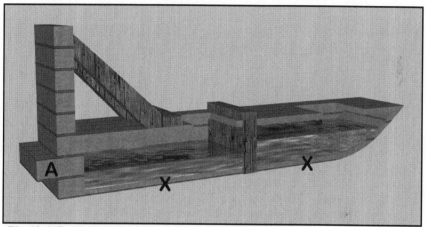

Fig 10.4 Cross-sectional view of a tipping barge. There are two watertight
compartments in this barge's specialized hull. One is toward the front and
the other is in back. Water can be added or removed from these
compartments independently allowing the barge to pivot as well as raise
and lower. The location of the valves allowing water to enter each of the
two compartments is designated by the letter (X). The heavily built ledge
which will support the back edge of a casing stone is located at (A).

Astonished I asked the foreman, "How did they lower
the barge?"

"Easy kid," was his reply. "We have many different
barges to do specific tasks. This barge and those like it have
a valve in the bottom to let water in which lowers the barge.
When the barge is lowered the proper amount, the valve is

closed. Now that's a pretty slick way to move that heavy stone off of the barge!"

I agreed, but I didn't see how they raised the boat back up so I asked, "How did they get the water *out* of the boat?" I know water is heavy and to move it out of the boat must be a chore.

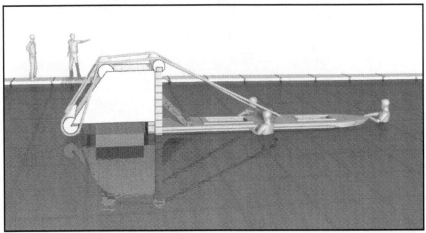

Figure 10.5 While the casing stone is resting on the supports it is attached to a tipping barge. The tipping barge is partially filled with water which causes it to float low in the water. A sleeve is placed on the sharp front edge of the casing stone as well as on the top edge. This allows the casing stone to be secured to the barge with ropes without damaging the casing stone or the ropes.

"Even easier kid," he instantly responded. "Those guys at the edge of the construction pond have a hose full of water with a valve on the end of it. They place the end with the valve over the side of the pond and the other end they put in the boat. Opening the valve on the hose quickly siphons out the water from the boat and it is as good as new. The water that was once inside the barge goes over the edge of the construction pond." I was so impressed all I could do was smile and shake my head. The massive stone was removed from the barge in just a few minutes.

As the empty barge was moved away, a very oddly shaped barge was moved so that one edge fit on the back of the casing stone. Then ropes were used to secure the casing stone to this barge. Workers attending this unusually shaped barge caused it to rise up enough for the casing stone to be lifted off the supports! This time I saw how it was done. The barge which was called a tipping barge was already lowered because it was allowed to fill with water. When the barge was moved under the casing stone the water was siphoned out over the edge of the pond and the barge rose up coming in contact with the casing stone. After the casing stone was secured with ropes to the tipping barge, more water was siphoned out and the barge with the casing stone attached to it rose up lifting the stone off of the supports!

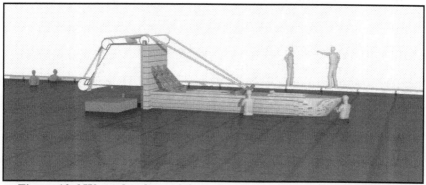

Figure 10.6 Water has been siphoned over the edge of the construction pond from both compartments of the tipping barge. This raises the barge and it is now supporting the casing stone. Controlling the amount of water in each compartment allows the barge to lift the casing stone and also allows the barge to float level in the water.

Now the casing stone was held up and secured to the front of a very oddly shaped, specialized barge. This barge was built with a very heavily constructed structure on one end. This structure allowed the casing stone to be attached to the barge. There was an extremely strong support that the back of the casing stone rested on. Securing the casing stone to the barge with ropes only took a few minutes and a few workers.

Workmen wading in this pool of water moved the specialized barge with the casing stone to the edge of the pond right near where we were standing. It was to be set on top of casing stones already in place. I saw a layer of glue or paste or some bonding agent being applied to the horizontal and vertical surfaces where this stone would be set in place. The casing stone supported by the tipping barge was gently and easily positioned to just above its final resting position. Then the casing stone that I rode up with from the Nile was gently lowered and set in place. When the casing stone was lowered onto the wall of casing stones the tipping barge was moved away.

Then with the use of another strange barge the casing stone's position was carefully and quickly adjusted so that it fit as perfectly as the others. This strange barge which I heard someone call a positioning barge was able to quickly and accurately position the massive casing stone. The bonding agent allowed the casing stone to be easily adjusted so that it was positioned perfectly. It happened just that fast. It was obvious these workers had experience doing this delicate procedure.

I asked my foreman another question. "That stone is very heavy. When it is tipped onto the wall of casing stones why did it move so smoothly? I was afraid it would fall with a crash but it didn't."

My foreman told me, "The specialized barge acts as a counterweight when the stone is set in place. This barge is designed and made specifically to accomplish this task. The tipping maneuver is a delicate operation and requires care to move the stone with no damage. This barge acts like an extremely large lever with water as a counter weight allowing for a very gradual and controlled placement of the casing stones. With a little experience, it is a piece of cake!"

"Where do these beautiful casing stones come from and how are they made to such perfection?" I asked my boss.

He paused for a moment, lost in thought then finally he answered me. "I have been to the quarries. If you think this building site is a place of wonders you should go to the quarries if you ever get a chance. The quarries are filled with specialized equipment just as this building project is. These stones are quarried with the use of special machines and the workers operate the machines. There is virtually nothing done by hand. Could *YOU* create this degree of precision by hand?" he asked me.

I shook my head no.

Pointing at the casing stone he is standing on he demands, "Have you ever seen a surface this large and this accurate ever made by hand?"

I again shook my head no.

Continuing he explains, "These stones are made to very high precision so the joints will be strong and watertight when the bonding agent cures. No one can create this incredible precision by hand. No one can and no one ever will. In many respects the quarries are a lot like here. Specialized machines do the work, and the workers operate the machines. All activities are done using specialized devices which are needed to achieve high precision and high production."

As we stood near the edge of the pond on the wall of casing stones, I looked over the edge. I could see down the side of this building to the blue canal that encircles it. The sides of this massive building were white and smooth, and looking over the edge made me dizzy. There is no cliff near my home village as high as this.

Standing on the casing stones I could also see that the side of this structure was wet where water was siphoned out of the barges. I marvel, realizing that five hundred strong backs could have never moved and placed the stone I just saw moved.

Looking down I could see the artificial duct which supplied water to the building. Yet even at this great height I couldn't see where the water came from. Part of the canal bringing water to the building site was underground. All I knew on this first day of my being at this great marvel was maybe it somehow came from the Nile River or even a lake which is too far away to see. I could not tell were the source of the water was coming into the enclosure pond keeping it full.

The foreman beside me looked out at the magnificent view of the surrounding countryside and started talking to me again. "Look over there." He said pointing down to the moat surrounding the building under construction, "You will be working on the barges in the canal circling the pyramid. This is where the barge maintenance is performed. You will be on a crew and they will show you what to do. They are a good bunch of guys who do excellent work. You'll learn a lot from them."

Pointing to another set of buildings he informed me, "Out there are your sleeping quarters and the mess hall. The food on this project is very good as you will find out shortly. And over there is a place to pick up your personal supplies. It is called the company store and things are kind of expensive there but hey, that's the way it is."

"What is going on over there?" I asked pointing at a very large boat near the middle of the lake.

"Watch and you'll see." The foreman told me. The boat was very long and narrow, with a long high bow and equally long, high stern. The bow and stern were joined together with a strong rope. As a carpenter I could see this boat was built well and very strong. It was also lashed together so that it could be taken apart!

I had never seen a boat like this. There was a strong rope attached to the bow and it hung down to a stone on a barge. Many men holding weights in their hands walked back and forth on this boat. When they walked to the rear of the boat, the front rose up. The rope on the front of the boat lifted the stone on the barge in the air! The barge was moved out of the way by workmen wading in the water. The men on the boat moved to the front of the boat causing the front to slowly move down. The stone moved down in the water and rested on the bottom of the pond. This process set the stone in place.

The foreman went on, "That's how the rough cut interior stones are set in place. This building is made mostly of this type of interior stones. The boat-crane pivots forward and back which picks up and sets interior stones as fast as they are brought up." Proudly he said, "Yet the boat-cranes have a hard time keeping up with water lock crews! These large boats were here at the first of the construction and make easy work of moving the interior stones off the barges lowering them down to their final designated locations."

I asked another question, "When you are finished with this level how do you get the big crane boats up to the next level? Do you take them apart and reassemble them on the next higher level?"

Shaking his head the foreman said, "Of course not! When this level is finished the pond is simply raised to the next level and the boat-cranes rise with the pond. When the pond gets too small to use the boat-cranes they will be disassembled and removed from the pond."

"Why don't they move casing stones in this same manner as the interior stones?" I asked.

He anticipated my question and replied, "Interior stones are only about 2 ½ tons and most casing stones weigh much more. The weight of the casing stones is greater than the capacity of the boat-cranes. Every type and size of stone isn't moved the same way. Interior stones are moved from the barges by the boat-cranes, and the casing stones are moved in the manner you just saw using specialized barges made just for each step of the process. There are stones in this structure which are even larger by far than the casing stones and they are moved using even different procedures."

He went on, saying, "The techniques fit the application. You are a carpenter. You use a small knife to whittle but a big ax to chop down a tree. Both processes cut wood but the different applications require different tools and procedures to get each job done. Am I getting through to you kid?"

Fig. 10.7 Work on the passages and chambers is completed level by level. Just as the precision cut casing stones are placed above the construction pond the precision cut interior stonework is place just above the construction pond. The Grand Gallery, vents and other interior precision stone work is completed level by level.

"Yes sir!" I responded learning as fast as I could. The foreman continued, "The building is ahead of schedule and with the machinery and specialized tools doing most of the work, we are under budget too!" he told me with a proud smile.

"What are the stone islands in the lake for?" I asked.

The foreman said, "This building is completely solid except for a few pressure chambers and conduits for water. Those passages and chambers are built, level by level, just as the casing stones are set in place level by level. Those islands are the level of these passages currently under construction. As the building progresses level by level, the construction of these passages also progress level by level."

I told my foreman, "I am amazed the work involved is mainly operating the equipment. No one is hauling stones around. In my small village far away we use muscle power when we build our temples."

"That's what everyone says who visits this construction site." My boss told me. Then he added, "It's *not* like this because the engineers and people running this project are benevolent. It is done in *this* manner because doing a job like this by hand or by hauling the magnitude of stones involved by hand is simply impossible. Listen up kid; it cannot be done that way. Everything here has a purpose and a reason for being as it is. Everything has been thoroughly planned and thought out. Nothing is haphazard or ornamental. The casing stones are made with such precision and joined together watertight so we can use a pond for each level. That is the reason which necessitates the extreme precision of the casing stones. Water's property of buoyancy actually does the work of lifting the stones on barges so they can be moved with extreme ease. Water locks on the north face of the structure bring the stones on barges to this pond. As each level is finished then the pond is raised up one level and another water lock is added to the locks on the north face."

Watching me ponder all I have seen my foreman and teacher continues saying, "Allowing water to enter a barge lowers the barge. Siphoning water out of the barge over the side of the pond raises the barge. Using all these techniques together allows us to manipulate extremely heavy stones in any manner we need to. This system is powerful, controllable and very fast!"

With so much going on that seems so foreign to me I question my foreman again. "I see barges coming up but I don't see any going back down. When are the empty barges taken down the water locks?"

Fig. 10.8 The empty barges are moved over the side of the structure. (A) An empty barge is moved into position. (B) Water is being siphoned through a hose into the holding tank causing the apparatus to pivot. (C) After the apparatus has pivoted, the barge has been moved over the edge and is being held by a rope. (D) A valve is opened by a worker allowing water to drain out of the apparatus which is what causes it to pivot back to its original position.

The foreman said, "Look over there and you will see what we do with the empty barges. The empty barges go over the side. This way we don't have to waste any time lowering the empty barges down the water locks. Water locks take quite a bit of water to operate. Lowering the barges over the side uses just a small amount of water. The main reason the empty barges go over the side is so that we do not have to stop production to move the empty barges down the water locks. Everything comes up the water locks. Anything going down goes over the side. It works very well!"

Fig 10.9 A barge is being lowered down the side of the pyramid where it will enter the water in the canal encircling the structure. The workers have wrapped the rope around the support which makes it easy to lower the barge down the side of the Great Pyramid.

I wondered out loud, "Why not have two sets of water locks, side by side so loaded barges can go up and empty barges can go down all at the same time." I was proud of my idea for improving the construction procedure until my foreman spoke up.

He said, "No, kid, that's not how it's done. It would waste water and it would require twice as many water locks. We don't need to use two flights of water locks sided by side. That would be way too complex. This system of using water locks to move materials up and lowering empty barges over the side is better than the complexity of pairs of water locks." Trying to make me feel better he added, "You were not the first to make that suggestion. Even though two flights of water locks are not needed in this application, at least it was a thought."

I looked at the far side of the pond and I saw the process of an empty barge being moved over the side of the wall! The barge was moved to the edge of the pond. Suddenly a platform came up from under the water which lifted the barge above the level of the pond. Workers slid the empty barge from the platform out over the wall of casing stones impounding the pond. Then the barge was lowered using ropes down the smooth side of the building until it was floating in the moat that surrounds the pyramid. The ropes which lowered the barge were coiled around a heavy column. The friction of the rope around this column made lowering the empty barge easy and controllable.

This process like the others I had the privilege to watch was efficient, easy, fast, and actually made sense! I can see now that they do not need two sets of water locks side by side. It was about midday and I was getting hungry. I smelled food way up here! Then I heard someone say, "Here comes the lunch barge!" The next barge entering the pond on top of the man made mountain had not only a stone but also many baskets of food and vessels of drink. There was bread and meat and many kinds of fruit. There was more food and drink than I had seen for years in my small village back home.

"Are they going to stop for lunch?" I asked.

"Don't ever say stop!" my foreman warned. "That is one thing we don't do. My job is to keep the process going nonstop! We never stop and if we do it means there is a problem. As foreman I see to it there are no problems."

"Do we work while eating?" I asked puzzled.

"No." the foreman explained. "Each crew is relieved with a few extra workers so everyone can have lunch. Every crew gets to have a nice lunch break but the lunch breaks are staggered. This way everyone gets a break but none of the work ever stops."

"Work stops at dusk, doesn't it?" I said, knowing it must.

"Not at all." The foreman told me, "With moonlight we can operate the locks all night long without any problem. We have been doing that for years. Many workers prefer working at night because it is cooler and there are fewer bosses and supervisors hanging around. Some nights when the moon doesn't shine we use a few torches and the work keeps going. At night we place mostly the rough interior construction stones. The precision work is done in the light of day, but we never stop. On this project we work continuously. Each crew is relieved after their work shift is over. Some work crews work during the day, others work in the evening and another shift of workers are on duty from late at night until the morning. This way the construction progresses every day and every night throughout the year! The way it is done here is a day and night are divided into three equal parts. The time you spend at work is short compared to many other jobs like farming or goat herding."

"My father is a farmer and he works all the time," Gonna-no lamented.

Pointing to the food on the barge my foreman said, "There is the lunch barge Gonna-no, get yourself something to eat. Go ahead and eat whatever you want, there's plenty."

Even though I was quite hungry and had not eaten that day I told my boss with pride, "I have not worked and to take food would be charity. I do not accept charity sir."

"Nonsense!" My foreman told me as he gave me a friendly pat on the back, "You have been hired and on the job since we met on the dock by the Nile. The trip up here is your orientation. This construction project is so unusual we need our workers to be aware of the building process. To understand what is going on helps our workers do a better job. Take your break, and eat lunch. After that we will go down to your work area at the enclosure pond and I'll introduce you to the barge maintenance gang you will be working with."

My eyes got big. I had never thought about going down. "How do we get back down?" I asked, afraid of the answer.

"I'll show you after you've had your fill to eat," the foreman said with a sly smile. Then he added, "When you're lunch break is over we'll take *another* ride!"

The food was as good as my foreman told me. I thought this feast was for a special occasion but the workers acted as if it was what they regularly ate. While dining on the top of a mountain of stone, I kept my eyes open seeing many things happening all at once. After lunch I got out of the way and was able to just stand and watch stone after stone being moved and set in place. What a wonder it was!

After the foreman finished some of his duties he came to me and said, "Are you ready to go back down?"

I nodded my head and followed him to a platform hanging over the side of the pyramid.

"Climb aboard." he said, as he and a bunch of workers stepped out on the platform. I did not want to, but I did and soon we were moving steadily down the side of this great construction project.

Seeing my worried expression, the foreman explained, "Workers leaving the construction pond at the end of their shift are lowered down the side on this type of platform like the empty barges. This way there is no interruption of production. This method is obviously quick, efficient, easy and consumes no massive amounts of water. Just as we rode up on barges, the workers hitch a ride on barges traveling up the water locks. At the end of the work shift we and the workers leave by going down on this platform. Don't worry; there is no back breaking work here."

I should have kept my mouth shut but I said, "Well, lowering the platform may be easy but to pull it back up would be hard work. I am glad that is not my job."

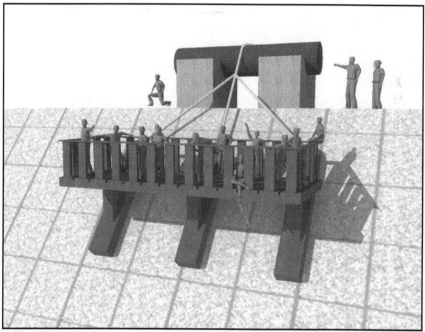

Fig. 10.10 Workers are lowered down the side in a similar manner to the empty barges. The platform the workers are lowered on is made to be easily disassembled and brought back up the water locks on a barge.

The foreman shook his head in disapproval saying, "Dragging that type of platform back up the side of the Great Pyramid would be a daunting task to be sure. It would be hard work and I sure would not want to do it either! This specialized platform is lowered onto a barge and disassembled into sections. Then the barge, with platform, is brought back up the water locks. This platform is made so it comes apart into sections, placed on a stone laden barge and returned up to the construction pond using the water locks. That way, it does not reduce production by even one stone! It is reused every shift. Just keep your eyes and mind open and you'll soon get it figured out."

So that afternoon on my first day, my new boss and I rode down the platform on the side of a manmade mountain accompanied by a number of workers who actually built the Great Pyramid. Safely and efficiently being lowered down the side of the half finished Great Pyramid, with the gentle breeze and the bright sun shining, I stood elbow to elbow with a bunch of happy productive workers ending their work day.

As the platform moved lower, ever closer to the enclosure pond, my mind was filled with wonder of how these workers built mankind's greatest wonder!

Chapter 11
Stone Moving Details

The previous two chapters were written in story form to provide an overview of the activities involved in this truly unique construction project. Gonna-no's story of his initial work day gave an account of his first impressions of what he saw and his limited understanding of the unique procedures used to move the stones and assemble the Great Pyramid. It is now time to analyze these stone moving procedures in much greater detail.

In describing the activities of the workers performing their specialized tasks, allow your mind's eye to envision the overall sophistication of this construction process. Although radically different from anything modern mankind is familiar with, the use of water as a means to transport, lift and maneuver stones to build a tall, massive, solid structure is astoundingly versatile.

The versatility of water locks and walls of watertight casing stones to impound ponds used in conjunction with a massive water pump allowed the Great Pyramid to be built. Even at first glance in the previous chapters, the wide array of stone moving and manipulation techniques which are available using water is astounding. The many methods to harness the powerful force of buoyancy are endless. Using water and its characteristic of buoyancy was used in so many special ways to build the Great Pyramid. The detailed analysis provided in this chapter concentrates on just the most obvious methods to move stones. There is no doubt in my mind the Original Builders used these methods as well as many other sophisticated and efficient stone moving procedures utilizing water's powerful force of buoyancy.

To answer how I know stones were moved in the manner described in these chapters, I tell people the following. This book describes a number of very simple techniques which utilize water's property of buoyancy as a powerful and versatile force to lift and move very heavy payloads. For a civilization that could envision and build a structure as ingenious and magnificent as the Great Pyramid, the few stone moving methods discussed here are blatantly obvious.

It is apparent to me the Original Builders were geniuses and these straight forward methods would be immediately apparent even before construction started. This systematic utilization of water to lift and move materials is adaptable, controllable, powerful, fast and with the integral massive construction pump, available. It is consistent with reason, the direct physical evidence, as well as the research conducted at the Pharaoh's Pump Foundation that the Original Builders of the Great Pyramid utilized all of the immediately apparent and self-evident advantages provided by the use of water to lift, manipulate and move stones. The procedures described in this book to move and lift stones were not only apparent to the Original Builders but are obvious to any open-minded researcher.

I marvel at the genius of the Original Builders! Moving and placing the stones in this sophisticated manner was the *easiest* aspect of the entire construction project.

In building the Great Pyramid, forklifts, large diesel power trucks or even modern steel cranes were not needed, except of course in one important exception. That exception is in Egyptologist's feeble demonstrations to substantiate the ramp/strong-back hypothesis.[1] Unlike Egyptologists the Original Builders, who were geniuses, did not use or need a forklift made of metal. Instead they used water to do the lifting and moving. The use of water with all its versatility was the prime mover utilized by the Original Builders to transport, lift and place stones accurately at an incredibly fast rate.

We live in an age of diesel trucks and trailers, rail road cars and air freight. The versatility of using water to move and *lift* cargo is generally unfamiliar and unappreciated knowledge in our age. The descriptions offered here are just a few simple, readily apparent applications of using both water and simple but specialized equipment, combined with efficient procedures to accomplish ALL of the pivotal stone handling tasks required in constructing the Great Pyramid.

Any method of moving the stones of the Great Pyramid must meet several important criteria.

- The method must be fast. The huge quantity of stones requires a system which will move a very high number of stones. Any system which is slow is not the system used by the Original Builders.

- The method must be able to accommodate the largest stones. If a method cannot be demonstrated to accommodate the rapid and precise movement of 70 ton payloads then, it is not the system used by the Original Builders.

- The method must be able to move stones without any handling scars. No chipped surfaces, no marks from chains, etc. If a moving system marks the stones or damages the stones, it is not the system used by the Original Builders.

- The stone moving method must be highly controllable. The method used by the Original Builders allowed for the extremely accurate movement and placement of 16 ton casing stones as well as 70 ton precision cut stones. If a proposed method cannot accomplish these tasks with great accuracy, then it was not the system used by the Original Builders.

- The stone moving method must fit the direct physical evidence provided to us by the Great Pyramid. If the method is inconsistent with the evidence of the Great Pyramid, it is not the system used by the Original Builders.

All stone moving and placement techniques offered by any researcher, author or college professor must meet the above criteria. The detailed stone moving techniques described in this chapter meet these requirements in full.

The brute force and ramp hypothesis fails to meet these same criteria. Using brute force and ramps to move a virtual production-line of massive payloads cannot be adequately demonstrated. Therefore brute force and ramps were not the method used by the Original Builders to assemble the Great Pyramid. A gargantuan ramp populated by human beasts of burden is an incorrect assessment of how the Great Pyramid was assembled.

Historical context is an interpretation of evidence, not evidence in and of itself. This description of the Great Pyramid's construction does not match current conventional thought about how the Original Builders accomplished their mighty achievement. In that regard, experts who cannot demonstrate what *they* profess to be true, consider *this* interpretation of the physical evidence "out of context." This explanation of the Great Pyramid is "in context" with the remaining direct physical evidence, and that is what really matters. The "science" of Egyptology has offered their hypothesis as to the methods used. Their hypothesis cannot be supported by the scientific method. The science of Egyptology cannot even make one casing stone. Again, brute force and ramps is an unproven hypothesis which cannot be supported by valid demonstration.

Nothing in this description of stone moving is overly complex or out of the comprehension of a civilization who demonstrated their genius and abilities by building the Great Pyramid. Nothing in the description of stone moving defies the laws of physics or requires an ancient religious, cultural or hieroglyphic interpretation. This is an analysis of the movement of stones. Therefore no aspect is "symbolic" or needs religious interpretation. Every detail of the stone moving process meets the criteria of moving massive amounts of stone with extreme accuracy, controllability, ease and speed.

The Original Builders used the genius of their minds and did not strain their backs to build the Great Pyramid. It would be a wonder if modern humanity could acknowledge this fact.

The movement of the massive amount of materials used to build the Great Pyramid is a very interesting and highly controversial subject. Many books written about the Great Pyramid address this very important topic. Can an infinite number of strong backed Bronze Age ramp walkers accomplish the specific tasks of transporting the massive volume of stone and arranging it to become the Great Pyramid? Orthodox Egyptologists, the world over, say yes, and claim their assertions are true based on their authority. Most alternative experts say no. Herodotus, as well as the 5th century B.C. "priests" he talked to at the Great Pyramid would be counted among the No-Ramp group.

The stones used to build the Great Pyramid come in all different sizes and shapes, yet in very basic terms there are three general weights of stones which were used as components to build the Great Pyramid. The largest weigh roughly 50 to 70 tons in weight and comprise the ceiling of the King's chamber and a relatively few other extremely large stones. The next general weight range is the large precision cut casing stones weighing up to 16 tons. The third size is the 2½ ton rough cut interior stones which comprise the overwhelming majority of the structure.

Basically, these three general sizes of stones comprising the Great Pyramid. These three basic sizes of stones required differing methods to move them. The largest stones are moved differently from the smaller stones.

The movement of the interior stones was touched upon in Gonna-no's story, when he reached the top water lock and saw the pond on top of the half finished building.

Among much activity, he saw large ships on the pond. He watched as they were used to lift and move interior stones.

There are a number of pits around the Great Pyramid which held boats of various sizes. One of these boats is now housed in a museum on the Giza plateau and there is another large boat still buried at the Giza plateau.[2] These so-called "Sun ships" or "solar barges" have been interpreted by traditional Egyptologists as having the purpose of giving the Pharaoh's carcass one last ride on the Nile to his final resting place.[3]

There is another interpretation of the same direct physical evidence. Based on extensive research by Hungarian researcher and author István Sörös, the purpose of these controversial and oddly configured ships is that they were designed, built and used as boat-cranes.[4]

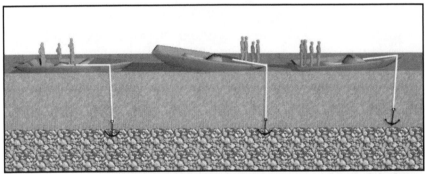

Fig 11.1 To free a stuck anchor the passengers move to the front of the boat. Then the rope is pulled taught and tied off. The passengers walk to the back of the boat pulling the anchor free. Tremendous pulling power can be achieved using this technique!

These long boat-cranes were used as powerful floating fulcrums. I live in western Oregon and when our small boat's anchor gets stuck in the bottom of the lake everyone moves to the front of the boat. Slack in the anchor line is taken up and the line is tied to the cleat. Then everyone walks to the back of the boat and the tremendous force of leverage pulls the anchor free. It works very well. The boat acts like a lever with its fulcrum supported by water. It is a simple, easy and fast process to exert a great deal of pulling force on the anchor line.

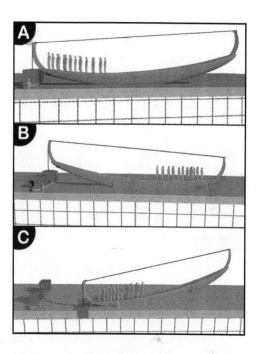

Fig 11.2 These images show how an interior stone was lifted off a barge and set in place. The large boat is a stylized depiction of the so-called solar barge or sun boat found on the Giza Plateau. (A) Workers walk to the front of the boat and a rope is attached to the stone. (B) Workers walk to the back of the boat lifting the stone. (C) Then after the barge crane is moved into position the workers walk to the front of the barge which allows the interior stone to be placed into the construction pond and placed at its final resting place.

This same idea was used in moving the 2½ ton interior stones. The long boat-cranes worked in a similar manner. These boat-cranes were well built and had a high prow and aft connected with a strong rope.[5] Workers on the barge (possibly carrying weights) move towards the front of the boat-crane. A line is attached from the bow of the boat-crane to the 2½ ton interior stone on a barge. The workers then move toward the back of the boat-crane raising the bow enough to lift the stone off the barge. The barge is moved out of the way by workers wading in waist high water. The boat-crane is held in the correct position by workers standing in the pond. Then the workers on the boat-crane move to the front of the boat. This gently lowers the stone into the construction pond setting it in place.

This fast and efficient method was used to place the vast majority of the interior stones of the Great Pyramid. The rough cut interior stones were lifted off the barge and lowered to its final resting place in the construction pond as fast as the water locks could deliver stones.

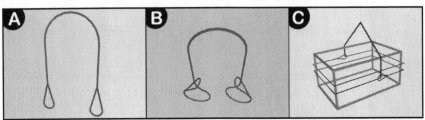

Fig. 11.3 These images depict the way ropes are attached to the rough cut interior stones. (A) A rope has an eye in each end. (B) These eyes are used to make a loop on each end if the rope. (C) These two loops are placed around a block. This allows the rough cut interior stones to be lifted and set in place by the boat cranes. Using this method, the ropes were attached easily and quickly before the stone was lifted off the barge and removed just as easily and quickly after the stone was set in place.

The method of setting in place the 2½ ton interior stones is extremely water efficient requiring no consumption of water to operate the boat crane. It is amazing to realize these building blocks are used to fill up the pond. Each time a stone is moved from the barge into the pond, the pond gets smaller and there is more water available to use. Let me repeat that because it is so fascinating. Replacing water with interior construction stones removes volume from the pond and results in a net gain in water available for use. This represents another example of efficiency inherent in this unique construction process.

The boat crane had the lifting power to raise an empty barge over the casing stone wall which impounds the construction pond. If empty barges were backing up on the construction pond a boat-crane could help lift the empty barges over the side. After the empty barge was lifted over the edge of the construction pond it would have been lowered down the side of the pyramid in a similar manner as described in a previous chapter. Versatility, adaptability, speed and power are all hallmarks of this fascinating construction method.

While water locks universally operate around the clock, so do the boat-cranes. Traditional Egyptologists grudgingly admit the dangerous stone transportation method of a mega-ramp could only have been used during the light of day.[6] Using water locks and boat-cranes allowed for a much shorter length of time to build the Great Pyramid than estimates using the notion of a ramp.

The specifics of the boat cranes are examined in exquisite detail in the book, *Pyramids on Water, Floating Stones* by István Sörös. I highly recommend this well-illustrated book in regards to its analysis of the solar barge designed and built as a boat-crane to move stones. Although efficient and fast these boat-cranes are not the entire answer to moving all the stones of the Great Pyramid. The capacity of the boat-crane is insufficient to move 70 ton payloads. Even István Sörös acknowledges this moving method is not viable for the movement of the largest stones encountered in the Great Pyramid.[7] Other movement and placement techniques and procedures need to be employed to accommodate the extreme weights of the casing stones and King's chamber ceiling stones.

Again, Gonna-no's story touched on the method used to move and set Great Pyramid casing stones. The payload on the barge he rode up on was a casing stone. He watched it being set in its final resting place. Although this procedure was described in a general way in his story, now is the time to analyze the way in which casing stones are moved and set in place. The Original Builders were able to quarry, move and place casing stones over a hundred thousand times and yet the "science" of Egyptology cannot duplicate this same feat even once. In the last 200 years the "science" of Egyptology has not made a casing stone like the remaining

Great Pyramid casing stones nor has it moved a casing stone like the remaining Great Pyramid casing stones in the manner they say they were moved. Egyptology with unlimited resources cannot demonstrate what they profess to be true.

Fig 11.4 The barge supporting the casing stone is moved so that the casing stone is above the mound of bonding agent. The workers will allow water to enter both compartments on the barge gently lowering the barge and casing stone onto the mound of bonding agent. As soon as the casing stone is set down on the mound of bonding agent the ropes and other supports are quickly removed.

Gonna-no described how a casing stones was set down onto the wall of casing stones and then positioned in place. We need to examine this procedure closer to appreciate how it was accomplished.

Just before lowering the casing stone onto the wall of casing stones, the bonding agent is applied to the area where this stone will be placed. This bonding agent is applied to the horizontal surface as well as the vertical surface of the casing stone which is next to the one being placed. While applying the bonding agent, a worker applies what at first glance appears to be a large mound of this material where the casing stone will be placed. It would seem to be too much, but this mound serves an important purpose.

Now it is time to lower the casing stone down on the casing stones already in place. This is accomplished by re-introducing water into the forward watertight chamber. This lowers the tipping barge as well as the casing stone. Both the filling and removing of water from the aft chamber in the tipping barge controlled the exact angle of decent. This causes the long tipping barge to act like a pivot so that the casing stone is lowered flat and not at an angle. By controlling the water in both of the watertight compartments, the tipping barge slowly and carefully lowers the casing stone down exactly flat onto the mound of bonding agent.

This procedure allowed for the casing stone to be placed very close to its final resting place. The casing stone is a few inches away from the casing stone it sits next to. This is because there was a rope in the way which attached to the sleeve at the front of the casing stone. Also the casing stone was placed back about a foot or less to accommodate the shelf which supported the casing stone.

From the quarries to being set on the existing wall of casing stones, no torturous, gut wrenching, pulling up a ramp was performed. The casing stone was set down near its final resting place but it is still not exactly where it needs to be. And what about the sleeve at the front edge of the casing stone? How was it removed with 16 tons of weight on it?

To finish the casing stone placement, two more tasks must be accomplished. These are the removal of the sleeve at the front lower edge of the casing stone and then positioning the casing stone exactly to within 100's of an inch. At first glance it would seem impossible to remove a heavy duty sleeve from the front of the casing stone after it already has been set on the mound of bonding agent. This sleeve must be removed without damaging the sleeve or more importantly without damaging the casing stone. There are a number of ways to easily accomplish this step in the procedure which would be obvious to the Original Builders. I will describe just one of these.

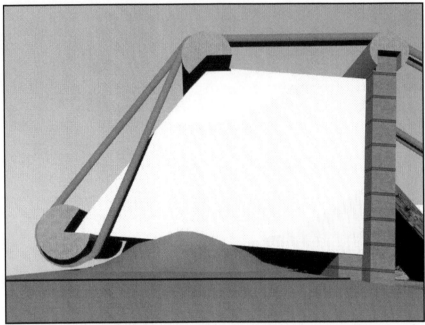

Fig 11.5 Detail of the process used to set a casing stone down. The mound of bonding agent is used to support the casing stone long enough to remove the sleeve and all the ropes and rigging.

There was a purpose in using a large mound of bonding agent placed strategically where the casing stone was to be placed. This purpose was to support the casing stone just long enough to remove the sleeve! After the sleeve was quickly removed the casing stone would settle down, flattening out the mound of bonding agent. The copious amount of bonding agent was used for this purpose as well as creating the all important watertight seal between the casing stones. Excess bonding agent which oozed out from between the joints was scraped from the joints and saved to be reused right away on the next joint, limiting waste.

Virtually all Egyptologists and researchers say the material between the joints helped in easing the final exact placement of the casing stones.[8]   The bonding material, when it was still wet, acted like a lubricant to allow the casing stone to be moved easier than without it.

Fig 11.6 The process of moving and placing the casing stone is almost completed. This image shows the directions that the casing stone has to be moved to reach its final resting place. Both the joint below and beside the casing stone have been coated with a strong bonding agent. This will make the horizontal and vertical joints watertight.

The final step in placing a casing stone is to precisely position the exquisitely cut stone to its exact position to within a few 100's of an inch. Although they can't show us, Egyptologists feel this was accomplished using the motive power of back muscles.[9] There is no way workers could have pushed with enough force to move the casing stone up against the next casing stone to squeeze out the bonding agent and force the casing stones together to within 1/50th of an inch. With a very limited working area as well as the extreme weights involved, Egyptologists assertions are unprovable. Egyptologists cannot accomplish this task but the Original Builders could by using a much different procedure. With available water, the maneuvering was done in a systematic, fast, extremely powerful and accurate manner.

Fig 11.7 The positioning barge finished moving the casing stone to its final resting place. The main barge would be filled with water allowing it to sink to the bottom of the construction pond. This provided a very strong support for the two heavy duty pivoting arms on the positioning barge. Filling the two smaller barges would cause them to pivot and pull on the ropes. This force would move the levers which would move the casing stones with exact precision and powerful force. The upper support for the pivot post is not shown for clarity.

Egyptologists cannot and never have lifted a 16 ton payload for even a few inches using only back muscles. Let's see how the geniuses this book calls the Original Builders finished moving a full size casing stone to its final resting place.

The utilization of water allowed this final step to be accomplished in a variety of ways. This system of using water to build the Great Pyramid is so versatile the methods of accomplishing this final positioning task are endless. I will describe just one method to whet the appetite of the inquisitive mind yet there are many other ways to accomplish this same task.

Another very specialized barge called the positioning barge was moved near the casing stone and quickly filled with water allowing it to sink to the bottom of the construction pond. While the other barges never sank so far as to touch the bottom of the pond, this barge was loaded with large stones acting as heavy ballast and was allowed to sink securely to the bottom of the construction pond. The main distinguishing feature of the positioning barge was that it had a heavily built structure called the pivot post used as a pivot for two levers. Also, it had two smaller barges which attached to the main barge so that they could pivot. The positioning barge with its two pivoting barges would be placed as the illustration shows.

The positioning barge finished moving the casing stone to its final resting place. The main barge would be filled with water allowing it to sink to the bottom of the construction pond. This provided a very strong support for the two heavy duty pivoting arms on the positioning barge. Filling the two smaller barges would cause them to pivot and move the levers which would move the casing stones with exact precision and powerful force. The upper support for the pivot post is not shown for clarity.

When the positioning barge was lowered and in place, its two massive levers were ready to serve their purpose. One lever was at the back of the casing stone and the other was at the side of the casing stone. A heavy duty lever was positioned behind the casing stone. Its fulcrum was the pivot post. Each lever was attached using rope to a pivoting barge. All of this was accomplished in a systematic manner and then everything was ready to move the casing stone to its exact final placement.

To move the newly placed casing stone up against the casing stone next to it, the valve was opened in the pivoting barge attached to the lever, which was against the side of the casing stone. Lowering the pivoting barge would cause it to pivot. This pivoting action would pull on the rope exerting tremendous force on the lever. This force would move the lever against the side of the casing stone and move it in that direction.

To move the casing stone in the other axis was just as easy. Simply allow water to enter the other pivoting barge, causing the lever to push the casing stone to its final resting place. These two levers acted in unison, moving the casing stone precisely to its exact final position. They were not powered by back muscles. The force needed to press the casing stone up against the stone it abuts is more than can be provided by back muscles.

The subject of using short wooden planks to build the Great Pyramid was discussed by Herodotus and the Priests on the Giza plateau.[10] This author feels that the short wooden planks were doors for the water locks and not levers. Yet this is one of the very few applications where the planks are used as levers. This is made possible by the lubricating effect of the bonding material, as well as the very short distance the stones are moved in this manner. Even so a specialized barge is needed because this operation is beyond the force which can be provided by back muscles!

Just as soon as the casing stone is positioned using the levers of the positioning barge, this specialized barge is quickly re-floated by using siphon hoses draining water over the nearby perimeter wall of the construction pond. Another casing stone is already waiting on the tipping barge to be set in place. The excess bonding material which oozed out of the fine joints of the casing stone which was just positioned into place will be used to prepare the site for the next casing stone.

The construction process continues nonstop. Stone after stone is moved and set in place in a systematic process. All of these procedures and specialized barges are able to do what Egyptologists cannot do. The Original Builders using water, specialized barges and systematic procedures effectively and efficiently moved and placed the stones which comprise the Great Pyramid.

The Original Builders could do it and so can the nonprofit research foundation I am involved with. Imagine how interesting it would be to see this process today. It would surely make an interesting TV documentary. To move and set in place a full size 16 ton casing stone in this manner would be more interesting and much more valid then watching a gang of people herniate themselves dragging a 1½ ton stone up a three foot high ramp. A documentary demonstrating the movement of even one full size casing stone would supersede everything the entire "science" of Egyptology has ever done in regards to showing how the Great Pyramid was built.

The movement and placement of both the 2½ ton rough cut interior stones and the casing stones have been described. This leaves the largest stones. How were they moved and set in place? That very important and fascinating subject is addressed in a following chapter. But first, a thorough investigation of the water locks and casing stones is necessary.

---

[1] This Old Pyramid, dir. Michael Barnes, perf. Mark Lehner, Roger Hopkins VHS Nova 1994.
[2] Mark Lehner, The Complete Pyramids (Thames and Hudson 1997) 118-119.
[3] Ibid.
[4] István Sörös, Pyramids on Water, Floating Stones (Mandorfi 2001) 38-39.
[5] Ibid. 34.
[6] Gerard C. A. Fonte, Building the Great Pyramid in a Year: An Engineer's Report (Algora Publishing 2007) 113.

7 István Sörös, Pyramids on Water, Floating Stones (Mandorfi 2001) 98.
8 Leonard Cottrell, The Mountains of Pharaoh (Rinehart 1956) 240.
9 Gerard C. A. Fonte, Building the Great Pyramid in a Year: An Engineer's Report (Algora Publishing 2007) 137.
10 Herodotus, The Histories. (5th century B.C.) Translated by Henry Cary (G. Bell 1885) Book 2, Chapter 124 page 131

Chapter 12
Water Locks and Barge Moving Techniques

The construction of the Great Pyramid continues in a steady, uninterrupted process. It is efficient but efficiency in and of itself could never be responsible for the creation of this mighty structure. Remember, Egyptologists are efficient, but cannot actually do anything in the real world regarding moving or making components of the Great Pyramid. Efficiency in conjunction with the processes and procedures described in this book as well as using specialized equipment is what made this structure become a reality.

Construction pond crews starting their day (actually their shift) of work would hitch a ride on a barge ascending through the water locks. This trip up would be fast and much easier than climbing up along the series of water locks. Also, the trip would be much faster than most modern people spend traveling to work. The workers going up will replace the workers which will travel down the side of the pyramid after their work shift is completed.

As for evidence of a platform which was used to move workers down the side of the Great Pyramid during construction, there is none. There are no artifacts, hieroglyphs, written records depicting or referring to any such platform to move people down from the side of a half finished Great Pyramid. It is interesting to note that there is no physical evidence at all, specific to the Great Pyramid, that barges were used to move stones from the quarries on the east bank of the Nile River to the building site. There are no artifacts, hieroglyphs, written records, or drawings of any barge used to move stones for the Great Pyramid. Even though there is no evidence for barges at all in regards to the Great Pyramid, most traditional and untraditional researchers acknowledge and agree barges existed and were used to move stones from the quarries across the river to at least the catch basin in the Nile.

There is certainly no evidence by the demonstration of creating a casing stone equaling the precision of the casing stones of the Great Pyramid using bronze chisels or bronze saws by hand. It has never been demonstrated, yet this unsubstantiated notion is held near and dear to the heart of every traditional Egyptologist. The foundation I founded is so interested in this story to be subjected to the scientific method that there is a $50,000 research scholarship being offered to provide funding for such a demonstration. Please refer to Appendix A.

Just try to imagine what it would have been like working on the construction pond filled with water, barges and workers. Try to envision the choreographed orchestration of organized activity up on the construction pond. Imagine you are wading in a cool clear pool of water moving barges. You watch in fascination as workers on boat cranes walking back and forth as stones are lifted off barges and set in place. Work consists of operating valves and lock gates. Instead of working as animals hauling stones up ramps, water does the lifting. Instead of being beasts of burden, workers are signaling to each other and operating specialized barges and equipment.

This understanding of the construction process is based on the physical evidence of the Great Pyramid. This research concentrates on the stone moving methods and the technology involved in building the Great Pyramid. There could not be a greater contrast between this understanding of the building process, and the dry, dusty, outdated, and undemonstrated stories we are told by traditional Egyptologists who will remain high priests of the Ramp Cult until the day they die.

At the end of a shift, workers are relieved by another crew which starts their shift. The relieved shift heads for the platform which is ready for their trip down the side of the man made mountain. And the orderly, efficient construction process continues nonstop.

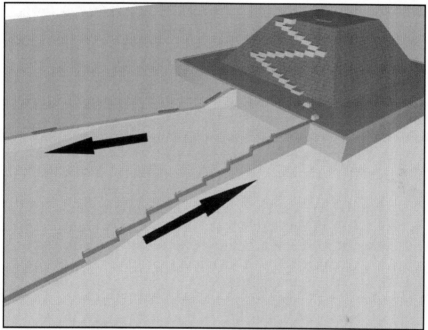

Fig 12.1 Loaded barges travel up the water locks in the foreground. Empty barges travel down the side of the Great Pyramid and then over the enclosure wall and down the causeway back to the Nile. The enclosure wall is about thirty feet high.

The empty barges must be returned to the quarries to transport another stone. This journey starts as they are moved over the edge of the construction pond and lowered down to the canal that surrounds the Great pyramid. But how do they get from the canal down to the Nile River? Possibly there were two sets of water locks between the building site and the Nile River as virtually all canal systems use. This would allow for the empty barges to move back down to the Nile. That is the most obvious possibility.

But there is another possibility which is much more elegant and is consistent with the direct physical evidence. These unloaded flat bottom barges may have been moved down the causeway (a large inclined plane) that goes from the building site to the Nile. Its original purpose may have been to return the empty barges to the Nile. To move an endless supply of *empty* barges *down* a ramp is much easier than to move an endless supply of loaded sleds up a ramp.

The purpose of using the causeway instead of using water locks is efficiency in water use and enhanced simplicity. Using the causeway eliminated the need for an entire flight of water locks to move empty barges from the enclosure pond back down to the Nile River. This idea is offered as just another possibility available to the efficient and ingenious Original Builders.

In figure 7.2 and figure 7.3 the enclosure wall is shown to be relatively short. This was true in the very early stages of construction. Even the Empire State Building during early stages of construction was less than ten feet high. The enclosure wall ultimately rose to a height of approximately thirty feet. The height of the construction of the enclosure wall coincided with the height of the construction of the casing stones until the enclosure wall was its full height. This allowed the material for the enclosure wall to be brought in on barges. As the casing stones rose level by level, so did the enclosure wall until the enclosure wall was at its full height of about 30 feet.

The use of water locks relating to the assembly of the Great Pyramid is conceptually a radical leap away from the familiar but unsubstantiated assertions of a gargantuan mega-ramp. Unfortunately, in our age, few people are intimately well versed in the operation, advantages, power, versatility and speed of systematically moving cargo through canals and water locks. The glory days of the canal and water lock era of the 19th century has long been over, and few people now have seen a water lock operate or have ridden in a boat being lifted by a water lock. The methods and advantages of transporting, lifting, manipulating and setting in place massive stones using water and water locks was what made the Great Pyramid's assembly possible.

In our age, the Great Pyramid is a tattered remnant of its original condition. The primary ravages and destructive violations to the most enduring wonder of the world created by man has been at the hands of mankind. Be it striping of casing stones, blasting with black power, tunneling in hopes to find treasure, the Great Pyramid is now just a dry, lifeless hulk, only a former shadow of its original condition.

In our age the Great Pyramid is dead, but it once was alive. It was alive with purpose, function and fulfillment for the culture that planned designed and built it. Even during construction the Great Pyramid teamed with life. Now this lifeless pile of rocks sits on a dry, dusty plateau overlooking the muddy Nile on one side and a seemingly endless desert rising up on the other. It was not always this way.

The primary difference between the Giza Plateau now and when construction was under way was water. It was water, the fluid of life, which transformed the Original Builder's vision of the Great Pyramid into reality. Water, in all of its wondrous properties and applications was the life-giver to the Great Pyramid. Water was utilized in a uniquely designed water pump to lift this powerful fluid to great heights. This lifted water, supplied a series of water locks allowing stones on barges to ascend the north side of this manmade mountain.

Water, impounded by precision made walls of watertight casing stones, was used in a series of waist deep ponds of ever increasing heights to move stones to their final location. Water, whose buoyancy is stronger than ten thousand legions of men, lifted stones on barges without human muscle power. Water was used to move and manipulate an endless precession of massive stones with ease and speed beyond the ability of man's puny muscles.

We have all been told the Great Pyramid is a symbol relating to death. We have been taught this monument is a tombstone, showing everyone including tomb robbers where the Pharaoh's body has been interned. The official story we have been told is that this structure is the high water mark of a bizarre, nonsensical, burial cult, built to hold a dry dusty mummy for eternity. Nothing could be farther from the truth concerning the Great Pyramid's construction and purpose.

The Great Pyramid is not a symbol or monument to death, it is all about life. Just as a hydroelectric dam does not have mythological, symbolic meaning to our civilization, the Great Pyramid was not "symbolic" but instead was functional. The Great Pyramid was not built to entomb death but to enhance life. I mean real life, not ritual mumbo jumbo to maintain order of the KA or as a symbolic Ben-Ben stone but the actual, tangible, daily lives of the Original Builders of the Great Pyramid.

Even when under construction the Great Pyramid was teeming with life. It was alive with workers manning the gates and valves of the water locks. Barge handlers, water-crane operators, stone placers, and so many other specialized workers all performing their respective specialized tasks.

Just as all large public works projects, the assembly process continued day and night 24 hours a day, 7 days a week, all year long. There was no need to stop with the setting of the sun. Canals and water locks all over the world have always operated around the clock. The exacting placement of the casing stones would surely be done in daylight but the interior 2 ½ ton stones could easily be moved up the locks and to their final resting place with the bright moonlight or the light of torches.

For the ancients, using water and barges to manipulate stones and water locks to lift stones were liberating, effective and empowering building concepts. But for many in this day and age these same concepts and processes are a stumbling block to understanding the Original Builder's method of constructing the Great Pyramid. In our age of air travel, railroads, diesel trucks with trailers, canals and water locks are looked down on as being archaic, slow and obsolete. Nothing could be father from the truth.

When mentioning water locks in the same sentence with the Great Pyramid I get a lot of objections. Some of these objections are from people who have read books saying the ancients were not smart enough (or definitely not as smart as us) to be able to figure out something so "complicated" as a water lock. The reality is, modern man cannot even duplicate even one casing stone like those at the Great Pyramid by using hand tools, so there is much we have yet to figure out about how the Original Builders accomplished their advanced technological feats.

Other people, who I call the number people, email me with loads of computations as to how much water would be needed to be pumped for this system to work. They explain to me if a water lock holds 10,000 gallons to move a stone up to the next lock and if every level has it's own lock just to get to the twentieth level you would need 200,000 gallons! They tell me moving one stone at the slow rate of one every ten minutes would have drained the Mediterranean. They contend that no pump would be able to supply the necessary water needed for the water locks. They want to know how I answer that.

I laugh and ask them, if a Jet airliner uses 10,000 gallons of fuel to take a passenger from New York to London, how much fuel is used if two people are flown from New York to London? The usually answer: If they take two planes, 20,000 gallons of fuel is used, if they go on one plane, 10,000 gallons are used. Then they say, "But that is different."

No it is not different. The analogy holds true. Just as the same fuel is used to move two passengers or a whole plane load of passengers, the same water is used to move stone laden barges over and over again. Contrary to what most people would guess, it takes about the same amount of water to move a stone up one water lock as it does to move a stone to the top of a flight of 20 water locks! In this application there are stones in barges in every water lock up the north side of the Great Pyramid. Each time the uppermost water lock is filled a stone on barge emerges into the construction pond. The next time the uppermost pond is filled another barge enters the uppermost pond.

Look at it this way. Imagine there is a flight of twenty steps and you need to take bricks up to the top of the stairs. Suppose it takes 6 minutes to go from one step to the next higher step and you carry one brick. How long does it take to carry a brick to the top of the stairs? That is easy. It takes 20 times 6 minutes which is two hours. Wow, that does seem slow. If a system takes twenty minutes to deliver every stone from the base of the Great Pyramid to even half way up, then that system is invalidated by being too slow to move the number of stones needed to accomplish the building project.

The real question in regards to our stairs and brick analogy is: how long does it take to deliver the next brick? The answer to this question is pivotal to understanding the validity of water locks in this application.

When I ask this question some respond by saying that it would take two more hours to deliver the next brick up to the top of the steps. Other people say it would take over four hours. It would take two hours to go back down the steps to get the next brick and two more hours to go back up the stairs with the brick. I am truly amazed at how many people I encounter, who consider themselves knowledgeable, who give answer such as these. It is just a relatively few who give the correct answer.

If we lived in 1850 in a town along the Erie Canal such as Lockport, New York, everyone would know the correct answer. They would see firsthand every day and night demonstrations which validate the correct answer. But in our modern age, we live in different times. In today's world, this type of information is not common knowledge. The correct answer is not two hours or four hours to bring the next brick to the top of the stairs. The correct answer is a time duration which is shorter. Much shorter!

Fig 12.2 The speed of material flow using water locks is illustrated by the workers moving bricks up stairs. If it takes six minutes for a worker to move up one stair, then every six minutes a brick is delivered to the top of the staircase. After the brick is delivered to the top the worker moves down the ladder instead of traveling down the steps. This is analogous of the empty barges being lowered down the side of the Great Pyramid instead of back down the flight of water locks. Material flow is rapid and water usage is very efficient.

Even though it took two long hours to take the very first brick to the top of the 20 stairs, it would take only six minutes to bring the next brick to the top! The third brick would be delivered six minutes after the second. The forth brick would be delivered six minutes after the third. After the first brick each successive brick would be delivered to the top of the stairs at a rate of one brick every six minutes.

This is accomplished simply by having a person holding a brick on each step. When the first person with the first brick moves up a step, another person with a brick moves up right behind him. This continues until there is a person with a brick on each step. Then each time a person with a brick exits the flight of stairs at the top the person behind him moves up one step. Then the next person moves up a step and the next person behind him moves up a step all the way down the flight of steps. After every six minute interval another brick is moved to the top of the stairs! That is a rate of 10 bricks an hour around the clock. What if each person carried two bricks or even three? If each person carried three bricks then the delivery rate would be one brick every two minutes twenty-four hours a day! The rate of one stone every two minutes would be true for barges carrying three, 2½ ton interior stones! Using water locks, instead of stairs, the speed of delivering payloads is just as rapid. It is a fast system to raise heavy payloads.

Let's look at it another way. The famous flight of five water locks on the Erie canal was built at Lockport, New York. The town that sprung up around these locks was named after this engineering feat of the early 1800's. This flight of water locks did not cause a traffic jam or bottle neck through the canal. The reason is that the *flow* of traffic through five water locks is virtually the same as through a single water lock. Even as the Great Pyramid rose to the sky and the flight of water locks increased, the *rate* of the flow of materials was not significantly diminished.

Remember, every aspect of the strength and speed of moving and raising very heavy payloads with water locks has been demonstrated hundreds of thousands of times in the real world. Dragging one 70 ton payload up a dirt ramp has never been demonstrated. Not in the modern age or even during the construction of the Great Pyramid.

People still object to this line of reasoning. They point out after just a little while there would be a lot of people at the top of the stairs. They would have to stop the movement of bricks to allow the people at the top of the stairs to move back down. This would greatly hamper the movement of bricks up the stairs and reduce efficiency. But in our analogy after each person took his two hour journey up the flight of stairs and delivered his payload he then went down the fire escape and was ready to haul up additional bricks without slowing down progress in any way.

This analogy shows how this author contends the movement of stones to the needed height took place. Stones on barges moved up a series of water locks on the north face. These water locks were in effect a one way road going up. Each lock had a loaded barge in it and every time the uppermost water lock was filled a loaded barge entered the construction pond. When emptied of their payload these barges were removed from the pond by lowering them down the side of the Great Pyramid into the enclosure pond surrounding this structure.

With the enclosure pond encircling the entire building site, the barges would be able to be lowered down any side of the structure to the construction pond. That is, except the north side with the water locks. Whichever side was chosen at any given time would be based on which side would be the most convenient. This is just another facet of the versatility of this construction method.

Not only is time used efficiently, so is the water. Water is used efficiently and repeatedly because the water is reused each time it goes down the series of locks. The water goes down the water locks filling each successive water lock. This raises each stone laden barge one water lock. The series of water locks raises a continuous chain of stones on barges. As the building rises there is no large increase in demand for water to supply the ever lengthening flight of water locks. As water works its way down through the water locks, barges with stones work their way up the water locks. A flight of water locks is a very efficient use of water to raise cargo.

In most canal systems including the Erie Canal, the Panama Canal, and the Saint Lawrence Seaway, two sets of water locks are utilized. These side by side pairs of water locks allowed traffic to travel both directions at the same time. Construction of the Great Pyramid did not require two sets of water locks going up the north face to allow a route for the empty barges to go back down. This would have caused unnecessary complexity and water consumption. Moving the barges over the edge of the construction pond and then down the side of the pyramid eliminated unneeded complexity and excessive water usage. As always, the construction procedures used in building the Great Pyramid are the epitome of sophistication and efficiency.

Seventy tons is a heavy load to be sure. It has been demonstrated hundreds of thousands of times that a 70 ton payload on a barge can be moved through canals and water locks. The Erie Canal was originally built to a water depth of about 4 feet.[1] The barges were enlarged to handle a payload of seventy tons.[2] There were weigh scales with the capacity to measure 70 ton payloads, and bills of lading charging for the hauling those 70 ton payloads on barges. It is water and water locks that allowed the movement of these large payloads during the canal era of the 1800's and it was water and water locks that allowed the movement of these largest stones when the Great Pyramid was built.

Working people in the 1800's were able to move 70 ton payloads. Egyptologists in the 1800's right up to the twenty-first Century are unable to move a seventy ton payload even one inch!

People often disagree about this research, telling me the barges holding the largest stones would require a series of water locks which would be much too large to fit on the side of the Great Pyramid. They also object because they maintain the barges for the largest stones would be too big and too cumbersome to lift over the side of the construction pond and lowered down the side. These issues were easily resolved by the geniuses who built the Great Pyramid and are described in a later chapter.

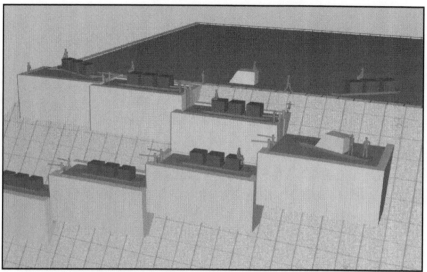

Fig 12.3 Detail of a water lock switchback. Switchbacks are used by railways as well as mountain trails to traverse a steep grade. The sloping side of the Great Pyramid is a "steep grade." Barges enter the switchback on the same end they exit. Notice that the barge entering this switchback is traveling stern first but will exit the switchback water lock traveling bow first.

The water locks zigzagged up the face of the Great Pyramid. At the top of each individual flight was a specialized water lock which allowed the stone laden barges to snake their way up the water locks. These water locks were distinctive in that barges would enter and exit on the same end of the water lock. In modern times these water locks would be called switchbacks.

Railways often employ the same concept when traveling up steep grades. In effect the side of the Great

Pyramid is a "steep grade" even for water locks so the ancient geniuses who built the Great Pyramid utilized switchback water locks to their full advantage. Just as in trains traveling through railway switchbacks, the barges would be traveling stern first part of the time as they traveled up the side of the Great Pyramid. This did not cause any problems whatsoever.

Yet, as amazing as it seems the most massive stones were *not* raised to their final resting place passing through water locks up the north side of the Great Pyramid. As described in a later chapter, these relatively few extremely large monoliths were moved from the Nile, up to the construction project and raised to their final resting place in a manner which is efficient and appropriate for the most massive components of this structure. This was accomplished without the need for extremely large water locks on the north face of the Great Pyramid.

I am often asked the exact dimensions of the water locks. The exact size is under scholarly debate. More research is needed to be conducted in the area between the catch basin and the Nile up to the building site. Also additional onsite research is needed to examine the north face of the Great Pyramid. When these areas are examined with water locks in mind, additional direct evidence will emerge indicating the size of these locks. To indicate an exact size without all the data would be inappropriate.

The need for this additional research has resulted in much scholarly debate as to the size, configuration, and location of the water locks on the north face. Research is ongoing but much can be surmised. Being a flight of water locks they were of similar dimensions and held about the same amount of water. Also, the height of lift was probably similar for each water lock. My assessment is that each of the water locks lifted the barges about the height of the first level of casing stones.

But there was not a water lock for each level of casing stones. Some levels of casing stones only had a height of eighteen inches. It would be impractical to use water locks that would raise a barge such a short height. To solve this, the Original builders simply used two or even three levels of shorter casing stones to build up the wall of casing stones for the height of the next water lock. This served the purpose of efficiently using shorter casing stones instead of wasting that material. Several layers of casing stones were used to create the walls for one level of construction pond. Again the Original Builders used construction methods which epitomized efficiency in the use of available material.

The first level of casing stones is about five feet high (all dimensions are approximate). The Great Pyramid being about 450 feet tall, there would have been about 90 water locks. Creating ninety water locks is less work to build and use than building a massive ramp with a volume larger than the Great Pyramid. Ninety water locks seems like a lot, but it is comparable to the number the Erie Canal had when it was first built.[3]

Another question I am asked is how much water could the subterranean chamber and related passages pump. The short answer is enough to build the Great Pyramid. Using water saving techniques, like lowering the barges over the side which requires very little water consumption and using the construction cranes requiring no consumption of water, helped in using the pumped water efficiently. But the exact gallons per minute needed to maintain the construction process is unknown in our age. The answer to the volume of water pumped was certainly known during construction.

The construction pump is gargantuan and its output considerable. The massive subterranean water pump cut into the solid bedrock, would have easily met all the demands created by the water locks and all other construction requirements.

To help answer these questions and others, the nonprofit organization called the Pharaoh's Pump Foundation is conducting research and experimentation to fully understand the operation of this unique and important water pump. Our foundation is dedicated to the redevelopment of this lost ancient, but high technology to be used in our modern, yet troubled era.

During construction it is estimated the water locks are delivering stones on barges to the construction pond about every 4 to 6 minutes, 24 hours a day. Although there is scholarly debate on this issue, each barge held possibly three to four rough cut interior stones. These same barges would handle just one of the largest casing stones. Boat cranes are moving the 2½ ton interior stones quickly off of the barges. Stone placers are placing the next row of casing stones. Empty barges are being lowered down the side of the pyramid. Everything is happening quickly and simultaneously.

Research indicates the construction process was very rapid. Most people have not spent much time in factories or witnessed the efficient construction of massive public works projects. To get an idea as to the huge amount of work which can be accomplished when workers operate machines I will tell of a recent experience I had with something that may be more familiar to people in our age.

I was recently at the home of my brother-in-law who is an avid firearms enthusiast. He was telling me he was going to do some cartridge reloading. Never having seen this done I asked, "What does it take to reload a cartridge?" As he was telling me all the numerous precision operations involved in reloading a cartridge I realized how labor intensive the process was. I asked how many cartridges he was going to reload? About 200 was the answer. "All that tedious, repetitive and exacting work will take days!" I exclaimed.

"Let me show you." He said as he took me down to his basement. At his reloading bench there was a funny looking blue machine bolted to the bench.

The most prominent feature of this machine was the large lever in the front. Telling me how cartridges are reloaded, he placed an empty casing in the machine. He pulled the lever and placed another casing in the machine. He did this several times then behold; a finished completely reloaded bullet (more accurately termed a round) came out of the reloading machine.

Continuing to operate the machine by simply moving the lever, he told me it was a progressive reloader. Each time he moves the lever once, several distinct and progressive steps in reloading are performed by the machine. As soon as the machine had a casing in each progressive step of reloading, every single time the lever is pulled a completely reloaded cartridge exits the machine. I watched with fascination as he kept pulling the lever and adding empty casings. Complete, perfectly assembled rounds came out of the machine. The exquisite precision of the mass produced product was astounding. Precision and fast work was performed by the machine the worker operated, but not by the worker.

As with a progressive reloader, so it is with the Great Pyramid. Each time the uppermost water lock (of the level being worked on) is filled, another barge enters the construction pond. While this was happening, workers move to the back of a boat-crane causing a 2 ½ ton interior fill stone to be lifted off a barge. When the workers move towards the front of a boat-crane a 2 ½ ton interior fill stone is quickly set in place. At the same time one barge has its stone (or stones) removed, another empty barge is being moved over the edge of the construction pond. All the while stones on barges are moving up the flight of water locks. Each step is an increment of the entire process and each step of the process happens simultaneously. It is just like the progressive reloader.

All researchers, either traditional or alternative, ponder the question of how much energy it took to move and place the stones. Traditional Egyptologists, who only move the most diminutive size of stones to attempt to convince people how the largest of stones were moved, ponder how many backs of sweaty slaves-taxpayers-volunteers it took to move the stones. Their edict is that it took a great many sweaty strained backs. That edict is not accompanied by a demonstration.

Less traditional researchers ponder how many priests had to worship sacred crystals to move the stones. Others ponder how many voices were used to "sing" the stones into place using the power of sonic waves. Still others wonder what energy source "aliens" used or try to comprehend the profound and secret energy force of pyramid power.

I know how much energy it took to move the largest of the stones of the Great Pyramid of Giza. I know how much energy was consumed to move the 70 ton megaliths comprising the ceiling of the King's chamber. I know how much energy it required to move the largest stones weighing as much as a diesel locomotive. It took 1,500 watts to move the most massive stone of this great building. 1,500 watts is the energy it takes to light 15 one hundred watt incandescent light bulbs. If you have 15 one hundred watt incandescent light bulbs illuminated in your home, you are using the same force it took to move a 70 ton stone of the Great Pyramid.

Does that make sense? Does that sound outrageous? Does it seem even farcical? Prove it you say! I don't have to prove it again because it has already been proven in the real world thousands, actually hundreds of thousands of times. The Erie Canal was built to be the same depth as the construction pond; between four to five feet deep.[4] The Erie Canal was used to move 70 ton payloads on barges. The payload was coal or wheat, not monolithic stones, but nevertheless 70 tons of payload were moved on a single barge. The method the loaded freight barges were moved along the canal was usually by the force exerted by two horses.[5] One horsepower equals about 750 watts making two horsepower around 1,500 watts. A working man can exert about ¾ of one horsepower therefore moving a 70 ton payload on a barge would be easy work for ten to twenty men.

Fig 12.4 Two horses walking on a towpath were used to move a barge with a seventy ton payload. Traditionally children were often used to lead the horses. If children can and did demonstrate the movement of seventy ton payloads what is the reason that Egyptologists cannot demonstrate how they think it was done? The reason is they are wrong.

Yet with the physical evidence supporting water as the lifting medium and water locks to lift the stone laden barges, people still object to water locks as being cumbersome, slow and unable to deliver the huge volume of materials needed to build the Great Pyramid. Again, look to the Erie Canal as an example. This 4½ foot deep, water filled ditch with over 75 water locks lifted payloads as large as 70 tons vertically over

500 feet. This is higher than the height of the Great
Pyramid.

The weight of the Great Pyramid is estimated to be
over 5 million tons.[6] The Erie Canal in 1846 moved almost 2
million tons of cargo.[7] This is nearly a third of the entire
weight of the Great Pyramid and it was moved in one year.
Water locks were just one key to the mystery of the lost
technology used in the construction of the Great Pyramid.
What is lost is modern mankind's knowledge that this
structure was built using water locks.

You can think whatever you want about the viability of
moving large amounts of heavy payloads using water locks.
You can maintain the opinion of water locks being hopelessly
antiquated; their usefulness superseded by modern man's
"advanced" technology. If that is what you think, then the
Chinese would contest your opinion. As I write these words
the Chinese are constructing the largest structure ever built
by mankind. In the valley of the Three Gorges River they
are constructing a mega-dam which will be used for flood
control and the largest producer of electricity on earth. This
dam incorporates structures instantly familiar to canal age
people. The world's largest structure will utilize water locks
to allow the passage of ships up past the dam into the large
reservoir it will impound.

Recently the Panamanians have decided to modernize
the Panama Canal because so many ships are being built
larger than this modern wonder of the world can
accommodate. Plans are in the works to build larger water
locks so that this canal will be able to handle much larger
ships. In the 21st century water locks are the most effective
system our greatest engineers choose to move our largest
objects.

The engineering minds of modern mankind use water
locks as the best choice for moving extremely large payloads.
They are successful in moving heavy payloads. The
engineering minds of the canal era used water locks as the

best choice for moving extremely heavy payloads. They were successful in moving heavy payloads. The engineering minds of the ancient geniuses who designed and built the Great Pyramid used water locks as the best choice for moving extremely heavy payloads. They were successful in moving heavy payloads. Egyptologists tell a story of sweaty backs moving extremely heavy payloads. They are successful in telling the story but forever unsuccessful in moving extremely heavy payloads. The reason is obvious. They cannot validate their stories using the Scientific Method.

The value and operation of the numerous examples of modern 21st century water locks being built around the world would be instantly understood by both canal age people as well as the Original Builders of the Great Pyramid.

What if, instead of just thinking about and pondering the idea of moving a couple of million very heavy payloads to a height of over 400 feet, you really had to do it? From the level of the Nile River or even the quarries at Giza to the top of the Great Pyramid requires moving the majority of stones vertically over 400 feet. What if, instead of sitting in your chair or standing in front of your college class, you really actually had to do it. If instead of just simply developing a conceptual model or a hypothesis presented as fact and then pontificating about it you really had to accomplish the goal of moving over two million very heavy payloads to great heights, how would you do it?

As you ponder that question consider the following excerpt from the book, Operations Carried Out on the Pyramids of Gizeh by Richard Howard Vyse. He wrote this passage when he was near the Pyramid of Illahoon.

This building is situated about two miles to the northward of the village, and at no great distance from the cultivated plains, which extend to the banks of the river. It is also near the commencement

of a strip of land, along which the
principal road passes to the Faioum, and
which is rendered productive by the
admission of water through a lock, erected
about five or six years since, apparently
upon ancient foundations.[8]

That excerpt is from his book published in 1842. Vyse
was describing a recent water lock which was constructed on
an ancient foundation. I submit to the reader that if this
ancient foundation was of a design which accommodated a
water lock in an era contemporary with Howard Vyse then it
is not unreasonable to contend that the ancient foundation
would accommodate a water lock in ancient times.

If you could not use or did not want to use modern
machinery like railroads, diesel trucks and trailers, cranes
with steel cables or any other similar modern machinery but
you were responsible for actually accomplishing the
movement of over two million very heavy payloads how
would you do it? What if you ventured into the unfamiliar
realm referred to as the real world, where competence is
defined as accomplishing genuine goals and achieving
tangible results? While you were in this uncomfortable
realm you really had to move the massive amounts of
materials the Original Builders of the Great Pyramid
unquestionably did. If you ever did achieve the goal of
moving so much material I already know the process you
would use.

If you would actually demonstrate success in the real
world, you would use water locks.

---

[1] Frederick Haynes Newell, Water Resources, Present and Future Uses
(Yale University Press 1920) 266.
[2] Ronald E. Shaw, Erie Water West: A History of the Erie Canal, 1792-
1854
(University Press of Kentucky 1990) 96.

3 Ronald E. Shaw, Erie Water West: A History of the Erie Canal, 1792-1854 (University Press of Kentucky 1990) 87.
4 Ibid.
5 Clifton Johnson, Highways and Byways of the Great Lakes (Macmillan and co., ltd. 1911) 20.
6 Charles Piazzi Smyth On the antiquity of intellectual man, from a practical and astronomical point of view (Edingurgh Edmonston and Douglas 1868) 469.
7 Peter L. Bernstein, Wedding of the Waters: The Erie Canal and the Making of a Great Nation (W. W. Norton & Company 2005) 376.
8 Richard Howard Vyse, Operations Carried Out on the Pyramids of Gizeh, Vol. III, Appendix, p. 81.

Chapter 13
Casing Stones

There is as much controversy and interest in the casing stones of the Great Pyramid as there is in just about any other feature of this fascinating structure. For centuries learned minds and dedicated researchers debated the very notion of the Great Pyramid being covered by a smooth layer of precision cut stones.[1] This century long debate ended in 1837 when Colonel Howard Vise discovered a few remaining casing stones still where they were placed by the Original Builders.[2] His discovery, made while removing the rubble from the base of the Great Pyramid, instantly ended the controversy of whether or not there was at one time a covering of smooth stones over this structure.

While that controversy is essentially over, everything else about the casing stones is hotly debated in our age. Every aspect of these magnificent finely crafted masterpieces is subject to raging and unending debate. In our age these casing stones are encased in a swirling whirlwind of controversy. Yet, at one time there was no mystery or controversy about how they were made, why they were made and how they were moved. There was no controversy about these things when the Original Builders were building the Great Pyramid.

The quarrying and moving procedures of the casing stones are not fully understood by modern science. Egyptologists cannot substantiate their assumptions, speculative guesses and preconceived, opinionated conjecture with experimentation which would validate their hypotheses. When dealing with the technology required to actually build the Great Pyramid, Egyptology cannot leave the shadowy realm of wide eyed storytelling and venture into the bright dominion of the Scientific Method. With all their education and resources Egyptologists can only provide lofty verbiage about the casing stones but cannot back up their words with demonstrations which would provide verification.

Egyptology cannot and will never reproduce even one casing stone in the manner their stories tell us it was done. They have yet to even demonstrate the creation of a *single* accurate surface of one casing stone to the same size and precision as the original artifact. If they cannot even get one casing stone right, maybe there is a lot they have not gotten right. Diametrically opposed to highly educated and highly trained Egyptologists, the Original Builders were people who exhibited an ability to create, transport and set in place casing stones over and over again.

Each and every time they created a massive precision casing stone it was a demonstration of how it was actually done. Construction of the Great Pyramid required over a hundred thousand casing stones.[3] Working people quarried the casing stones, finished them to perfection and then set these masterpieces in place. It is the working people who by actually *demonstrating their expertise* showed they were the real experts. If the creation and moving of casing stones were left to the responsibility of Egyptologists, the Great Pyramid would have never been built.

How these massive and exquisite stones were quarried to extreme precision and moved to their final location is the subject of endless heated debate. This debate is fueled by no expert providing compelling demonstrations to back up their words. Egyptologists, archeologists and all other experts have their own highly regarded opinions (which are nothing more than stories) on the quarrying and movement of these specific stones. Yet without demonstrations, these stories are all that modern day highly educated experts have to offer. How fascinating it is that every transporting and lifting requirement has already been demonstrated using canals and water locks.

As interesting as how the Original Builders created and moved the casing stones is the question of why. Every feature of these precise and massive stones elicit the question of why. Why did the Original Builders need the casing stones to be extremely large and seemingly difficult to move? Why did the Original Builders need the casing stones to be among the most precise stones of the entire Great Pyramid? Why did the Original Builders make casing stones to a greater degree of precision than the so called "coffer?" Why did the Original Builders need to bond the vertical and horizontal surfaces of adjoining casing stones with an ultra-strong bonding agent? Why did the Original Builders expend the extra effort to construct each of the four faces of the Great Pyramid so there is a crease along the center of each face? As we wonder about the Great Pyramid, the casing stones require us to ask the question of why.

Every feature of these casing stones fits the design requirements of the Original Builders. They knew what they were doing and did everything to fit their needs. The challenge to modern mankind is to understand how these design features fit into the overall construction process, as well as, why the Original Builders chose these design features for the casing stones.

Using water, locks and ponds to move and lift heavy payloads on barges is consistent with the available direct physical evidence. This is why the casing stones are created with such precision and bonded together. These features are necessary to create a watertight enclosure. Water locks and water are not a problem but a solution to every stone handling challenge met by the Original Builders. The construction pump, (built into the solid bedrock) water locks and watertight casing stones are the answers to all material transporting tasks required to build the oldest and most significant wonder of the ancient world.

If water is to be impounded by each level of casing stones to create a construction pond then the casing stones must be watertight. These casing stones must have precision made joints and the joints between stones must be bonded together. Not only must the vertical joints between casing stones be watertight, the horizontal joints between each successive layer of casing stones must also be bonded together.

Precise watertight casing stone construction is consistent with the available direct physical evidence. Both the feature of extreme precision as well as cemented vertical and horizontal joints impervious to water are critical for this construction process to be feasible. All of these required design features of the casing stones are found in the direct physical evidence.

The Great Pyramid's casing stones were not intended to be a good roof to keep the pesky Egyptian rain out as some have suggested, to be "profoundly symbolic," or to show the pride the workers had for their king. The casing stones had a design function. That function was to impound water. The physical evidence supports this assessment of purpose for the Great Pyramid's casing stones. The horizontal and vertical joints between the remaining casing stones are still watertight!

There exists much misconception as to the nature, design and placement of the Great Pyramid's casing stones. For almost a millennium, the vast majority of the casing stones have been separated from the rest of the Great Pyramid. Some Egyptologists and other researchers are of the opinion that generally, in pyramid construction, the interior stones are set in place first and then the casing stones were in essence a finishing layer placed over the rough cut interior stones.[4] Many maintain all of the rough cut interior stones were set in place first, and then a "sheathing" of casing stones was set in place over the rough cut interior stones.[5]

That order of placement is incorrect. That order of placement differs from the order of placement used by the real experts referred to in this book as the Original Builders. If you are of the opinion the Great Pyramid was built similar to what we see now, and then the casing stones were set in place to cover the structure, then you are wrong.

Think about it for a minute. Why would they move and position in place a covering of massive casing stones over the rough cut stones that are exposed today? Remember, full-sized 15 ton casing stones are so large and heavy it is beyond the entire science of Egyptology to lift even one a distance of one inch.

Fig 13.1 This image shows that if the builders just wanted to cover the pyramid so that it looked pretty there would be no need to use casing stones which were even larger and heavier than the stones they are covering. They could have used casing stones which were much smaller to achieve this same objective. Each course of interior stones could have easily supported the small casing stones. The Original Builders purposefully chose not to use small casing stones. Their construction procedure dictated the necessity of very large casing stones.

238 Lost Technologies of the Great Pyramid

It would seem that the casing stones are out of proportion if their purpose was to just cover the pyramid for a religious or cultural purpose. Look at it another way. Having an extremely heavy-duty covering is like having the paint on your car thicker and stronger than the automobile's chassis. Another example of a covering out of proportion would be the shingles of the roof on your house being thicker and stronger than the walls.

There is another explanation for the massive scale of the casing stones. This explanation gives a purpose and justification for the casing stones being more massive than the stones they are covering. In fact the casing stones had to be of massive proportions to accommodate every aspect of the fascinating building process used to construct the Great Pyramid. What follows is a thorough explanation of the building process focusing on the need for the casing stones to be components created on such a massive scale.

The Great Pyramid was built level by level. The bottom level was built first, including casing stones, then the next higher level and so on. Each level's casing stones were set in place when that level was under construction. Furthermore, the casing stones were set in place for the level under construction before the interior stones were set in place. I will say this again for emphasis. Each level's casing stones were set in place before that level's interior stones were set in place.

Although this order of placement is diametrically opposed to the ideas of most modern Egyptologists, the venerated father of Egyptology, Sir Flinders Petrie was of the expert opinion that the order of placement is as I have described. Late in his career as the premier Egyptologist in the world Flinders Petrie, wrote about this order of placement. In the 1930 article published in the prestigious periodical titled *Ancient Egypt,* he strongly maintained the Great Pyramid was built level by level and the casings stones were set in place as each level was under construction. He even wrote the casing stones were set in place not after but *first* before the interior stones were set in place for each level under construction.[6] Regarding the order in which the casing stones and interior stones were set in place, Flanders Petrie is in total agreement with this book. Other prominent early Egyptologists were in agreement with Flanders Petrie but their opinions have lost favor with contemporary Egyptology.

In that same article, Petrie was unsure of the exact method of how the Original Builders transported the interior stones over the wall of casing stones as each level was completed.[7] One of the purposes of this book is to explain how the Original Builders accomplished that task as well as other tasks during the construction process of the Great Pyramid.

The Great Pyramid was not just a bunch of loosely fitted stones with a layer of casing stones covering it up to make it look pretty. The casings stones, backing stones and interior stones were assembled allowing the Great Pyramid to become one massive, cohesive unit. This design feature made the Great Pyramid virtually as strong as if it was a solid structure.

The base of each side of the Great Pyramid is approximately 766 feet. The four walls of watertight casing stones rise up and converge at a single point about 45 stories high. Based on the construction procedure detailed in this book, the four casing stone sides of the Great Pyramid impounded water. I know of no solid concrete dam 45 stories high which is only about five to seven feet thick. Any dam built so incredibly thin and weak would burst by the pressure of the water behind it. The casing stones are not just a thin sheathing placed on a roughly built pyramid. The Great Pyramid is much more sophisticated than that.

In earlier chapters casing stones placement was described in reference to moving and placing stones during construction. Now a detailed examination is in order, focusing on how the sides of the Great Pyramid were assembled with sufficient strength to withstand the tremendous hydrostatic force of water as this structure was built.

During construction, the four sides of the Great Pyramid acted as four dams impounding a central body of water. Even though the construction pond in the center of these four dams was only about four feet deep the hydrostatic pressure on the walls of the structure is determined by the height of the structure during construction.

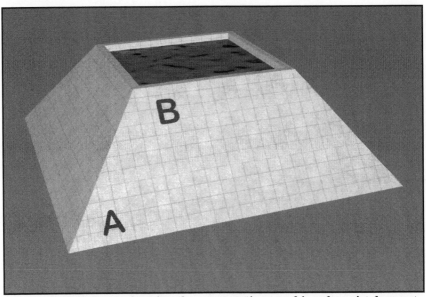

Fig 13.2 In this simple drawing the construction pond is only waist deep yet the hydrostatic pressure exerted at A is greater than the pressure on the walls at B.

When the structure is 200 feet high the construction pond is only about 4 feet deep but the pressure on the base of these four dams equals water 200 feet deep. This is because water exists between the cracks of the interior stones all the way down to the base of the Great Pyramid. Water pressure from the height of the construction pond exerts an ever greater force as the elevation of the pond increases, and as construction progresses higher and higher.

Thus each of the four walls of the Great Pyramid was required to be both watertight as well as extremely strong to resist the massive hydrostatic pressure. How was this strength maintained for the construction process to continue? When the construction of the Great Pyramid reached 300 feet high the water pressure on these walls acting as dams must have been tremendous! How could the Original Builders create the strength required to meet this necessity?

Instead of being a covering over a roughly constructed pyramid, the Great Pyramid's casing stones were an interconnected, integral and intergraded part of the structure. Although rarely discussed, between the rough cut interior stones and the finely cut casing stones were relatively well-cut stones called backing stones.[8] These backing stones were an interface between the rough cut stones and the fine cut casing stones. The casing stones, backing stones and rough cut interior stones were placed in such a manner that they interlocked and unified the entire structure. This interlocking arrangement and the cementing together of the casing stones added tremendously to the strength and integrity of the entire structure.

The first level of casing stones were set and cemented in place. These massive stones were about 5 feet high and at least 5 feet thick. They are undoubtedly strong enough to impound a pond about 4 feet deep. But the issue is how could the four walls of casing stones act like four dams and resist the tremendous force of the hydrostatic pressure when the pyramid was under construction?

Essentially the Original Builders ingeniously integrated the casing stones, backing stones and interior stones into a cohesive, unified structure. When the Great Pyramid was nearing completion the hydrostatic force on the lower portion of each of the four sides was tremendous. But the interlocking design of these three types of stones was more than adequate to resist this pressure. By using casing stones which were massive in scale and by integrating these huge components into the rest of the structure, the walls were more than adequate for resisting the force of the water inside the structure.

The hydrostatic pressure near the top of each of these four dams is relatively minor. As the construction progresses, the integration of each successive layer increases the strength of each of these four dams. So the effective strength of the four "dams" with this integration process is much greater than simply a relatively thin sheathing of casing stones.

The difference between this explanation of the casing stone placement and the explanation given in early chapters is this explanation provides greater detail. First, one becomes familiar with the general assembly procedure focusing on movement of stones and the order of placement. Then the integration procedure is included to more fully understand how the casing stones were strong enough to withstand the tremendous hydrostatic force from within the structure.

There is more to consider while examining the issue of hydrostatic pressure as it relates to the construction process. Again, consider the Great Pyramid nearing completion. The level of casing stones at the construction pond was not integrated into the structure. The beauty of this system is they did not have to be. At the construction pond level the water pressure on the casing stones was the very least. But just several levels below the construction pond the casing stones were firmly integrated with the backing stones and interior stones into the virtually solid structure of the Great Pyramid.

As construction progresses the integration of stones is completed as the hydrostatic pressure increases. The

Original Builders were truly unparalleled geniuses! I am forever amazed at the superiority and sophistication of the minds that envisioned and created the Great Pyramid. I am forever shocked and dismayed at the hellish and unworkable construction procedures and wasteful purpose this structure has been assigned by modern day "experts."

Another feature of the Great Pyramid that receives an enormous amount of interest is the sides bending slightly inward. When the casing stones were still covering the Great Pyramid there was a slight bending inward of each of the four sides from the apex down to the middle of the base. This crease in the casing stones is mirrored by the required indentation down the center of each rough face on the Great Pyramid which can still be seen today. Some say, including this author, the Great Pyramid has eight sides not counting the bottom. This design feature added complexity to the structure and it served a purpose important to the Original Builders. What that original purpose was is up to debate by numerous experts all with their own theories.

There are a number of purposes which have been presented to the general public as to why the Great Pyramid has this feature. It has been suggested this feature enhances the sunlight reflected off the casing stones in some profound way.[9] Others suggest the indentation was constructed by the Original Builders to tell us they knew the number of days in a solar year and wanted to tell us what they knew in this profound way.[10] Another proposed purpose for this feature was to provide a way to align the faces of the structure during construction by some undemonstrated method.[11] In the book, *the Giza Powerplant* it was asserted this feature helped the sides of the Great Pyramid act as a type of antenna to send and receive interplanetary, or at least extraterrestrial, electronic signals in some undemonstrated way.[12]

This author's interpretation of this design feature of the faces of the Great Pyramid is that it added strength to the structure. The four sides of the Great Pyramid acted like large dams impounding water. The very slight crease in the four faces in effect caused the faces to be "bent inward" providing additional strength to the walls impounding the construction pond. The pressure of water impounded by these four dams put the casing stone in compression. Stone is very strong when stressed in compression.

When I say this, I get a lot of objections. People look up the different types of dams on the internet or books and say that a curved dam must have abutments to absorb the pressure of the water impounded by the dam. People even send me pictures showing this. They say the four sides of the Great Pyramid do not have large abutments like canyon walls to take the pressure so the crease in the walls are not designed to help with impounding water.

We are analyzing the Great Pyramid which embodies the genius of the Original Builders. They did things differently than modern mankind does. I do not know of any arched dam which looks like the sides of the Great Pyramid. Arched dams like the famous Hoover Dam in the southwest United States of America are typified by having a beautiful curved arch which transfers the force of the impounded water into the canyon walls on each side. This is what gives arched dams their strength.

The sides of the Great Pyramid are much different than any arched dam I have ever seen. To simply compare an arched dam with the sides of the Great Pyramid to prove water was not part of the construction process is rather shallow research. It is the issue of the abutments a modern arched dam incorporates, but the Great Pyramid does not have. A number of people cannot get a handle on this.

Let me explain.

The four sides of the Great Pyramid and arched dams are very different structures. The casing stone walls of the Great Pyramid are integrated into the rest of the structure. Although constructed of components of very large stones, the

Great Pyramid, when completed, was literally as strong as if it were a solid structure. This is why it retains its structural integrity after over forty centuries. Even though it was built of blocks the construction procedure resulted in an extremely strong structure.

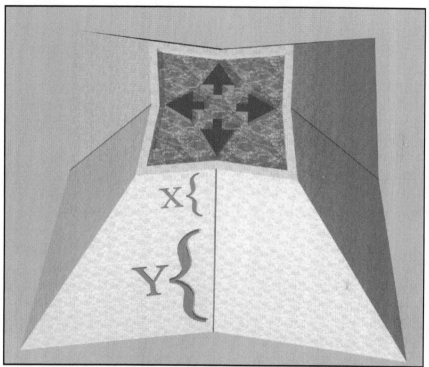

Fig 13.3 The hydrostatic force of the water pushes against the casing stones. In the area X the crease down each side caused the casing stones to be stressed in compression by the moderate water pressure increasing the strength of the sides. Yet in area Y the hydrostatic force is much greater but the integration of the casing stones with the backing stones and rough cut interior stones is complete. This provides the strength to withstand the tremendous hydrostatic pressure exerted on the four sides of the Great Pyramid. The crease down each face is shown out of scale to help convey how the water pressure acts on the casing stones.

At the height of the construction pond and a few levels below it the force of water pushing on the sides is at its minimum, but it is still a force to be considered. To help resist this force, the four walls of casing stones have a crease, or to put it another way, are bent in slightly. This puts the casing stones of the construction pond and the associated joints between these casing stones in compression. Stones stressed in compression are very strong.[13]

Yes, that compressive force pushes out towards the four corners of the pond. There are two important things to remember. The first thing to remember is the hydrostatic pressure at the level of the construction pond is relatively small. There is not enough water pressure pushing out at the construction pond level or even several layers below the construction pond to burst out the sides of the Great Pyramid.

The second thing to remember is just a few layers below the construction pond, the massive casing stones are completely integrated into the entire structure and are bonded in place with an extremely strong bonding agent. After integration, the water pressure is insufficient to move the casing stones even one millimeter. The pressure exerted towards the corners of the construction pond are absorbed by the structure itself.

The inward crease does add strength but it is only needed until the integration process is completed. It is just the level of the construction pond and a few layers below it that benefit from the inward crease. Yet several layers below the construction pond, the structure is just as strong as solid rock. The structure itself absorbs the pressure exerted on the four corners of the construction pond. The part of the four walls utilizing the crease to increase strength is only a few levels below the level of the construction pond.

A number of people have had difficulty with this concept. Looking at books on different types of dams they cannot point to a picture which is exactly the same as the structure of the Great Pyramid. They do see a picture of an arched dam with abutments. Some people have trouble visualizing how the crease incorporates into the construction process and it is a stumbling block for them.

Let's look at it again in another way. Imagine if a structure was under construction today shaped like the Great Pyramid. Imagine it is nearing completion and incorporates a construction pond. Today the structure would be built as a solid structure made of poured concrete. Instead of the pond being only waist deep let's have the pond's depth be several levels to where the integration process would have strengthened the walls. This would be about three levels down from the construction pond.

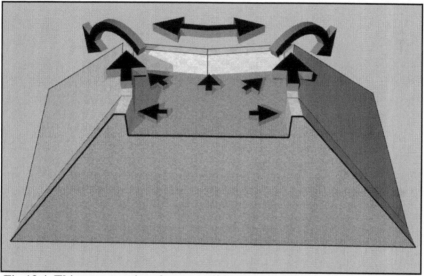

Fig 13.4 This cross-section shows a solid pyramid shaped cement structure with a pond on top. Water pressure pushes out on the walls of the pond. The crease on each side causes the water pressure to push the sides of the pond in compression. This exerts pressure towards the four corners of the pond. That pressure is absorbed into the solid structure. Although the structure of the Great Pyramid is made of massive components, their size, how they are interlocked, and the bonding together of the casing stones are features that contribute to the casing stones being able to resist the water pressure. The casing stones, backing stones and interior stones act as one cohesive unit impervious to the high water pressure.

What we have is a solid pyramid shaped structure with a flat top. That top has four walls extending up maybe 15 feet impounding water over the entire top of this structure. The structure below the pond is solid and extremely strong but the walls are not as strong. How could strength be added to the walls of the construction pond?

An excellent way would be to have the walls of the pond bend in ever so slightly putting the concrete in compression making the part of the structure which impounds the water stronger. The pressure pushing towards the four corners would be easily absorbed by the solid structure itself. The solid structure, as well as the relatively low height of the walls being strengthened by the crease, allow the structure itself to absorb the force directed toward the corners of the pond.

The walls of casing stones impounding the construction pond and a few levels below the construction pond are not as strong as the walls that have been integrated into the structure. This crease helps strengthen the walls at the level of the construction pond until the integration process provides enough strength to make the wall impervious to the increased water pressure.

Again, the crease in each face temporarily helps strengthen the walls of the construction pond until the integration process is complete. Pressure towards the four corners of the pond is absorbed by the structure itself. Exterior abutments are not necessary. The entire structure is virtually solid. The totality of the structure holds the water in.

This is a difficult concept for many. If all you can do is point to a page in a book about dams and say, "See there are no abutments on the Great Pyramid." then you will have trouble understanding how the function of the indented faces was incorporated into the ongoing construction process.

This crease is just another example of the direct physical evidence indicating the sophistication and advanced design the Great Pyramid possessed. The sophisticated construction procedure of interweaving the stones together like every aspect of this advanced engineering project points to the advanced intelligence of the Original Builders. To appreciate their sophisticated intelligence by understanding every aspect of the construction procedure requires some independent thinking on your part.

---

[1] Charles Piazzi Smyth, Life and Work at the Great Pyramid (Edmonston and Douglas 1867) 207-210.

[2] Ibid. 209.

[3] George R. Riffert, Great Pyramid Proof of God (Kessinger Publishing 2005) 38.

[4] John Anthony West, The Traveler's Key to Ancient Egypt: A Guide to the Sacred Places of Ancient Egypt (Quest Books1995) 205.

[5] Worth Smith, Miracle of the Ages: The Great Pyramid of Gizeh (Kessinger Publishing 2005) 61.

[6] Flanders Petrie "The Building of a Pyramid." *Ancient Egypt* June 1930, part ii pp. 33-39.

[7] Ibid.

[8] Craig B. Smith, How the Great Pyramid Was Built (HarperCollins 2006) 112.

[9] D. Davidson, Great Pyramid Its Divine Message (Kessinger Publishing 1992) 8.

[10] H. W. Badger, Great Pyramid and Talks on the Great Pyramid (Kessinger Publishing 2003) 2.

[11] Roger Herz-Fischler, The Shape of the Great Pyramid (Wilfrid Laurier University Press 2000) 264.

[12] Christopher Dunn, The Giza Power Plant: Technologies of Ancient Egypt (Bear & Company 1998) 221-222.

[13] David Dernie, New Stone Architecture (Laurence King Publishing 2003) 64.

Chapter 14
An Engineering Challenge

The civilization of the Original Builders, as well as our modern civilization, has left evidence of moving big objects. In this regard, our two civilizations are alike. A fundamental difference about these two civilizations is the manner in which big objects were moved. This difference in how our modern civilization and the very ancient civilization which built the Great Pyramid moved heavy objects has become a pivotal focal point of fascination to many historians, scholars, and researchers.

The Great Pyramid incorporates a number of massive monolithic stones in its construction. Most notable are the stones which comprise the King's chamber ceiling. Some authors describe these stones as being over 50 tons and some authors attest they are near 70 tons.[1] This author will not quibble as to their exact weight. There are other stones of the Great Pyramid which are of Herculean size. The large stones of the relieving chambers above the King's chamber, the ceiling stones in the Queen's chamber, as well as the two massive stones near the original opening of the descending passage, are the largest and heaviest known components of the Great Pyramid.

Many of these stones are fine granite from the Aswan quarries 500 miles upstream and on the opposite side of the Nile from the Great Pyramid construction site.[2] All traditional Egyptologists agree these granite stones were brought from the quarries and close to the construction site with the use of barges at least to the catch basin in the Nile.[3] This is true even though there is absolutely no remaining evidence of the barges which were used to move these specific massive stones. It is an accepted fact these massive stones on barges were at one time at or near the catch basin of the Nile.

These same experts, known as Egyptologists, cannot quarry nor finish a stone like the original ceiling stones of the King's chamber in the same manner as they say the ancient Egyptian working people did. Even though it is beyond the education and expertise of the "science" of Egyptology to recreate a King's chamber ceiling stone, they should be able to at least confirm their assertions of how the stones were moved by moving a payload equal to the weight of a King's chamber casing stone. Yet, their entire "science," which specializes in understanding ancient Egypt, cannot move even one payload the weight of these very massive components in the manner they say the ancient Egyptian working people did.

Our modern civilization has available for demonstration many heavy objects to move. Although Egyptology cannot create a King's chamber casing stone, our civilization has many 70 ton objects available to move allowing Egyptology to at least show the world how moving these huge payloads was done. Seventy tons is comparable to the weight of a railroad locomotive.[4] All Egyptology has to do is take the wheels off a locomotive and drag it up a dirt road. When they have dragged it up a dirt road about 20 stories high then it would at least lend some credence to their hypothesis and provide a measure of substantiation to their stories. Moving a 70 ton object is truly a monumental task of which the Original Builders were capable of. Working people could do it. The evidence is in the Great Pyramid. Yet it seems evident this same task is impossible for the "science" of Egyptology.

What then gives them the authority on this subject and why are they considered the definitive world experts on things they cannot do and will never do? I know they can discuss the hat styles of pharaohs, they can divine meaning from a bit of broken pot, and of course they can find and remove items as well as corpses from old graves they have disturbed. They can also say Imhotep, RA, and Ben-Ben quite often. Evidently, it is these peripheral abilities which make them the world's premiere experts on moving massive stones yet they cannot move massive stones. To be sure they can move relatively little stones. That is what they seem to concentrate on in the few demonstrations they have attempted. But in reality, a proposed stone moving method is validated only by a demonstration of moving the largest stones, not the smallest.[5]

Actually the real experts were the designers, engineers and common everyday workers who undeniably accomplished on a daily basis the movement of very heavy objects. It is their demonstrated expertise in successfully moving a mountain of big objects which truly made them the real definitive experts. To use a common catch phrase, the Original Builders didn't just talk the talk, they walked the walk. It is their actions and accomplishments which speak infinitely louder than the words in books and lectures of college professors. These Original Builders, by their impressive actions, demonstrated how the massive stones were quarried and moved. The Original Builders were the real scientists because they validated their stone moving methods by extensive and repeatable demonstrations. Those demonstrations resulted in the construction of the Great Pyramid. My endeavor is to understand how the Original Builders, who could and did move heavy objects, actually moved them. It does not lead to true understanding to accept the method of moving objects from people who find it impossible to move them.

This book has asked the reader to engage in several mental experiments. These mental experiments are a tool to help use one's imagination to visualize the events which resulted in the construction of the Great Pyramid. Use your mind's eye to visualize the process of moving the most massive stones on barges from the catch basin in the Nile up to the building site.

With your imagination, I ask you to engage in this mental experiment by transporting yourself back to the time when the Great Pyramid was under construction and place yourself as the respected engineer responsible for the task of moving the largest stones!

Imagine you are down at the catch basin and can hear the water splashing against the sides of the stone laden barges. You can see the finely cut King's chamber ceiling stones as they rest on barges. These massive stones were created in the quarries, and floated on barges down the Nile to the catch basin near the building site. From your vantage point on the edge of the Nile you can look up to the building site which is the final destination for these massive stones. You are faced with and *required* to accomplish the task of moving these largest stones to the building site. This engineering challenge is your job and your responsibility.

Are you up to the challenge?

This engineering challenge is the definitive challenge of the entire construction project. The largest and heaviest stones are considered the most difficult to move and set in place. The Original Builders met this challenge with unquestioned success but are you able to equal their performance in this mental experiment? These ancient engineers were faced with this exact same problem, which you are now faced with. They achieved their important objective.

There have been a number of suggestions as to how this seemingly formidable task was accomplished. It has been suggested by some traditional Egyptologists that the barges were brought even closer to the construction site than the catch basin by taking advantage of the yearly inundation of the Nile River. With the rising of the Nile, the barges would be allowed to get closer to the building site, reducing, but not eliminating the need to drag the stones with brute force of slave/volunteer/taxpayer back-muscle power.

Essentially, Egyptologists maintain that the 70 ton monoliths were moved on barges when the Nile was at its most treacherous. Then, when the barge was as close as it could get to the building site the stone was somehow offloaded from the barge into the muddy edge of the inundation. From the mud it was dragged up a dirt ramp towards the building site until it reached a presupposed nonexistent mega-ramp. Then the monolith was dragged up the dirt or possibly tafla ramp which, had it really existed, was arguably the largest structure ever built in ancient Egypt. Ultimately these 70 ton payloads were somehow muscled in place without any handling scars.

That is the story which is near and dear to most traditional Egyptologists hearts, and it is consistent with their belief system. Their faith in this tenant knows no bounds. After 200 years, the "science" of Egyptology has provided no demonstrative corroboration of this story. To Egyptologists, this often repeated article of faith is their only available option to explain the movement of these large stones.

Other researchers strongly maintain these stones were moved by a highly trained ancient priesthood who touched the stones and sang or hummed. It is proposed that this process allowed the stones to be somehow effortlessly moved. We are told, this mysterious stone moving technique accounts for the oral traditions and myths which refer to the stones being somehow "floated" into position.[6] It is the contention of this book, that the stones (on barges) were floated not by humming priests but by the buoyancy of water.

Some have assumed these largest stones on barges were simply and easily moved up the existing series of water locks from the Nile up to the building site. Then these monoliths were moved up the water locks on the north side of the Great Pyramid. As surprising at it seems, no, these largest monoliths were not moved to the building site in this manner for several reasons.

To move a 70 ton payload of coal or gravel or even a single monolithic stone requires a water lock the size of the ones used in the Erie Canal. The Erie Canal accommodated barges which handled seventy ton payloads.[7] These water locks measured 15 ft wide and 90 ft long. Only a relative few stones, less than one hundredth of one percent necessitated a water lock of this huge size. The vast majority of the Great Pyramid's components were much smaller requiring a water lock of much smaller dimensions.

Efficiency epitomized every aspect of this construction project, especially the aspect of stone moving. To construct water locks this large to move just a few stones is not efficient. To have a flight of water locks of this huge size going up the north face of the Great Pyramid was not feasible. To build colossal water locks to accommodate just a couple dozen massive stones is not an efficient use of water locks or water. It certainly does not seem reasonable to have an entire series of water locks that large for a few dozen stones.

Detractors of this theory of construction say it is nonsensical to have water locks of this immense size to move the largest stones to their final destination. They say it is absolutely impossible to build water locks up the north face which could accommodate barges for these largest stones. Therefore, detractors of this research contend that since the largest stones cannot be moved to their final resting place in this manner, the entire theory is invalidated and debunked.

I agree that enormous water locks were not built up the north face to move the most massive stones but, I do not agree this invalidates any of this theory. It is because of the valid technical reasons stated previously, the largest stones did not travel up the series of water locks built from the Nile to the building site, and did not travel up the water locks built into the north face of the Great Pyramid. There are many ways to skin a cat and there was another way the Original Builders moved the largest stones from the catch basin up to the building site.

So the Engineering problem remains. In this mental experiment, you are faced with the challenge of transporting these massive stones to the building site. You can only use what was available to the Original Builders to solve this engineering problem and accomplish your goal in order to fulfill your responsibility. There is only one force which is now unavailable to you but was available to the Original Builders. This powerful force, more powerful than all the back muscles of ancient Egypt, is what you as engineer must recreate in this challenging mental experiment. The force I am referring to is the undeniable genius of the minds of the Original Builders. Are you up to the challenge?

Remember, the use of large steel cables, motorized forklifts, tall gasoline powered cranes and flatbed trucks are all allowed in the movement of heavy stones of 1½ ton to the gigantic size of 2 tons. Naturally, this is only true if you are a modern day Egyptologist and these needed devices are out of the view of the cameras filming the "valid demonstrations" recreating how the ancient Egyptians moved stones.

Yet for you, in this mental experiment, the *engineering* problem remains! You are an engineer and you are still faced with the engineering problem of moving the 50 to 70 ton stones on barges which are in the catch basin of the Nile up to the building site. Each of these stones is the weight of a locomotive! Have you solved the problem yet?

You could do a number of things to assist in solving this engineering problem. You could hunt for mummies and take them and the booty buried with them to museums. You could spend years studying the Book of the Dead. You could interpret the shards of broken pots. You could become familiar with hieroglyphs in tombs which were written over 1,000 years after the Great Pyramid was built. You could write your doctorial thesis on the "all-important," Opening of the Mouth Ceremony. You could say words like Imhotep, mastaba, KA, Du'at, Ben-Ben, and Osiris an inordinate number of times when you lecture or write your book. You could learn about various "gods" which were worshiped and battles which were fought in ancient Egypt. You could be an authority on King's Lists or the hat styles of pharaohs. You could do any of these things or all of these things. You could do all of the above and more, but you would still be faced with the *engineering* problem.

That engineering problem is how to move very heavy payloads which are on barges from the Nile River up to the building site.

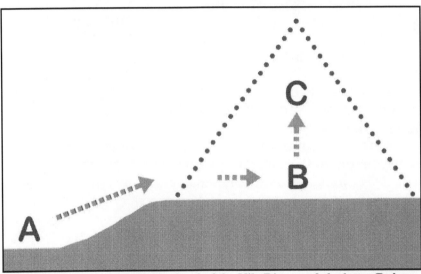

Fig 14.1 The letter A shows the level of the Nile River and the letter B shows the level of the building site. The letter C indicates the final destination of the largest stones of the Great Pyramid. To move the stones from point A to point C is the engineering challenge you are faced with.

It is time. As you stand on the dock at the catch basin with the wind in your hair and the sun beaming down, the 70 ton stones are still on their barges floating in the Nile River. The workforce around you is patiently waiting for your instructions. As chief engineer assigned to solve this problem you are required to accomplish this task on time and within budget. That is your job! What is your workable answer to the problem of moving numerous 50 to 70 ton monolithic stones from the catch basin of the Nile to the building site?

Remember in this mental experiment you are a proud and capable engineer. Unlike Egyptologists, engineers are trained to produce tangible results and solve physical problems in the real world. Don't tell a story; solve the problem. Leave the storytelling to Egyptologists.

This exact definitive stone moving challenge was solved by the Original Builders. The challenge to you is to solve the very same *engineering problem* faced by the Original Builders.

There were human beings a very long time ago in the place we call the valley of the Nile. Those human beings were just like us and they were faced with the same problem and challenge I have presented to you. But unlike people today, those human beings, without any question, accomplished the goal of moving those massive stones to the building site. To them it was not an academic amusement, mental experiment, a classroom lecture or a story in a book written by an Egyptologist. They were achieving a monumental accomplishment. They were faced with this problem and met the challenge. It was these advanced, ancient engineers who were the experts because they demonstrated their expertise.

Their minds were challenged by this same challenge you faced in the above mental experiment. Their genius solved this Herculean feat. You can see and touch the massive components which prove they solved the engineering problem. You can have faith and believe in ramps if you want to or need to. That is your prerogative. You are a sovereign being and I will not invade your sovereignty. If, for some reason, you need the ramp and brute force crutch to explain the existence of the Great Pyramid, it is your choice. If you need the unverifiable ramp and brute force story to conform to your preconceived paradigm of mankind's ancient past, again, that is your choice. If that is your preference, you have my condolences. I do know this. At least you have unwavering faith! Yet, your children or even their children will read this book with an unbiased open mind and make their choice as well.

What matters now is, the engineering problem still remains. I contend the massive stones on barges did not travel up the flight of locks and were not dragged up to the building site or up to their final resting place. What possibility remains which provided the solution used by the Original Builders?

The Great Pyramid does not easily fit the convoluted presupposition of tomb because it has many chambers and vents but the man-god only had one corpse and one spirit. Therefore, Egyptologists say there were a number of design changes in mid-construction. This author contends from the same direct physical evidence that the Original Builders actually knew what they were doing, from beginning to end. The Original Builders built the Great Pyramid with no change of plans as interpreted (a fancy word for guessed) by traditional Egyptologists.

To support a 70 ton payload be it coal, grain or even a single massive stone, requires a rather large barge. In the Erie Canal, barges which could handle a 70 ton payload required water locks to be 90 feet long and 15 feet wide. Instead of using a single enormous barge to carry just one of the most massive stones, research conducted by the Pharaoh's Pump Foundation, indicates that the Original Builders used a different method. They used several barges that supported a single stone.

There were a number of advantages to this method. Instead of a large stone on a single long skinny barge several barges were placed side by side. This arrangement allowed the series of temporary water locks to be both shorter and wider because the barges would be concentrated under the stone. Also it would allow these stones on multiple barges to be stored on the construction pond taking up less space. Plus the barges could be easily maintained as they floated on the construction pond.

Fig 14.2 Utilizing several barges, as shown, to support the largest stones has a number of advantages over using just one large barge.

Research conducted by the author in conjunction with the Pharaoh's Pump Foundation indicates that each of the largest stones were floated on several barges. This permitted barge maintenance workers to remove a single barge which needed repairing and replace it with a repaired barge. These largest stones, supported on multiple barges, were easily maintained when any repair was needed. The large ships Egyptologists call Sun Ships were constructed to be completely disassembled into parts.[8] It is not unreasonable to contend an ancient civilization can utilize several barges to support a massive stone.

During the initial stages of construction, even before the first layer of casing stones was set in place the activities to bring the largest stones to the building site were undertaken. There was no change of plans in mid-construction. The Original Builders knew there would be what we call a King's chamber with massive ceiling stones before construction began. These largest stones were quarried and shipped on barges to the catch basin during the *very* early preparatory stages of construction.

The topography between the catch basin and the building site is an inclined plane. This inclined plane rises up to the height of the building site. It has already been explained how a series of relatively small water locks were used to move the vast majority of the stones to the building site. But these water locks are too small to transport the largest stones. The Original Builders created temporary water locks designed to allow the movement of the very few largest stones on barges from the Nile to the building site.

There are numerous advantages of building this additional series of large temporary water locks. To build only extremely big water locks, large enough to allow the transport of the few largest stones would not be an efficient use of water or water locks. To build extremely large water locks to transport the few largest stones up the side of the Great Pyramid would be virtually impossible.

The Original Builders dug an enclosure near the shore of the catch basin at the Nile. The exact size of this large enclosure is unknown in our age. It could have been large enough to hold many of the massive stones on multiple barges or just one set of barges supporting a single 70 ton stone. For the sake of simplicity, we will say the enclosure was built to hold barges supporting a single 70 ton payload. The depth of this enclosure would have been about 4 to 5 feet below the level of the Nile. The Erie Canal was 4 to 5 feet deep and it accommodated barges holding 70 ton payloads.[9]

No, the stones on barges would not have been buried in this pit for thousands of years so Egyptologists could dig them up looking for amulets and mummies to take. This enclosure had an opening to the Nile so that the set of barges with a 70 ton stone could float into the enclosure. This enclosure would become a temporary pond capable of holding a single set of barges supporting a massive stone.

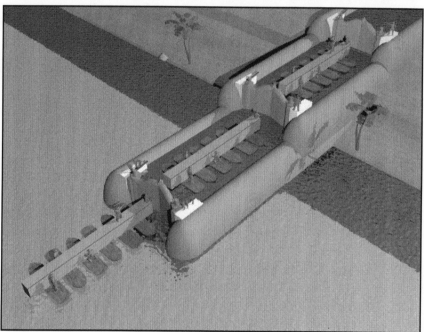

Fig 14.3 shows a series of large temporary stepped ponds separated by watertight doors on pivots allowing the movement of the largest stones up to the building site. The most massive stones on barges would enter these large temporary stepped ponds from the Nile River and travel up to the building site. The first temporary water lock would be built so that it had enough depth to allow the heavily laden barges in the Nile River to start their journey up to the building site.

Large burms or earthen walls about 4½ to 5 feet high were built along both sides of the temporary pond. This process was repeated several times creating a series of large stepped ponds up the incline to the building site as depicted in Fig. 14.3. Material for these earthen walls was dug out of the incline and from the areas of the temporary ponds. Between the temporary stepped ponds were large doors on pivots and the precision stonework necessary to support those doors.

The Original Builders had already provided a water source which supplied ample water to the building site. The enclosure pond impounded by the enclosure wall was full of clear, cool water. This water was directed to flow into the series of temporary stepped ponds creating a series of large temporary water locks! The water supplied to the building site kept the enclosure pond full. These barges carrying the largest stones were elevated up this series of temporary stepped ponds to the building site.

The process continued. These large barges traveled up the temporary stepped ponds. Walls were created as well as depressions in the inclined plane. The depressions helped in providing material for the walls and created depth for the ponds. Masonry was used only to provide a seal for the watertight doors between the temporary ponds, as well as pivot points for the doors to open and close.

These stepped ponds allowed massive stones on barges to march their way up to the building site. Once these temporary stair-stepped ponds reached the enclosure pond, the stone laden barges were allowed to enter the enclosure pond. The powerful lifting force of buoyancy was available and utilized in every successive pond. Behind this first set of barges in the enclosure pond were more barges in each of the temporary stepped ponds. They formed a procession of barges, and massive stones moving up a series of large scale temporary earthen water locks.

As with many water locks around the world, the method used to control the water levels in the stair-stepped ponds was obvious. Valves built into the watertight doors between successive ponds would provide water level control. In short order this procession of massive stones on barges moved through these temporary large ponds until they reached the enclosure pond. The water, already available at the building site, was used to keep these temporary water locks supplied with all the water they required.

Research indicates that once the process started, moving a 70 ton stone on barges from the Nile River to the building site took less than one day! That is a very conservative estimate for the time it took to complete this fascinating process. Certainly time and expense is involved in building water locks. Yet the tremendous advantages to water locks justify the work to construct them. That was true to those who built the Erie Canal and still true to the people currently constructing massive additional water locks for the Panama Canal.

Egyptologists reject virtually everything about this research including the utilization of water locks to build the Great Pyramid. The real experts (working people) actually accomplished moving these colossal stones. The "science" of Egyptology can only demonstrate their prodigious power of pontification. Egyptology cannot offer an adequate explanation or valid demonstration to substantiate what they pontificate. The reader does not have to agree with the theory offered in this book but must acknowledge the dismal failure of Egyptology in their scholarly effort to explain the Great Pyramid's construction methods.

This procedure of moving the largest stones would have taken place during the very initial stages of construction. In fact, these massive stones would have been moved just after the first layer of casing stones were set in place. They would have entered the central portion of the construction pond in an area designated for them. There, these huge stones, still on their barges, would have floated, waiting until these stones would be needed much later in the construction process.

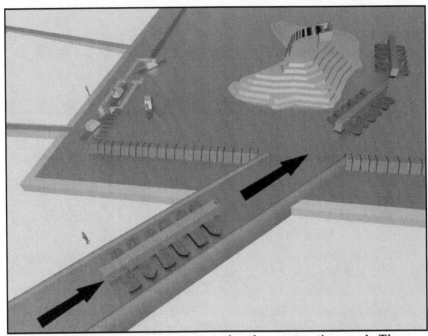

Fig 14.4 The largest stones are entering the construction pond. They traveled from the Nile River up the large temporary water locks to the construction site. Although these stones are the largest used in the construction of the Great Pyramid, moving them to the construction site was relatively easy. These massive stones were simply stored on their barges and rose up with the construction pond until they were at the level they were needed. Then they were only a few feet away from their final destination.

The approximately two dozen massive stones supported by barges would have been stored floating on the construction pond inside the wall created by the first level of casing stones. These massive stones on barges would have rose with every level of the construction pond until each stone was needed. When the stones were to be set in place, they were already available on the construction pond just a few feet away!

As the largest stones were stored on the construction pond for an extended time, occasionally their barges would need maintenance. The process of removing and replacing an individual barge out from under a 70 ton stone was very simple. The first step of this process was to provide extra support under the barge to compensate for the barge being removed. This was accomplished by partially flooding (which lowered) an additional barge and moving it under the 70 ton stone to provide additional support before a barge was removed for maintenance.

After the additional barge was in place water was siphoned out of that barge and over the edge of the construction pond which raised the additional barge. This provided supplementary support for the stone. This process would be done in a similar manner used with other specialized barges which were raised and lowered by letting water in a barge or siphoning it out over the edge of the construction pond as needed.

Then the barge needing repairs was partially flooded which allowed it to be lowered away from the stone and moved out of the way. The stone is still adequately supported by all of the other remaining barges plus the additional barge. The next step was to replace the barge needing repairs with a reconditioned barge which is already lowered by being partially flooded with water. When the reconditioned barge was in place water was removed from the reconditioned barge by the technique of siphoning, using a hose over the side of the casing stone wall. This allows the barge to become fully buoyant and rise up to again assist in supporting the massive stone.

The individual barge which was removed is now ready for repair. Every step in keeping these barges in excellent condition, which support the largest stones is quick, easy and labor efficient. There is no reason it wouldn't be.

As soon as all the barges with stones too large for the regular water locks were in the enclosure pond, the temporary series of ponds were not needed. These simply constructed and temporary ponds consisting of some masonry and mounds of earth, after thousands of years, left little if any direct evidence to prove their existence to the most obstinate "modern" minds whose faith focuses on the mythical mega-ramp. Eons of time and the shifting sands have obliterated these temporary structures which were built before the Great Pyramid. No excavations in this area have ever been conducted to look for remains of water locks or earthen walls used as stepped ponds.

So, how did you do in this mental experiment? As an engineer, it was your job and responsibility to complete the mission of moving the 70 ton monoliths up to the building site, as well as twenty stories above the building site. Did you succeed? Did you figure out the answer to the problem as well as fully appreciate the genius of the Original Builders? I hope you did.

I hope you now know how this monumental feat was performed. The Original Builders built a few relatively cheap and simple walls. The Original Builders built an artificial duct which provided a supply of water to the building site. The Original Builders built the enclosure wall around the construction site for the Great Pyramid. The Original Builders set in place the first level of casing stones. With the introduction of water as the powerful lifting force, dozens of massive monoliths already on barges were moved to the building site through a series of temporary water locks. No handling scars, no damage to the precious freight and the mission was a complete success.

We know the Original Builders were successful, I just hope the mental exercise was as successful. Placing yourself in the position of engineer, instead of Egyptologist, I hope you understand there is no other way to complete the engineering task of moving the largest of the components of man's first wonder, the Great Pyramid.

As the description of the construction process continues, these largest stones on barges are now floating on the ever rising construction pond at the Great Pyramid construction site. For the sake of simplicity and clarity the process of moving these largest stones to the building site was not included earlier.

In unison with the construction pond these massive stones effortlessly rose higher and higher. When construction progressed to the stage that these massive stones needed to be set in their final resting place, the stones were ready and available. But how was each of these massive stones moved *from* their barges and set in their designated final resting place? That is the subject of the next chapter.

---

[1] Ivan Van Sertima, Egypt Revisited (Transaction Publishers 1989) 149.
[2] David Hatcher Childress, Technology of the Gods: The Incredible Sciences of the Ancients (Adventures Unlimited Press 2000) 248.
[3] Craig B. Smith, How the Great Pyramid Was Built (HarperCollins 2006) 50.
[4] Ivan Van Sertima, Egypt Revisited (Transaction Publishers 1989) 149
[5] Edward J. Kunkel, Pharaoh's Pump (Warren, OH: Kunkel, 1977) 22.
[6] David Hatcher Childress, Lost Cities and Ancient Mysteries of Africa and Arabia (Adventures Unlimited Press 1990) 131.
[7] Henry Wayland Hill, An Historical Review of Waterways and Canal Construction in New York State (Buffalo Historical Society 1908) 444.
[8] Peter Lacovara, The Pyramids, the Sphinx: Tombs and Temples of Giza (Bunker Hill Publishing, Inc. 2004) 48.
[9] Ibid.

Chapter 15
Placing the Largest Stones

The worldwide escalating debate as to how and why the Great Pyramid was built rages on. This ongoing heated argument among experts in numerous disciplines, authors and professors seems irresolvable. The subject of the moving method of the most massive monolithic components of the Great Pyramid becomes more controversial every day, slipping further away from any expert consensus. This heated dispute encompasses all the mutually exclusive theories proposed by every type of expert. There is more controversy about transporting and placing the biggest stones of the Great Pyramid than sand on the Giza plateau.

Egyptology has done nothing to quench this raging fire of controversy. As Egyptologists shake their heads in disgust at this ongoing debate, the world craves real answers as to how this monumental structure was assembled and why. Egyptology has done little more than propose their yarn as a "solution" to how this structure was built. They have offered nothing more than their heightened ability to tell stories of ramps and perspiration, both on a massive scale. Their "science" does not engage in the Scientific Method by adequately demonstrating any aspect of how these largest stones were quarried to extreme precision, transported and set in place. Egyptologists have so far just told tattered tales as to how this was done.

Egyptology is described as the modern, scientific study of ancient Egypt. This discipline is about 200 yeas old. To put this in perspective, Egyptologists tell us that the three large Giza pyramids, massive construction ramps, various causeways and temples were built within the span of less than 200 years.[1] Egyptology has existed longer than they say it took to build the structures on the Giza Plateau.

The irony is Egyptology has yet to engage in the Scientific Method by recreating virtually any of the engineering tasks they say the ancient Egyptians did to build the Great Pyramid. The "science" of Egyptology has declared an edict proclaiming the precision casing stones were chiseled by hand.[2] They can't even show how a single 5 foot by 7 foot surface was hand chiseled to perfection let alone an entire casing stone. In Egyptology, tangible results of experimentation are secondary to storytelling. Their expert opinions are validated not by valid scientific experimentation but by "authority" and their own brand of expert interpretations. Engaging in the Scientific Method is foreign to this "science." If they are unable to provide validation to their ideas with a demonstration creating one casing stone then there is certainly *much* they are wrong about concerning the construction and purpose of the Great Pyramid.

The Original Builders were very different from Egyptologists. The Original Builders were able to demonstrate every single unique task which together resulted in the construction of the Great Pyramid. This included their grand demonstrations of quarrying, transporting and setting in place the largest stones of the entire structure.

The previous chapter explained how these massive stones were transported on barges into the construction pond. This chapter's description of how the Original Builders placed the largest stones starts with these most massive stones of the Great Pyramid, resting on barges, floating in the construction pond. In first analyzing the preparatory stages of construction early in this book, the description of moving these largest stones was not included. This was for the sake of clarity and simplicity. Now that the reader is familiar with the basic construction procedure it is time to address how the ancient geniuses responsible for this feat were able to place the largest stones which are still where the Original Builders set them in place.

In the previous chapter you took on the role of being the engineer in charge of moving these largest stones to the building site. Our attention is now focused how these massive stones were set in place.

The King's chamber ceiling stones, and other monolithic stones, are already at the building site. They float on barges in the construction pond impounded by the casing stones. Already brought to the building site during the initial stages of construction, these large barges are tethered together and float patiently waiting like mothballed battleships for their call to duty.

As each consecutive level of the Great Pyramid is completed, these barges with massive payloads rise up as the construction pond rises to the next level. Some of these stones will be placed over 20 stories high. They make this vertical journey to their final resting places as the Great Pyramid systematically rises toward the sky. It is the synthesis of the genius of the minds of the Original Builders combined with the buoyancy of water and the operation of the construction pump deep in bedrock which make the vertical journey of these massive stones so elegantly simple.

There was no massive ramp. There was no unnumbered multitude of back strained wretched humans straining on ropes pulling 70 ton stones up a dirt ramp. The Original Builders did not do that then, just as Egyptologists cannot do it even once now. The most massive stones simply floated on barges as they rose with the construction pond.

Each successive construction pond was a buzz of organized activity. Along with all the other specialized tipping barges, positioning barges, crane-boats and workers performing their specific tasks, there were the largest stones on barges patiently waiting to be put in place. These barges did pose a problem. When a level of the Great Pyramid was being completed with rough cut 2½ ton interior stones, these large barges were in the way of completing the level just below them. This seemingly difficult problem of these large barges blocking the completion of a level was easily solved by real people who were ancient geniuses.

When it was time and everything was ready, raising the construction pond to the next level solved the problem of placing the interior stones below these barges supporting the largest stones. The construction pond at the newly raised height provided sufficient depth to allow the barges supporting the largest stones to be floated out of the way. Then the crane-boats were used to place the rough cut interior stones which were previously blocked by the barges holding the largest stones. This simple procedure was completed as each level of the Great Pyramid was finished. On each level they must be moved out of the way to allow the rough cut interior stones to be set in place. This short journey happened at each level of the construction pond until these barges arrive at their final resting place. This additional step in the building process allowed each level to be completed and ensured adequate depth in the pond for the barges holding the largest stones. When these last rough cut interior stones are set in place that level is completed!

This simple modification of the assembly process was not included in the construction description of early chapters for the sake of simplicity. This additional simple modification of the construction process allows for the movement of the massive stones up, as construction of the Great Pyramid progressed. No sweated brow or strained back was required to move many 70 ton stones up twenty stories high. All that was required was the genius of the Original Builders to solve the engineering problem.

These massive stones floated for years on the ever-rising construction pond as the Great Pyramid rose higher and higher. One of the jobs workers had to do was maintain the barges supporting the largest stones. This was an extremely important responsibility. If one of these massive stones sank into the pond there would be no way to recover that stone. If Egyptologists cannot move a massive stone by hand, neither could the Original Builders!

There is no direct evidence of the barges which were used to move any of the stones of the Great Pyramid yet virtually all researchers and historians acknowledge barges were used. The once common knowledge of the exact shape, size or design of these barges is not known by anyone in modern times. As other barges for this construction project were used for specialized purposes in the movement and placing of stones in the Great Pyramid the barges used to hold the massive monoliths were also very specialized. These barges were designed specifically to support the massive stones of the Great Pyramid.

In the analysis of the Great Pyramid's construction process we are at the stage of placing the largest stones of this entire construction project. To set in place numerous 70 ton stones over 20 stories high seems to be the most difficult aspect of building the Great Pyramid. Egyptologists tell us, many of these stones originated as "living rock" in the granite quarries located 500 miles upstream and on the east side of the Nile River.[3] Egyptologists tell us, after being quarried and somehow placed on barges these stones made the journey along the Nile to the catch basin near the building site.[4] From now on, their journey to their final resting place is much different from what Egyptologists contend.

These massive stones have already traveled up from the catch basin at the Nile up to the building site. There they sat peacefully on barges as they made the historic yet effortless vertical journey up with the rising Great Pyramid construction project. This journey coincided with the punctuated raising of the construction pond. But now these stones are at the needed height and only a dozen feet away from where they will rest for eternity. All that remains of this epic journey is moving the stones from the barges to their final resting places.

To engage the reader in another mental experiment to determine the method used to set these stones in place is unnecessary. The procedure is so straight forward it is almost self-explanatory. The same powerful lifting force is used as before. Similar stone moving techniques are used except they are adapted for the specific task of moving these most giant of stones.

As is apparent, this book concentrates on the assembly process used to build the specific structure called the Great Pyramid. To understand the Great Pyramid, this author considers the Great Pyramid to be the direct physical evidence which needs to be understood. Egyptologists feel this is a flawed method of understanding because it somehow "rips" the Great Pyramid out of its contextual place in the evolution of pyramid construction. Yet this author contends, to understand the construction and use of the Great Pyramid the evidence of the Great Pyramid *is* the most "in context" evidence to be examined.

There is another large structure in the Nile Valley called the High Aswan Dam. To understand the technical aspects of how this structure was built and why, it would be a good idea to study the High Aswan Dam. It was financed, designed and built by the former Soviet Union. To understand how and why it was built do you have to learn to read, write and speak Russian? No. To understand how and why it was built do you have to be an expert on Carl Marx or be able to quote from his writings? No. To understand how and why it was built do you have to dig up a dead leader of the Soviet Union and take things from his grave? No. To understand how and why it was built do you need to be an expert on a "Leaders List" of the former Soviet Union? These peripheral things will not help you to understand the technical aspects of how the High Aswan Dam was built or how it operates as a machine.

Egyptologists abhor anyone who wants to know how a single pyramid and specifically the Great Pyramid was constructed who doesn't look at everything considered by Egyptologists to be somehow relevant evidence.

Egyptologists detest it when someone points to a 70 ton King's chamber ceiling stone and says, "How was that stone moved there?" Egyptologists despise specific questions about moving the largest stones because they cannot scientifically answer the question by showing how it was done. After 200 years of Egyptology with numerous displays of their priceless artifacts in museums, highly educated professors, large financial endowments, and a legion of respected authors all they can offer to anyone is to tell us a story!

They want everyone to look at how a 150 pound sun baked mud brick was moved to extrapolate how a 70 ton granite stone was moved. I have an idea. Egyptologists should engage in the Scientific Method to see if this is relevant. Get a 70 ton locomotive without wheels and move it in the same manner as they think a 150 pound sun baked mud brick was moved. If they can move the locomotive without wheels uphill on a dirt road in the same way as they say a 150 pound sun baked mud brick was moved, they will have succeeded in invalidating this entire book. If they cannot move a 70 ton payload in the same manner they say a 150 pound sun baked mud brick was moved then their story is not relevant evidence.

They want everyone to look at a hieroglyph of a few oxen pulling a rectangle on a sled and say that is evidence somehow relating to how 70 ton stones were moved. I have an idea. Egyptologists should engage in the Scientific Method to see if this is relevant. They should substantiate their story by getting a few oxen and a sled. Put a 70 ton locomotive, without wheels, in the sled and see if they can pull it uphill on a dirt road. If they can do it, this entire book will be invalidated. If they cannot move a 70 ton payload in the same manner they say a few oxen moved a rectangle, then their story is not relevant evidence.

They want everyone to look at a hieroglyph of a single large statue being pulled horizontally by ropes. Then Egyptologists will tell you this is how 70 ton stones, the weight of a locomotive, were dragged up a dirt ramp 20 stories high. I have an idea. Egyptologists should engage in the Scientific Method to see if this is relevant. Gather up all the Egyptologists the world over. Get a 70 ton locomotive with wheels removed and demand them to SHOW US how it was done. Then place the ropes in their soft delicate hands and yell pull! If they can pull the locomotive uphill on a dirt road and place the locomotive without damaging it to within a few millimeters of its final destination then this entire book will be invalidated. If they cannot move a 70 ton payload in the same manner they say a large statue was moved, then their story is not relevant evidence.

If they can do any of these tasks which they say the Ancient Egyptians did, then there would be no need for the buoyancy of water to do the heavy lifting and no need for a water pump. A growing number of dissatisfied people, are impatiently waiting for their relevant and valid scientific demonstrations. The results of their demonstrations must be consistent with the remaining direct physical evidence to be valid.

We have grown tired of their stories.

If you get nothing else out of this book I want you to fully understand the following two fundamental facts facing today's world. Fact one is: The Original Builders moved these massive payloads. The remaining direct physical evidence is irrefutable proof which validates this statement. Fact two is: Egyptologists cannot move these massive payloads. Although Egyptologists say working people moved these massive payloads on a daily basis, it has been over 200 years, and Egyptologists have failed to show a single recreation using full sized stones to substantiate their stories.

The reason why both of these facts are true is because the Original Builders used different methods than the methods told to us by Egyptologists. Egyptologists are fundamentally wrong about how the Great Pyramid was built. Their complete inability to demonstrate their proposed methods, with virtually unlimited funds and unlimited time, is a kind of proof that they are wrong.

This is why Egyptologists abhor anyone who wants to look at specific direct physical evidence. People point to a King's chamber ceiling stone and ask the engineering question, "How was *that specific stone* moved and set in place?"

When Egyptologists encounter someone with that engineering question, they want to take them by the hand and talk about sun bake mud bricks, a 4 foot high inclined plane somewhere in the Nile Valley and hieroglyphs made 1,000 years after the Great Pyramid. Then they will give explanations about mastabas, mummies, gods, gold amulets, KA, the hats of Pharaohs and Imhotep.

But as an engineering question, it is not only OK, but it is the most valid method to actually analyze the specific direct physical evidence available. That is the purpose of this book. Analyzing the most direct physical evidence available to understand how this specific structure was built does not rip the Great Pyramid out of some highly subjective, conceptualized latticework of ideas called context. If it is regarded as heresy and a thought-crime by Egyptologists to actually study the Great Pyramid, to understand the Great Pyramid, then so be it.

Had the Original Builders tried to solve specific engineering problems in the same manner as Egyptologists then there would have never been a Great Pyramid. The Original Builders would have been like Egyptologists, doomed to failure too. It is a wrong way of knowing to point to peripheral and unrelated shreds of data across the entire ancient Nile Valley, and extrapolate how one dissimilar construction task is somehow evidence of how another very different construction task was preformed. Especially when Egyptologists cannot substantiate their interpretations of evidence with demonstrations which recreate what they themselves hypothesize.

This inappropriate comparison of unrelated evidence is at the very least a flawed way of knowing and at worst it is a method which is disingenuous. Unlike Egyptologists the Original Builders were not wrong; they were right! The Great Pyramid demonstrates that. Unlike Egyptologists, the Original Builders were scientists and the Great Pyramid is the result of their demonstrations.

Although it is heresy to the "science" of Egyptology, I am going to describe the placement of a specific stone of the Great Pyramid. This specific stone is one of the largest used to build the Great Pyramid. This stone is the center ceiling stone of the King's chamber.

In discussing how this specific stone was set in place, I will not refer to any hieroglyph written 1,500 years after this specific stone was set in place. I will not say words like Duet, Osiris or Ben-Ben. I will not discuss the various hats worn by different Pharaohs. I will not tell you about Imhotep who never even saw the Great Pyramid. I will not refer to any gods worshiped by anyone. I will not refer to the "all important" Opening of the Mouth Ceremony or quote from the Book of the Dead. I will not show you a golden amulet removed from a dry corpse. I will not regurgitate the questionable story of how ancient Egyptians built mastabas which progressively grew in size and grandeur to the point that they were the shape of pyramids. I will not discuss a highly subjective and tenuous hypothesis about the evolution of pyramid construction.

In describing how this specific King's chamber ceiling stone was set in place I will not interpret symbolic, cultural, religious, and societal aspects of the Great Pyramid or any pyramid in the entire Nile Valley. I will not tell you a story about how the Great Pyramid maintained the Pharaoh's KA in the afterlife.

In understanding the technical and engineering aspect of the placement of this specific stone it doesn't matter what gods were appeased and worshiped. The gods didn't move the stone; people did. In understanding the technical and engineering aspect of the placement of this specific stone it does not matter what written or spoken language was used. Words did not move this 70 ton stone. It was people performing specific tasks and procedures which achieved the goal of moving and placing this specific stone.

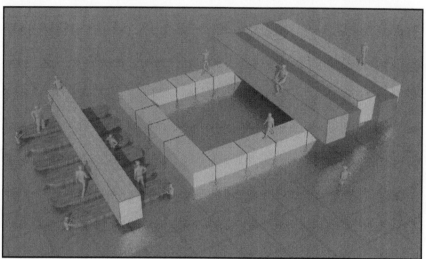

Fig 15.1 The construction pond is at the height needed to place the King's chamber ceiling stones. The pond is only waist deep. The next King's chamber ceiling stone is ready to be set in place. Some workers are wading in the pond moving barges. Other workers will be operating valves to let water into barges or siphoning water out of barges.

In understanding the technical and engineering aspect of the placement of this specific stone it does not matter what the cultural significance of the Great Pyramid or any pyramid was. Any symbolic or societal meaning ascribed to any artifact has no bearing on the engineering task of moving

King's chamber ceiling stones. In actually moving the 70 ton stone not one of these peripheral concerns matters then or now.

Instead of engaging in eloquent pontification about religious or symbolic meanings of golden amulets, I will do this. I will answer a specific engineering question. That engineering question is: How was the center ceiling stone of the King's chamber of the Great Pyramid moved to its final resting place? Egyptology has a grand story it will tell you about ramps and sweat maintaining the order of the Pharaoh's KA when they are confronted with this question. This book's answer to that specific engineering question offered to the general public is much different than what Egyptology has to offer. It is up to the reader to decide what best describes how the Original Builders answered this specific engineering problem.

The answer to how the Original Builders solved the engineering problem of moving and placing the center ceiling stone of the King's chamber is easier then transcending the mountain of misinformation about the Great Pyramid.

In describing the construction of the Great Pyramid we are at the point where the Original Builders had the center King's chamber ceiling stone on a series of barges floating in water just a few feet from its final resting place. The progress of the construction of the Great Pyramid is at the height which corresponds to the height of the King's chamber ceiling stones.

The ledge of a tipping barge was placed under the exposed end of the ceiling stone. This step was repeated on the other end of the ceiling stone so that there was a tipping barge supporting both ends of the ceiling stone. These tipping barges had the capacity of carrying at least 20 tons each. This is adequate lifting capacity plus a little extra to support a 16 ton casing stone which is the weight of the largest casing stone and together they were able to support about 40 tons! No sleeve was needed as when moving casing stones because the opposite end of the stone was supported by the other tipping barge.

But there is a problem. These two barges together can only support 40 tons and the King's chamber ceiling stones weigh up to 70 tons. More flotation is needed than what was provided by the two tipping barges. That additional floatation was supplied by several barges already supporting the King's chamber ceiling stone. These barges supplied ample additional flotation to support the center ceiling stone.

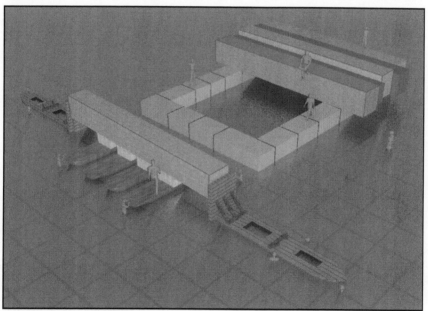

Fig 15.2 The King's chamber ceiling stone being moved is supported by a tipping barge at each end as well as several additional barges. These central barges have a platform between the ceiling stone and the barges.

Generally, when precision cut stones were to be set and cemented in place, the water level remained lower than where the stone was to be set. This kept water from interfering with the bonding agent as it cured.

Placing the King's chamber ceiling stones required a slightly different procedure. The next step in placing this very large stone was to raise the level of the construction pond up over the walls of the King's chamber. This would fill the chamber with water and the construction pond would be deep enough to allow the barge sections to float over the top of the King's chamber walls. This is an important necessity. There needed to be sufficient depth in the construction pond so that the center barge sections would be able to float over the King's chamber walls. This allowed the ceiling stone to be moved to a position which was just above its final resting place.

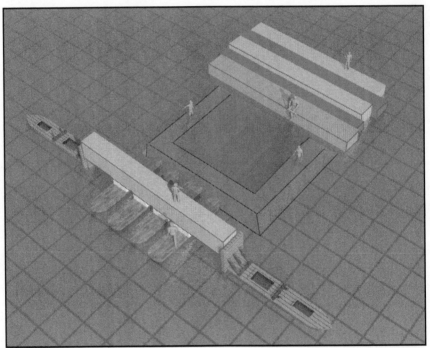

Fig 15.3 The level of the water in the construction pond was raised to the next higher level. It is impounded by the casing stones for the next level. The water is above the top of the walls of the King's chamber. The King's chamber ceiling stone and barges rose with the level of the construction pond. The next step in this systematic procedure is to move the massive stone nearer to its final resting place.

When this stone was positioned above its final resting place, the water in the construction pond was lowered below the level of the top of the King's chamber walls. Water in the King's chamber itself was kept level with the construction pond by using siphon hoses. Water was drained from the King's chamber into the construction pond keeping these two water levels equal.

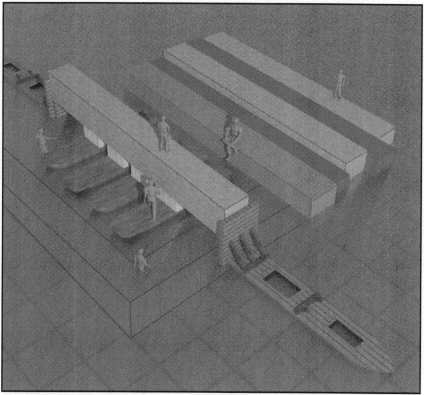

Fig 15.4 The massive stone and barges are moved close to the stone's final resting place. Then the water level in the construction pond is lowered. The platforms on the central barges allows the ceiling stone to be moved very close to its adjacent ceiling stone. The central barges move under the adjacent ceiling stone.

Now it was time to prepare the surfaces with the bonding agent where the ceiling stone will sit on the top of the King's chamber walls. This extremely strong bonding material was applied to the top of the King's chamber walls, as well as the underside of the ceiling stone to ensure a complete seal. Bonding agent was also applied on the vertical surfaces, where this stone will be joined to the ceiling stone already set next to it.

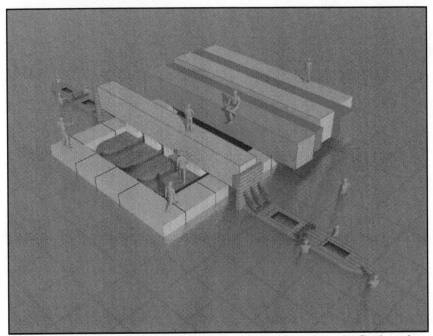

Fig 15.5 The King's chamber ceiling stone is one foot above its final resting place. There is also a gap between this stone and the ceiling stone adjacent to it. After a bonding agent is applied to the appropriate surfaces, water is allowed to enter all the barges and the massive stone slowly descends and comes to rest on the walls of the King's chamber! One step remains to position the King's chamber stone to its exact final location.

The King's chamber ceiling stone is floating about one foot above its final resting place. It is supported by specialized tipping barges on each end. Its center is supported by sectionalized barges. An extremely strong bonding agent has been applied to every appropriate surface.

The next step of this stone's incredible journey is lowering it carefully to where it will remain until the end of time.

Water is allowed to enter all the barges. This reduces their buoyancy and they sink in controlled unison. Watchful, expert stone placing workers perform this final task flawlessly as their supervisors watch with pride. Inch by inch the ceiling stone is lowered with several sets of hands used to guide the barge with accuracy to within a few millimeters. This massive ceiling stone continues its controlled downward movement until it makes contact with the top of the walls of the King's chamber. Finally this massive stone is placed on the King's chamber walls!

Additional water is allowed to enter the tipping barges as well as the barges used to place this massive stone. This process continues until the stone is free of all barges. The tipping barges are moved out of the way. The sectionalized barges floating inside the King's chamber stay in this chamber temporarily.

Then, positioning barges are moved into position and flooded so that they rest at the bottom of the construction pond. This allows for any final precision adjustment of the placement of this massive ceiling stone. Also, the positioning barges are used to push on the ceiling stone so that it is tight against the adjacent ceiling stone. This task cannot be done using back muscles.

There were a number of ways to remove the barges in the King's chamber. One way would be to leave the center sectionalized barges floating inside the King's chamber until the bonding agent cures. How long this takes is not known. The nature of this controversial but very strong bonding agent is under great debate. Only after the bonding material cures is the water of the construction pond allowed to, again move up over the tops of the King's chamber walls. When this is accomplished, the barges inside the King's chamber are floated out of the way and the next ceiling stone is moved into position.

Fig 15.6 Two positioning barges are being maneuvered into place. Just as they were used to position casing stones, they will push the ceiling stone tight against the adjacent ceiling stone. The positioning barges have been flooded and rest on the floor of the construction pond. This provides a sturdy pivot for the beam. Water is allowed to enter the barges connected to the positioning barges causing them to pivot. This pivoting motion pulls on the rope connected to the beam. The beam applies a tremendous amount of pressure against the ceiling stone causing it to move to its final resting place without the use of back muscles.

Another way to remove the barges from the Kings' chamber is to lift them out one by one with a large crane-boat. The crane-boat would be moved into position and the workers would move to the front of the crane-boat. Another worker would attach a rope from the bow of the crane-boat to the barge in the King's chamber. The workers would walk to the back of the crane-boat lifting the barge in the King's chamber out of the way. Whatever the method used to move the barges out of the King's chamber, the orderly process of placing each and every King's chamber ceiling stone is repeated.

This delay in waiting for the bonding agent to cure does not stop the overall construction progress. There is much more work to accomplish and rough cut interior stones to place while the bonding agent cures.

This systematic and ingenious process was the expression of the magnificent glory of the intelligence of the Original Builders! The ceiling stone, placed as it was is mute testimony to the brilliant intellect of those who moved it. There were no overworked sweat glands to make this engineering feat possible. There was no ramp.

Systematic, methodical, and orderly procedures were performed which allowed for the placement of all the King's chamber ceiling stones. Although these stones were the largest in size and weight, their transport and placement was no more difficult then placing any other stone. There is no reason it should be.

When all of the King's chamber's ceiling stones were set in place, what happened to the barge sections which were trapped inside this chamber? How were they removed? They were disassembled and removed from the King's chamber and the Great Pyramid through the passages and chambers after the entire structure was completed.

The creation, transport and placement of a payload like one of the King's chamber ceiling stones has never been accomplished to substantiate a hypothesis by any researcher of scientific discipline *in modern times*. That is; except for this explanation. The transport and lifting of a 70 ton payload using a barge and water locks in 4 ½ to 5 feet of water to a height higher than the Great Pyramid has been demonstrated over a million times in the Erie Canal!5

It is interesting how much evidence the Great Pyramid provides to support the movement and placing of these ceiling stones in the manner described. The ends of the ceiling stones of the King's chamber hang over the King's chamber walls.[6] These overhangs are still there and were needed to move the ceiling stone as described. These overhangs exist and were used to accommodate the ledges on the tipping barges. This important piece of direct physical evidence supports the moving method described in this chapter.

An enduring mystery of the Great Pyramid is the differing size and height of the casing stones. Generally the casing stones are largest at the base level and slowly decrease in size. This seems rational but in the 35th level the casing stones again become massive in size, comparable to the casing stones of the bottom level.[7] Many have pondered this odd arrangement of casing stones, wondering why the builders made the workers drag those big casing stones up to that height instead of just using those extremely large stones in a lower level.

Egyptologists would of course give cultural, religious, or societal reasons for this odd arrangement of casing stone sizes. They would suggest dragging these heavy casing stones so high was a way of paying a tax. I feel this placement of exceptionally large casing stones in the 35th level was for engineering reasons. They are there because they needed to be. Their purpose was to create a deep enough pond to maneuver and place the large Queen's chamber ceiling stones.

To maneuver these stones to the necessary angle and then placing those massive Queen's chamber ceiling stones in a gabled position, required a construction pond deeper than normal. The use of extremely large casing stones, roughly 50 inches high, was required to accommodate the placement of the extremely large Queen's chamber ceiling stones. How fascinating it is that the casing stones associated with this very level of construction are of massive size. The direct physical evidence must be this way to allow for the placing of the Queen's chamber ceiling stones. That is why the Original Builders used such large casing stones at that specific level.

The direct evidence supports this theory. This theory gives a functional meaning and purpose to the direct physical evidence. This explanation of the Great Pyramid's construction and the direct physical evidence of the Great Pyramid itself are in context with each other.

The ceiling stones were set in place using this systematic logical manner. There was no mythical mega-ramp. In contrast to the grand stories about an army of stone draggers, the placement of these massive ceiling stones was anticlimactic. Regular working people, using logical procedures in an orderly fashion, set these massive stones where we see them today.

Working people going about their everyday jobs, using the buoyancy of water and the power of their minds, placed the King's chamber ceiling stones. Oh how I wish Egyptologists were up to that same challenge!

The ceiling stones of the King's chamber, although among the largest stones of this structure, were simply considered to be components to the Original Builders. These ancient master builders assembled the largest components using a host of systematic procedures which utilized the powerful force of buoyancy.

The Great Pyramid is much more than the movement of just a few massive stones. It is the assemblage of millions of heavy stones moved to great height and positioned perfectly. To do this requires a production line of assembly and the Original Builders knew this. But that did not bother them because a production line capable of moving materials and assembling them was readily available by using water locks, specialized barges and the tremendous power of water.

---

[1] Craig B. Smith, <u>How the Great Pyramid Was Built</u> (HarperCollins 2006) 18.
[2] Ibid 90.

3 Ian McMahan, Secrets of the Pharaohs (HarperCollins 1998) 143.
4 Craig B. Smith, How the Great Pyramid Was Built (HarperCollins 2006) 112.
5 Frank H. Severance, (editor) Buffalo Historical Society Publications Volume Twelve (Bigelow Brothers 1908) 444.
6 Craig B. Smith, How the Great Pyramid Was Built (HarperCollins 2006) 190
7 William Kingsland, The Great Pyramid in Fact & Theory (Kessinger Publishing 1996) 25.

Chapter 16
Placing the Capstone on the Great Pyramid

The turn of the century was the dawn of a new millennium. To commemorate this once in a lifetime event, the people in control of the Great Pyramid had planned to install a replacement for the missing capstone on the Great Pyramid.[1] That is, if there ever was one. Brought to its resting place by a modern day military helicopter and lowered into position, this gold incrusted decoration would have adorned mankind's most endearing and enduring wonder. The ceremony associated with installing this ornament would have been replete with pageantry and showy ritual.

What a celebration this would have been with bands playing, fireworks exploding and speeches by both dignitaries and experts. A great throng of people from all corners of the globe would have been there thrilled to be eye-witnesses even though this media event would have been broadcast live everywhere on earth.

The true significance of this planned but cancelled event is debatable. Some saw it as fulfillment of prophecy or returning the Great Pyramid to its former "glory." Others thought the capstone would make the "unfinished" Great Pyramid symbolically "complete."

Would the new capstone help us understand how the Great Pyramid was built or why? No. Would the new capstone somehow, reveal hidden knowledge or important secrets of the ancients? No. Would the new capstone provide any tangible enlightenment? No. Would the new capstone compel Jesus Christ to reign on earth forever and ever? No. Would the new capstone help starving children or end droughts? No. Would the new capstone provide a cheap nonpolluting energy source for today's troubled world? No.

Would the new capstone act as a draw for tourists and increase revenues? Oh, yes! The new capstone would have served the same purpose as a new ride at Disneyland; bring the people back so they can spend more money. There is nothing wrong with that. I hope no one is kidding themselves in thinking there was ever any more to it than money.

The decision whether or not to place the new capstone on top of the Great Pyramid was in the hands of modern day high priests. These priests did not worry a bit about maintaining the order of the Pharaoh's KA or saying Ben-Ben or interpretations of hieroglyphs on temple walls. These modern day priests have their own religion and their own idols to appease. The religion of these priests is money and their idol is profit.

The effectiveness of advanced advertising was evaluated. Advice from world class promoters was gathered. The value of television rights was negotiated. Costs of the promotion and pageantry were estimated. Potential profit was projected. This data was analyzed with great concern by these modern high priests. The modern day priests announced their edict! There was not going to be enough money generated to make it financially worth it. The idol of profit would not be adequately glorified by placing the capstone on the Great Pyramid at the dawn of the new millennium. It is just that simple. Had there been enough profit generated, the Great Pyramid would have a modern gaudy trinket of a capstone on top of an ancient wonder.

Some say with unfailing confidence there was never a capstone on the Great Pyramid.[2] Others with equal confidence maintain the original capstone was set in place.[3] Still others "know" what the capstone was made of. Some say stone, others say solid gold, a few say electrum or even silver. Some say the capstone was an exquisitely cut jewel shining brightly in the rays of the sun. A few say it was an integral and important part of an exotic energy system.[4] Whatever you want the capstone to be made of or its purpose to be, you can find experts who will substantiate your opinion by their authority. This chapter will discuss how the capstone (if there was one) was moved and set in place based on this author's research.

From the remaining physical evidence of the Great Pyramid, there is nothing which conclusively proves there was or was not a capstone on this structure. No capstone from this structure has survived to modern times.[5] Through the last several thousand years, the writings of early researchers indicate the platform on top of this structure has increased in size.[6] In other words several of the top layers have been removed. This alteration of the pyramid was done by people dislodging the uppermost stones so they could enjoy the amusement of watching them tumble down the side of the pyramid.

To this researcher what the capstone was made of, be it stone or jewel encrusted gold is not important. It's ancient or modern religious, biblical, or prophetic significance (if any) is not important. I leave the interpretations of the capstone's "profound significance" to any number of researchers entranced by the esoteric. To this researcher, the significance of the capstone (if it ever existed) was how it was moved and set in place.

In striking contrast to the canceled, ridiculous event of placing a new capstone at the turn of the new millennium, what a show it must have been to witness the original capstone being finally set in place! That would have been something to see. That would have been an event worthy of real celebration. There probably was a huge commemoration by the very people who felt the satisfaction of their accomplishment. This celebration would be by the very people who accomplished what was celebrated. This long ago joyous time would have been much more genuine and significant than the crass epitome of sideshow hucksterism planned at the beginning of this millennium.

For those who are interested in seeing a real show, what a fantastic event that ancient show must have been! To move a precision cut stone to the pinnacle of the Great Pyramid must have been a feat to behold. Actually the process was not much different, or more challenging, than moving the stones the capstone sat on, or any other stone for that matter. The capstone was easily and systematically moved just as all the other stones were. Its only significance is that it was the uppermost rock (but not the last rock) to be set in place.

The construction pump (to be described in great detail in a later book) operated continuously keeping the ever rising construction pond full. Even at the height of the last few levels of the Great Pyramid, water was available to keep the construction pond full, and to supply the water needed for the water locks. How water was delivered to such a height will be the focus of an upcoming book by this author. The systematic assembly process continued nonstop, as this ancient skyscraper rose ever higher into the sky.

As construction of this structure advanced, each level would be finished more quickly than the level below it. Eyewitness accounts would say that the progress seemed faster as the Great Pyramid progressed up towards the point in the sky where the apex was placed. Each level is getting progressively smaller and is therefore finished faster than the level below it. This gave the impression that the rate of progress is increasing as the construction neared the top. In actuality, the rate of placing stones is progressing at virtually the same pace.

As the Great Pyramid construction project progresses, the construction pond rises higher and higher. This necessitates a progressively longer flight of water locks between the pond impounded by the enclosure wall and the construction pond as the building nears completion. Some would think that this would slow the rate of progress, but it does not. Additional water locks do not slow the movement of stone laden barges up to the ever rising construction pond. At Lockport N.Y. on the Erie Canal there was a flight of five water locks. This did not cause a bottleneck in the flow of traffic through the canal. The Panama Canal has two water locks on one end and three water locks at the other end. There is not a traffic jam at the end with three water locks compared to the end with only two water locks.

The main difference encountered as the building nears completion is the size of the construction pond. The higher the level under construction, the smaller the construction pond! Ultimately the pond becomes too small for the boat cranes to be used to lift the stones off the barges and set them in place. More than likely many boat cranes were used when the construction pond was large. As the construction pond became smaller, as each successive level was finished, fewer boat cranes were used or needed. When the decision was made that the construction pond was too small to use the last massive boat crane, the workmen disassembled it and the parts were lowered down the side.

Nearing the top of the Great Pyramid, the interior stones were relatively small compared to the majority of the rough cut interior stones.[7] One of the options of placing these smaller interior stones is to use smaller boat cranes than the large one which has been reassembled and placed in a museum near the Great Pyramid. There are smaller empty "boat pits" located very near the Great Pyramid which may have housed a smaller boat crane used in the construction of the upper levels of the Great Pyramid.

In constructing the top few levels of the Great Pyramid, the construction pond became very small. Often people have attempted to "debunk" this assembly process by saying that the construction pond would have been too small to finish the construction process. That would mean the complete system of construction described in this book is flawed. In the mind of many "debunkers" that is all it takes to dismiss this entire body of research. But we are dealing with much different minds than debunkers. We are dealing with the minds of the Original Builders, who were geniuses.

If you don't think the Original Builders were geniuses go to Giza (as I did) and see firsthand the result of their genius. I always wonder where all the debunkers run off to when an Egyptologist tells the story of extreme precision being created by using hand tools. Why are they afraid to debunk that??

Anyway, back to important matters. In the last few levels of construction, the construction pond was quite small. This necessitated the construction procedure to be slightly altered. There are a number of procedures that the Original Builders could have used to complete their wonder of the world. Interior stones in the top courses were of smaller size allowing for easier movement in tight quarters. A pivoting crane could have been used, supported on the casing stones. One end of the pivoting arm would be attached to the stone to be lifted. The other end of the pivoting arm would be attached to a large container which could be filled with water to counterbalance the crane and lift the stone. Other possibilities are endless, yet the method described below seems as efficient and interesting as any number of methods available to the Original Builders.

A temporary structure or wall was constructed around the top of the Great Pyramid. This wall was to impound a pond of sufficient depth to allow for the movement of the last few dozen stones on barges to finish the Great Pyramid. This *last* construction pond impounded by the temporary wall was supplied by the highest water lock, allowing stones on barges to enter this uppermost pond.

Nothing remains of this temporary wall that is known of in modern times. This wall was most likely built using timbers and made watertight by any number of materials. It could have been made watertight using animal skins glued together, using the timbers only for support. Possibly the timbers were constructed with precision and allowed to swell together when wet, making a watertight enclosure. What is important is the function of this temporary enclosure wall. Its function was to allow the completion of the last few levels of the Great Pyramid.

Fig 16.1 The temporary enclosure wall is on the top of the Great Pyramid. Stone laden barges enter the temporary enclosure from the uppermost water lock. This pond is waist deep. For clarity, the doors on the temporary enclosure are not shown.

After installation of this temporary walled structure, the construction process continued. Stones on barges arrive in this uppermost pond through the water locks. As always the stones are precut and ready for placement. In the last few levels, the construction pond is too small to accommodate a large boat crane. Therefore in these last few levels, the order of construction is reversed. The relatively fine cut uppermost *interior* stones are set in place first for each level then the casing stones are set in place for that level. The Great Pyramid is still constructed level by level but with the temporary enclosure impounding the uppermost construction pond the casing stones of these upper levels do not impound water.

The reason for this change in the order of placement of the stones is simple. Generally the casing stones impound the construction pond requiring them to be placed first. Then the interior stones of that level are set in place. But at the very uppermost levels, the temporary enclosure impounds the construction pond, allowing placement of the interior stones for a level and then the casing stones for that level.

When each level's cemented casing stone joints have cured, the water level in the temporary pond is allowed to rise to the next higher level and the process continues. The few relatively fine cut interior stones are set in place then the casing stones for that level are cemented in place. As this procedure continues up the last few levels, the available working area in the construction pond actually gets larger. This is because the levels are getting progressively smaller as construction reaches the apex. Work goes very fast in the final few courses of the Great Pyramid. The only delay in construction during these last few levels is the time needed for the cementing agent to cure before the next level is started.

As construction progresses the pond impounded by the temporary enclosure wall gets deeper and deeper. This requires the pond to be lowered back down to the level of the uppermost water lock when more stone laden barges are needed. Then several barges with stones enter the uppermost construction pond impounded by the temporary enclosure wall. The watertight doors are shut. Water is pumped into the enclosure causing the construction pond to rise to the needed level.

It is interesting to note most of the Great Pyramid was built from within where the final structure will be. That is except for the very first preliminary construction work. The first level of casing stones were set in place using an enclosure wall which was exterior to the Great Pyramid structure. Just as the first layer of casing stones were set in place from outside the structure with the help of a temporary enclosure wall, the last uppermost stones were assembled from outside the structure with the help of a temporary enclosure wall.

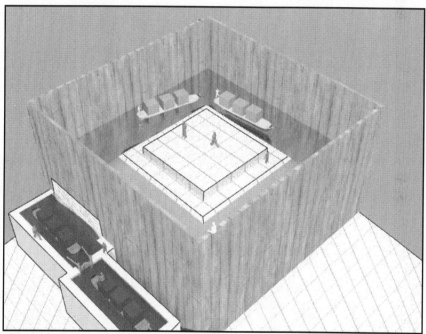

Fig 16.2 As construction progresses up to the apex, the construction pond impounded by the temporary enclosure has a larger and larger surface area and for the first time, becomes relatively deep. The water level is lowered down to the level of the uppermost water lock so that barges can enter this pond. Construction proceeds level by level as before but the interior stones of these uppermost levels are placed first, and then the casing stones for each level are set in place.

As it was in the beginning; so it was in the end.

Much of the movement and placement of the relatively smaller stones of the remaining upper levels was accomplished using the lifting force of water, as described before. Because of the diminutive size of the stones and the relative small number required in the last few levels, for the first time in the entire building's construction some very limited hand work may have been utilized. There may have been a small amount of levering of these smaller stones to move them off the barge into their final exact resting places. This minor levering of these smaller stones was probably more effort than the workmen were used to.

Just as the paving stones under the corner casing stones had a socket to align their placement, more than likely a socket was prepared for the capstone. Because the cementing agent was stronger than the stone a very shallow socket was all that was required.

The day finally arrived. All was ready. The final uppermost stone of this great structure was ready. The site for the capstone was over 40 stories high from the base of the building site. At the summit of the nearly completed Great Pyramid was a place prepared to receive this stone, revered in modern times, referred to by some in our age as the chief corner stone. At the building site, along with the workers, there were witnesses, scribes, dignitaries, holy men, officials, honored guests, scientists, engineers, and even the powerful leader of this advanced but ancient civilization. All were in attendance to witness this historic event.

All of the important personages gathered at the base of the building site which provided a view of the entire operation. Down below at the catch basin on the Nile is a barge with a faceted stone ready to make its monumental journey. This stone, a miniature mirror image of the structure it will crown, is the only stone of the entire building with this unique shape.

Just as when the first stone of this structure was moved, all in attendance watch as the mighty, wise leader gives a signal for the capstone to start its trip to its crowning destination. Then all eyes turn to the solitary gleaming stone on a lavishly decorated barge. The stone on barge makes its journey up the series of water locks, just as countless stones before it, from the Nile River to the enclosure pond encircling the Great Pyramid. Once the stone is in the enclosure pond, proclamations are given, speeches are made, hands are laid on the capstone accompanied by prayers, and the crowd and workers give a mighty cheer. When the ceremonies are completed the capstone continues it solitary journey.

Up the north side of the Great Pyramid the pointed stone on barge travels up the water locks. Each water lock acts as a step for this stone's historic climb. Heads tilt up as the stone zigzags up the flight of water locks to the summit of this brand new manmade mountain. As this stone reaches the temporary enclosure at the pyramid's peak, all minds ponder the significance of this stone's epic journey.

The capstone's barge enters the temporary enclosure and becomes hidden from all watchful eyes. The water pumping apparatus inside the Great Pyramid provides water to this great height, filling the uppermost temporary enclosure pond. Only those few workers chosen to place this stone are eyewitnesses to this monumental event. The same bonding agent is applied and the stone is allowed to slowly and effortlessly descend onto its rightful place of honor. Once this stone is in place, the usefulness of the temporary enclosure is over and the enclosure is disassembled and removed. It was probably made so that it could be disassembled just as the large boat cranes were made to be disassembled.

The honored dignitaries and impatient crowd had become restless waiting for the obstruction of their view to be removed. As the workmen remove this temporary structure the apex of the Great Pyramid is finally revealed. The roar from the crowd is a combination of pride, wonder, accomplishment, and awe.

I would give up everything and trade being a scholar of the Great Pyramid to be a workman on the pinnacle of the Great Pyramid that very day. To look down and view that long ago grateful assemblage surrounding this just-finished wonder of the world in all its newly built glory, would be an honor of which I am unworthy. What a privilege it would be to live in a time when leaders, experts, workers, and common people all understood the construction process, as well as the true purpose of the Great Pyramid.

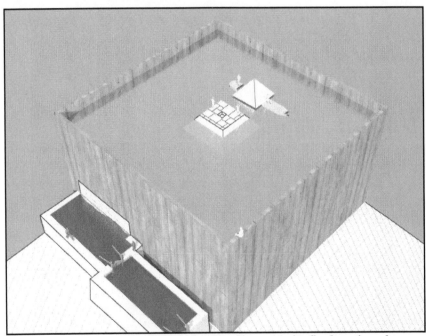

Fig 16.3 The capstone sits on a barge adjacent to its final resting place. This uppermost stone is ready to be set onto the Great Pyramid. After this stone is set in place the temporary enclosure wall will not be needed. This temporary wall will be removed revealing to the audience below the capstone crowning the Great Pyramid!

The capstone is in place but there is still much work to do. After the capstone was set in place, and the temporary enclosure structure was disassembled, the uppermost water lock was not needed. This water lock was filled in with smaller material.[8] The material to fill in this lock was brought up using the flight of water locks.[9] Even though the capstone was set in place water was still available to the uppermost water lock. This water came in from the interior of this structure, between the rough cut interior stones.

Casing stones were then brought up the series of water locks to replace the uppermost lock. The loosely filled area behind the casing stones allowed water to be available to the next water lock below. If this area was filled in with tightly fitting stone work, it would cut off the supply of water to the water locks. The only purpose for the water locks now is to bring the needed materials up to be used to fill in the locks. This process was accomplished from the top down.

After the uppermost water lock was replaced with fill and casing stones, the water lock just below it was subject to the same procedure. The materials were brought up to where they were needed by the water locks. Work progressed down the north side of the Great Pyramid until all the water locks were removed and the north side of the Great Pyramid was a smooth surface just as the other sides.

It was only after the replacement of the precision cut series of water locks with smooth casing stones that the Great Pyramid took on the monolithic, unornamented grandly simple and ultramodern appearance we imagine it had when new. These water locks, used to move millions of tons of stone had done their work and were no longer needed. These deceptively simple lifting machines, whose most memorable feature are the doors made of short wooden planks will live on enigmatically and cryptically in the oral traditions and legends of old. These water locks, now unneeded, were the antigravity devices used to levitate the stones with ease and "float" the stones ultimately to their final resting place.

Fig 16.4 As in all construction projects when the work nears completion workers are no longer needed. This is one such worker starting his journey back home. He is witnessing his last view, from the river, of one of mankind's greatest construction projects. The capstone is in place. The water locks which zigzagged up the north face are being removed and replaced with casing stones from the top down. The water locks from the Nile River to the construction site as well as the causeway, are not shown for clarity.

It was declared to Herodotus by the "priests" and he recorded that the Great Pyramid was built level by level from the bottom up, but was most assuredly finished from the top down.[10] His statement is accurate as explained in this chapter. Oh how I wonder how long it will take modern Egyptology to be as accurate as a 5th Century B.C. Historian!

Most researchers and authors have interpreted the statements of Herodotus in an incorrect manner. They incorrectly contend the casing stones were set in place after the interior structure was assembled. They also contend the outer surface of the casing stones was left rough when set in place.[11] So, many Egyptologists contend, after the Great Pyramid was covered in casing stones the outer surface of the casing stones was cut and polished smooth from the top down.[12] To corroborate their opinion, they point to Menkaure's pyramid.[13]

Yet in regards to the Great Pyramid, that is not how it was done. It has never been demonstrated using primitive hand tools that stone surfaces can be cut to the precision of the casing stones of the Great Pyramid. If you or any author or Egyptologist feels the stones were smoothed and polished by hand while in place, the nonprofit organization I founded is providing a $50,000 scholarship to help fund a demonstration proving your position. See Appendix A at the back of this book.

Another misinterpretation of the direct evidence is the sequence that the components were set in place. Many of the same authors and Egyptologists who are incorrect concerning creating smooth surfaces by hand, are equally wrong about the sequence of construction. They wrongly maintain that the interior stones were set in place for the entire Great Pyramid, then a sheathing, or layer of casing stones, were set in place to make a pretty covering for this structure.[14] That too is an incorrect assessment of the order of placement.

The construction process proposed in this book maintains the casing stones were, *finished on all sides*, before they were part of the assembly process. Then they were set in place first for each level under construction. Then the interior stones were set in place, finishing that level of the Great Pyramid.

The highly venerated Petrie wrote an article indicating the placement of the stones was in the exact order described in this theory of construction.[15] Regarding the Great

Pyramid, it was his expert opinion the sequence of stone placement was the same as in this theory.[16] How fascinating it is that the father of Egyptology, Flanders Petrie contended that the casing stones for each level were set in place first and then the interior stones were then set in place. But it took the visionary and genius, Edward J. Kunkel to figure out how that was done using water to float the barges, water in water locks, and water pumped up to supply the water locks!

The last step in creating the Great Pyramid was to finish filling in the water locks on the north face from top to bottom with smooth casing stones. Then the Great Pyramid, the greatest building project attempted and completed by ancient mankind was completed. It was finished as designed without any change of plans. This structure was built without any decoration or ornamentation and is complete inside and out.

Although made of stone, there seems to be nothing "stone age" about it. Although unbelievably antiquarian, this building is eerily ultramodern. The work is over, the project completed, and the society responsible for transforming a magnificent idea into reality is ready for their investment to make a profitable return by serving its purpose. This structure is utilitarian, and it serves as infrastructure, but what is its utility?

The brand new structure, the beauty and glory of the Nile Valley, sits as a solitary jewel rising from the glistening sparkling pond which surrounds it. Now it is able to give glory to where it rightfully belongs. The new Great Pyramid is designed, built, completed and ready to make the culture which created it better off than they would be without their new wonder of our ancient world. The Great Pyramid stands as an investment. It is an investment which heaped abundance, wealth, and leisure upon those who made the investment. This ancient yet high-tech marvel is ready to exhibit all the wonders of physics.[17] This ancient structure is the embodiment of lost ancient technologies which modern mankind desperately needs. The Great Pyramid is a dedicated machine built for one purpose only. It was built to be infrastructure for the civilization which constructed it. The Great Pyramid is a water pump.

---

[1] Vijay Joshi, "Great Pyramid to be topped off for new century" Associated Press San Antonio Express-News November 14, 1998.
[2] George R. Riffert, Great Pyramid Proof of God (Kessinger Publishing 2005) 99.
[3] Lytle W. Robinson, The Great Pyramid and Its Builders: A Study of the Edgar Cayce (Kessinger Publishing 2006) 7.
[4] Carole A. P. Chapman, The Golden Ones: From Atlantis To A New World (Lightning Source Inc. 2005) 126.
[5] Gerard C. A. Fonte, Building the Great Pyramid in a Year: An Engineer's Report (Algora Publishing 2007) 4.
[6] Everett W. Fish, Egyptian Pyramids: An Analysis of a Great Mystery (Health Research Books 2002) 78.
[7] Craig B. Smith, How the Great Pyramid Was Built (HarperCollins 2006) 112.
[8] Edward J. Kunkel, Pharaoh's Pump (Warren, OH: Kunkel, 1977) 19.
[9] Ibid.
[10] Herodotus, The Histories. (5th century B.C.) Translated by Aubrey de Selincourt (Penguin Classics, 1972) Book 2, Chapter 125
[11] I. E. S. Edwards, The Pyramids of Egypt (New Your Viking Press 1972) 207.
[12] Ibid.
[13] Craig B. Smith, How the Great Pyramid Was Built (HarperCollins 2006) 200.
[14] Ibid, 162.
[15] Petrie, 'The Building of a Pyramid' in Ancient Egypt, 1930, Pt II, pp 33-39.
[16] I. E. S. Edwards, The Pyramids of Egypt (New Your Viking Press 1972) 210.
[17] David Hatcher Childress, Technology of the Gods: The Incredible Sciences of the Ancients (Adventures Unlimited Press 2000) 259.

Chapter 17
Conclusion

Fifth century Greek historian Thucydides said, "Most people will not take the pains to get at the truth of things, and are much more inclined to accept the first story they hear."

The other day I went into the small neighborhood convenience store near my home to purchase a few items. The owner of this business (a friend of mine) was there and working at the checkout counter. As mutual friends do, we made small talk discussing each other's goals and recent activities as I handed him a 20 dollar bill to pay for my items. My friend took the 20 dollar note, and like all clerks do these days looked at it and then picked up a marker to determine if the bill was counterfeit. I stopped him and said, "Hey, what are you doing?"

"Oh, I'm just checking this 20 dollar bill, that's all. No big deal." He causally replied.

"I'm not trying to pass fake money to you." I declared.

"I know." he assured me as he continued to used the marker to check the bill I handed him to see if it is genuine.

Always being interested in how people decide what is true or not I pressed the point. Acting perturbed I said, "You told me you knew there was no problem with the money and you said you told me there was no problem with me, and yet you checked the money with that marker anyway! I want you to tell me why."

Looking me in the eye, he told me in no uncertain terms the reason he went ahead and checked the validity of the money I handed to him. As he finished the transaction and handed me the change he simply said, "Now I *really* know."

I was not mad at my friend but very proud of him. He took the responsibility and expended the effort to find out if the money I handed him was counterfeit or not. He made no assumptions, or extrapolations. He did not base his knowledge on anyone's authority, or worry about credentials. He simply performed experimentation on the 20 dollar note. My friend engaged in the scientific method to find out truth and is more of a scientist than any Egyptologist living today. That is an important lesson for us in a much broader spectrum because we live in a world containing both valid science and counterfeit science.

Much of scientific truth can and has been subject to repeatable and valid experimentation. This is the preeminent method to differentiate between what is true and not true in science. Unfortunately, much in the realm of science today has not, will not and never will be adequately verified as true by valid demonstrations. Instead of demonstrations and repeatable experimentations to validate what some authority contends to be true, validation is increasingly in the form of interpretation of evidence, extrapolations, unanimity of expert opinion and other forms of authority based verification. Counterfeit science has the opportunity to creep in when these alternative means are used to determine truth.

Thomas Jefferson said, "To maintain a free society, eternal vigilance is necessary." I feel this truism also applies to scientific inquiry. Just as the small businessman was vigilant in his pursuit of truth in his area of interest, it is everyone's obligation to be just as vigilant in their own quest in understanding the universe, the world and our distant past. Sciences involving valid and repeatable experimentation are less likely to be flawed with counterfeit science. The hardness scratch test used by geologists is reliable, repeatable and valid. We know this because it is verifiable.

How fascinating it is to me that when a science uses the scientific method by conducting repeatable experimentation there is generally a lack of controversy about the results of the experiment. There is no ongoing raging controversy about the scratch test to determine the relative hardness of rocks. In stark contrast there is ongoing raging debate surrounding much of what Egyptology says about the Great Pyramid. Heated controversy and debate go hand in hand with lack of scientific demonstration.

As of this writing, cold fusion has not been adequately validated by verifiable repeatable demonstrations. Because of this lack of demonstrations, the jury is still out on cold fusion's validity and rightly so. Yet for the life of me I cannot fathom why virtually the entire world has readily accepted what Egyptologists have told the world concerning how and why the Great Pyramid was built with virtually no demonstrations to back them up!

Unfortunately there is no felt pen to mark on the pages of this book or any book to see if it's content is genuine or not. There is no felt pen to put a mark on a theory to see if it is counterfeit or valid. There is no felt pen to use to validate or invalidate the results of a demonstration. There is no felt pen to use to make a determination if a particular theory is in context with the physical evidence. There is no felt pen to mark Egyptologists to see if they are simply blowing smoke. There is no all knowing magical felt marker to use to know what really happened so long ago when the Great Pyramid was being built. I only ask that this research be allowed the opportunity of open minded reflection.

Henri Poincare wrote, "Doubt everything or believe everything: these are two equally convenient strategies, with either we dispense with the need for reflection." This is exactly what I do not want you to do. The journalist Francois Gautier said, "Many live in the ivory tower called reality: they never venture on the open sea of thought." In understanding ancient mankind's greatest ancient achievement I do not grant you this luxury.

Some people tell me the ideas expressed in this book about the Great Pyramid, its construction method and that it pumped water, are all incorrect. They tell me I am wrong because these ideas and interpretations of evidence are all in direct contradiction of "expert" opinion in these fields. When people say this, they imply the end of science. However every discipline of every science is just getting started. Lewis Thomas writes, "In real life, every field of science is incomplete, and most of them — whatever the record of accomplishment during the last 200 years — are still in their very earliest stages." Science—the pursuit of truth—is only beginning, especially sciences requiring subjective interpretations of evidence which supersede the use of valid demonstrations as in the "science" of Egyptology.

Others who object to this book's direction of investigation say this research is folly and unfounded. To quote Alfred North Whitehead, "Almost all really new ideas have a certain aspect of foolishness when they are first produced." Nothing was more laughed at and resisted by the experts then the notion of mold making ill people well. John Locke wrote, "New opinions are always suspected, and usually opposed, without any other reason but because they are not already common." Although the ideas in this book are very uncommon now, I feel they will become the norm in the future. They were when the Great Pyramid water pump was built and used as designed.

Arthur C. Clarke's First Law states, "When a distinguished but elderly scientist states that something is possible, he is almost certainly right. When he states that something is impossible, he is very probably wrong." Someone on earth will be the last person who goes to his grave fully convinced of the idea a massive ramp was used to build the Great Pyramid. I pursue truth and I wish that fate on no one.

Science is, for the most part, wonderful but it is far from perfect. It is generally not the impartial open-minded pursuit of truth we imagine it to be. The way of knowing we call science seems to work best when the increase of knowledge and understanding progresses in small steps. The astrophysicist Bernhard Haisch wrote, "Advances are made by answering questions. Discoveries are made by questioning answers." The brilliant researcher Edward Kunkel was questioning answers when he discovered in our age the how and why of the Great Pyramid. As always, truly revolutionary discoveries seem to be fought tooth and nail.

The exalted experts of every field of Science have hampered the progress of the pursuit of truth when the truth is revolutionary to the accepted paradigm. Alfred Wagner never lived to see the acceptance of his theory of continental drift. Alexander Fleming fought 20 years with the expert medical community over the validity of penicillin. The list is endless and ongoing. If a discovery is revolutionary instead of evolutionary it will always be rejected and fought by the scientific community.

Science does not just routinely reject revolutionary truth; it also readily embraces falsehood as truth. If a false discovery or incorrect interpretation of evidence complies with the underlying paradigms held by the scientist then what is false will often be embraced as truth. The underlying paradigms and presuppositions of scientists often hold a higher priority than truth. The shining example of this is the immediate acceptance of the Piltdown skull as a valid missing link. It took over forty years for the expert community to "see" the file marks on the human skull and nonhuman jawbone. To my knowledge no expert ever said, "I accepted the Piltdown skull as a valid missing link but now I understand I was wrong and acknowledge the Piltdown skull is invalid." The experts who accepted the Piltdown skull as valid maintained their expert opinion until they died.

The next generation of experts knew the Piltdown skull was invalid but neither group of experts changed their minds.

When will these revolutionary ideas about the Great Pyramid's construction be accepted as true by the experts? Max Planck wrote, "A new scientific truth does not triumph by convincing its opponents and making them see the light, but rather because its opponents eventually die and a new generation grows up that is familiar with it." He is also attributed to have said, "Science advances funeral by funeral." Unfortunately it seems that when revolutionary discoveries are made it is the experts who are the last to figure it out.

George Orwell wrote, "At any given moment, there is an orthodoxy, a body of ideas which it is assumed that all right thinking people will accept without question." The current orthodoxy concerning the Egyptian pyramids in general is they were constructed using primitive methods, to be tombs. With regards to the Great Pyramid this current orthodoxy is under intense debate and beginning to crumble. This book's explanation of how and why the Great Pyramid was built contradicts Egyptologists current orthodoxy but is consistent with the remaining direct physical evidence. Egyptologist's refusal or inability to show us how this structure was made with any convincing demonstrations has fueled this controversy more than any other factor.

Max Planck also wrote, "The man who cannot occasionally imagine events and conditions of existence that are contrary to the causal principle as he knows it will never enrich his science by the addition of a new idea." I feel this is why the pseudoscience of Egyptology has completely stagnated in its understanding of the technology used to build the Great Pyramid. It is interesting to note that although Egyptologists are unable to convincingly demonstrate any aspect of the Great Pyramid's construction, every aspect of this building's construction has been fully demonstrated!

This series of valid demonstrations of every pivotal construction process was conducted when the Great Pyramid was built. By building the Great Pyramid the Original Builders demonstrated every aspect of the construction procedure. What the world has not seen in modern times (the last 200 years) is a demonstration of what Egyptologists tell us, showing was the methods of how this building was built. H. Bauer wrote, "It is not uncommon for engineers to accept the reality of phenomena that are not yet understood, as it is very common for physicists to disbelieve the reality of phenomena that seem to contradict contemporary beliefs of physics."

Egyptologists are neither engineers nor physicists. It is the aspects of engineering and physics of their explanations of the Great Pyramid's construction that are under dispute.

H. D. Thoreau wrote, "A man receives only what he is ready to receive. The phenomenon or fact that cannot in any wise be linked with the rest of what he has observed, he does not observe." As much as anything this is what the Egyptologists are faced with. Arthur C. Clarke said, "It is really quite amazing by what margins competent but conservative scientists and engineers can miss the mark, when they start with the preconceived idea that what they are investigating is impossible. When this happens, the most well-informed men become blinded by their prejudices and are unable to see what lies directly ahead of them."

Indigenous cultures around the world are not primitive. They utilize their environments in sophisticated ways, creating medicines, artwork and commerce. They have sophisticated languages, cultures and religions. And yet they have difficulty in conceptualizing radically different technology outside their understanding or experience. There is a story about Magellan's historic voyages concerning his contact with indigenous cultures on various Pacific islands. The sailors kept pointing to the ship and using sign language, but the islanders couldn't see it. They couldn't see the ship even when the landing boats were used to take natives out to it. The ship was so different from anything they ever saw or experienced they were unable to comprehend it. This fascinating phenomenon even appears in Disney's movie Pocahontas, where the main character sees the ship as "strange clouds."

There are accounts of inhabitants of isolated cultures which have never even seen photographs and are unable to comprehend the moving two-dimensional images on a television screen. Being unfamiliar with this completely foreign technology they cannot comprehend it. This is not to say any culture is primitive or inferior. It is only to emphasize that when faced with a radically different technology than the familiar, many people have a hard time seeing it.

I am not saying Egyptology or any other isolated culture is primitive. I am only saying this book's explanation of the assembly of the Great Pyramid water pump transcends Egyptologist's interpretation of the evidence. Egyptologists will not contradict their mindset to accept what is in this book. Their narrow training and extensive indoctrination inhibit them from giving the information in this book an open minded consideration. Truth is most elusive to those who will not look, or have something to lose.

Egyptology is not a real science, validating hypothesis with experimentation. Egyptology is more like a devoted self-encapsulated culture or a college credentialed cult more interested in handing down from generation to generation the often repeated stories, myths and legends of pyramid origins. Egyptologists are like academic Moulas offering edicts which cannot be proven scientifically or even questioned. This modern appearing yet stratified and stagnated belief system has its own brand of high priests. New priests are indoctrinated into the faith by the high priests in rituals of elaborate college classroom initiations guaranteeing the survival of this modern day mystery religion. They have ensured that their brand of mythology is passed from one generation to the next. They even have sacred objects which they treat not unlike religious icons in lavish shrines (museums) around the world and pay homage to regularly.

People ask, "How can I know if this book's explanation of the Great Pyramid's construction is true or not?" I know how you will be able to tell if the information in this book is NOT true. Imagine if you will the passing of 200 years from the publication of this book. Also imagine in that time this understanding of the building process and construction of the Great Pyramid water pump is widely accepted. Visualize that this understanding is taught in all major universities with distinguished experts heading departments dedicated to the Great Pyramid being built using water locks. These wealthy departments would be funded by well healed donors who provided lavish financial support to the highly regarded science of Great Pyramid Water Pumpology. Every year book after book would be published in every language lining the shelves of university libraries all around the world providing explanation of every aspect of the Great Pyramid as a water pump.

Imagine the passing of 200 years of generous financial backing in a world where there are prestigious museums dedicated to the Great Pyramid being a water pump all over the globe. Imagine these museums to have in excess of billions of dollars of assets and funding as well as hundreds of millions of dollars in yearly income. Imagine the passing of 200 years and the science of Great Pyramid Water Pumpology to be a rich science and a powerful institution.

Then also imagine nowhere in the world is there an attempt to build a functioning water pump as a demonstration to show how the Great Pyramid water pump operated. This group of highly educated professionals, authors and educators make no attempt in recreating even one valid aspect of how full sized stones were moved or set in place or making a functional water pump. Imagine in this future time, no Great Pyramid water pump expert has any interest in showing the world what they profess to be true or having no interest in making the world a better place with this technology they profess the ancient builders possessed and demonstrated.

Imagine a world 200 years in the future which is highly polluted by its own addiction to fossil fuels. This world has ongoing wars in oil rich countries to liberate the subjugated people. (Liberate the people of their oil) The politics and finances of energy have created entire regions of desperate terrorists. The world is dangerous, hostile and unstable, clamoring for a cheap, clean energy source to power their homes and cities. And yet there is a legion of Great Pyramid water pump experts who say ancient mankind built and used a water pumping power plant which meets these very needs but they steadfastly refuse to develop this world saving energy technology.

If after 200 years this scenario comes to pass then you can rest assured what is in this book is wrong. If in 200 years no valid demonstrations are presented showing how the features of the passages and chambers relate to a functional water pump then that is a valid way of knowing this research is inconsistent with what happened so long ago on the Giza Plateau.

Some say the above scenario has already come to pass, with one difference. Instead of advocates of the Great Pyramid water pump theory of construction the experts are Egyptologists. If the fulfillment of the above scenario would be proof positive that the Great Pyramid was not built to be a water pump then why would the fulfillment of the same scenario with Egyptologist's theories be any different?

Modern Egyptology had its beginnings with Napoleon's savants. Egyptology has had over 200 years to validate their proposed construction methods by valid repeatable scientific demonstrations. They could have made one casing stone like the originals at the Great Pyramid to validate their assertions that these extremely precise stones were made by hand. They cannot show us. They could have moved a 70 ton payload, like a locomotive up a dirt ramp using back muscles to validate their assertion that these massive stones were moved in this manner. They cannot show us. They could have dragged a sixteen ton payload around a corner of a spiral ramp. They cannot show us.

They could do any number of the specific tasks necessary in the creation of components for the Great Pyramid or demonstrate construction methods to assemble the Great Pyramid. They cannot show us. If after 200 years no water pump can be demonstrated it will indicate the research is invalid. This same way of knowing holds true with the idea of extreme precision being created using hand tools as well as the idea of a ridiculous mega-ramp hypothesis.

There is a distinction between the ideas of Egyptology and the theory of this book. Egyptology has had generations to prove their ideas and this alternative understanding of the Great Pyramid is just getting started.

Just before establishing our nonprofit organization called the Pharaoh's Pump Foundation, I was lamenting the difficult task of getting an Egyptologist to listen to or consider this research about the Great Pyramid. I discussed this with a very good friend of mine who has earned my utmost respect. He is one of the most successful men I have ever met. He has a long-lasting successful marriage and wonderful, well adjusted productive children. He is well educated and extremely intelligent which are two entirely different things. He has a thriving business and is quite well off financially. He is confident, well-read, and a great asset as a friend.

His business involves the movement of heavy freight and very large pieces of equipment. He owns long-haul tractor-trailers, heavy cranes and all the necessary equipment to conduct his business. His competence, experience and accomplishments make him a leading expert in his field. Above that he is an astute man experienced in the ways of the world. He is known for his insight and wisdom as much as his business savvy.

His business involves very heavy construction of bridges, industrial sites, and large public works projects in the Pacific Northwest of the U.S.A. He is an expert in moving extremely large and heavy objects. In a recent conversation he helped me put in proper perspective the difficulty I face with the aversion to the acceptance of new ideas.

"Steve, let's look at it this way," he told me. "As an owner of a freight and heavy equipment moving business I have to moved hundreds, no make that thousands of tons of payload every year. If nothing else, I am an expert in moving extremely heavy objects."

I replied in agreement, "I can't debate that."

He continued, "Well, those ancient Egyptians also were known to have moved very heavy objects too. Isn't that right, Steve?"

I said, "Many heavy stones were moved in the valley of the Nile and that is an important aspect of my research." He went on, "Since I move very heavy objects, often times even heavier than the heaviest moved in ancient times, then that makes me an expert. Wouldn't you say so, Steven?"

I agreed, "Yes that is your expertise which you demonstrate on a daily basis. There is no doubt."

With piercing eyes he then asserted, "Well then, as an unquestioned expert in the movement of heavy objects, even though I use methods that are different from those used in ancient times, that expertise qualifies me as an expert in potsherds!"

Startled by his very odd statement I exclaimed, "You move heavy objects and heavy objects were moved in ancient times. You moved your objects differently than the ancients did but what does that have to do with potsherds??"

He replied with confidence, "My expertise in moving heavy objects is unquestionable. The builders of the Great Pyramid showed their expertise as well. Yes, we used different techniques and used different tools of the trade but we both moved fifty ton and heaver objects. Therefore I am an expert in ancient potsherds."

I finally admitted, "Yes, you and the Ancients moved heavy objects even though different methods were used. But you lost me on how that makes you an expert in potsherds."

He reasserted his position, "Moving extremely heavy objects is what makes me an expert in potsherds."

Not know where this is going and still puzzled by how he connects his business and experience to potsherds I ask him a few questions as a way to gain understanding.

"Have you ever been on an archeological dig?"

He replied "No, but I am an expert on potsherds."

I asked, "Have you written a book or even read a book dealing on the subject of potsherds?"

He replied "No, but I am an expert on potsherds."

I asked, "Have you ever interpreted a potsherd?"

He replied "No, but I am an expert on potsherds."

I didn't know what else to say. I know he is trying to make a point but I am still perplexed. This is a no nonsense successful man that I admire and he is trying to make a point to help me understand so I continue. I simply told him, "You are unquestionably a modern day expert in the movement of heavy objects but I do not see how that would qualify you in any conceivable stretch of the imagination in being an expert in ancient potsherds. Even if you moved massive stones in the exact same manner as the ancients did, that would not help you in being an expert in potsherds."

He paused to let me think and then smiled. The next thing he said I did not see coming. It was the event which spurred me on to establish the foundation dedicated in understanding how the stones of the Great Pyramid were moved, set in place and why.

He finally asked me, "What about the other way around?"

"The other way around of what?" I replied still not knowing what he was getting at.

"If instead of getting my business degree and running my heavy freight and construction business, I studied potsherds in college and graduated with a fancy "Potsherdology" degree. Then went on Archeology digs, wrote books and articles on my subject of expertise and was renowned for my expertise in potsherds interpretation. Then would I be an expert in potsherds?"

Hesitantly I said, "Yes of course you would be."

As only a boss can, he demand, "Explain to me how that would make me an expert in operating the fleet of equipment I own or make me an expert in moving extremely heavy payloads? Tell me!"

I finally understood what he was talking about. Smiling back I said with renewed confidence, "I can't answer you because it wouldn't. It wouldn't because they are two very different areas of education and experience with virtually no overlap."

Slapping me on the back he said, "Well you finally got it! Just because an Egyptologist studies what is in a tomb doesn't mean he knows how a pyramid was constructed. By studying how Priests embalmed mummies does not make a person an expert in moving heavy payloads. The two disciplines are not related now and never were. That is like saying, because a Pharmacist knows how to fill a prescription he knows how to build and run the factory which made the pill."

My freight moving friend often speaks in the vernacular of truck drivers yet he eloquently conveys his thoughts. He continued, "Yes, Egyptologists have done some serious smoke blowing. So much so even they believe it themselves. I worked on some pretty big projects all over the Pacific Northwest and have moved some very huge and expensive payloads. I have done a lot of job interviews for my business looking for qualified employees. Imagine if someone came in for an interview saying his qualifications were interpreting potsherds or reading hieroglyphs. I would ask if he has ever moved the massive objects we move every day. If he would tell me no, but his qualifications in potsherds makes him an expert in moving heavy objects I would laugh him right out of my office. I wouldn't let him check the air pressure on my truck tires or even wash the road grime off the tractor trailers. I wouldn't risk having an incompetent person like that around my business."

He went on telling me, "Yes, I move very heavy objects differently than was done in ancient times but I feel a real kindred spirit with those ancient builders. They and I are judged by our ability to get the job done. As far as Egyptologists go, I have never met, read about or heard of any one of them who has done any moving on a par with the master movers of ancient times. In terms of moving extremely heavy objects, or the accomplishment of any tangible goal, Egyptologists are actually in an arena of activity where results are neither demanded nor even expected."

My friend said to me, "Let's look at it another way. Imagine if any Egyptologist was transported back to the time when the Great Pyramid was in the planning stage. The Leader of that ancient civilization, whose goal was to create that large public works project, would need competent people to produce the desired results. The Egyptologist would proclaim his vast expertise and request an audience with whoever was in charge."

The leader would ask the Egyptologist, "Can you help in completing this large public works project?" The Egyptologists would pontificate on his education and mummy extraction qualifications. The Leader would ask again, "Do you have any knowledge or abilities which will help me with my important goal of actually constructing my massive public works project?" The Egyptologist would insist he is an expert even though he has never moved any heavy payloads and has never created a single full sized precision component needed for the Leader's construction project.

The Egyptologist would offer to demonstrate his expertise in the specialized field of moving heavy objects by telling the Leader of this ancient culture to smash the pot by his throne. With great confidence the Egyptologist would assure the leader of his authority in building techniques of massive structures by divining an interpretation of the pieces of the broken pot.

"Steven," my friend asked me, "Do you know what this Leader would say?"

"No," I responded.

My freight moving friend said, "I do, because I too am a leader and I have expertise in this field. I have demonstrated my abilities to accomplish extraordinary goals in massive construction projects. I deal with people who expect Herculean goals accomplished on schedule and on budget. I spend my life, where results are the measure of competence, not interpretation of other people's accomplishments. I am a doer and I only get paid when something gets done. This is what that long ago Leader, whose goal is to get the project completed, would have said to the Egyptologist."

The leader would have said, "You may know about broken pots but that won't help me get my large public works project constructed. In regards to the extremely specialized work of moving very heavy objects you are an imbecile. Guard, get this simpleton out of my sight!"

Being a busy and productive man with constraints on his time my friend had to cut our talk short. As he walked me to the front door of his lavish home he said, "When considering the absolute lack of any meaningful research conducted by Egyptologists, the field you are studying is wide open. There is much work ahead of you as well as resistance to your research but don't let that bother you in the least. It is what you will discover in your research which will make the journey worth-while."

I will always be indebted to my friend for his clarity of understanding.

A time will come when people will have the advantage of not having to unlearn what they have been taught to embrace the information in this book. If they want to know about the Great Pyramid they will go to the library and this book will be right beside the books that talk about sweaty mega-ramps. They can come to know both explanations with equal footing. They can weigh in their minds the relative validity of each description and make their assessment. That goal is one of the major reasons for writing this book.

In reviewing this manuscript a traditional Egyptologists slammed it on my desk and said, "I don't believe a word of it!" I casually responded, "That's OK with me. By the way, did you let your teenage children read it?" His only response was a puzzled expression.

It is the young people who matter and will be responsible for creating the world in which they will live. I hope they will embrace this book in both understanding their fellow human's abilities in distant antiquity, and how that information will help them shape a better world for themselves and for the lives of their children in their future. That is what the Great Pyramid was about, and that is what this book is about.

This is not the conclusion of this research, it is just the beginning. We are only getting started. Robert Goddard said, "It is difficult to say what is impossible, for the dream of yesterday is the hope of today and the reality of tomorrow."

I have often had the opportunity of giving a presentation about this research at various gatherings, research workshops or lectures at colleges. Afterwards there is always a question and answer session. I am forever barraged by debunkers, skeptics and experts who explain why this research is flawed based on their understanding of the Great Pyramid's "context." Also they tell me why this book is wrong based on the books they have read and the interpretation of evidence with which they are indoctrinated. They even follow me out to the parking lot to my vehicle explaining why I am wrong based on their idea of the sequence of the construction of the pyramids or based on the primitive technology of the Great Pyramid builders yet they themselves cannot substantiate their claims with valid demonstrations.

For fun I ask the crowd around my vehicle if any of them consider themselves Egyptologists. Several will proudly raise their hands. I'll pick out the stuffiest or most annoying one and say, "I've never met an Egyptologist who could find a water pump even if he looked right at it. My vehicle is stock from the factory and has a water cooled engine under the hood. Just to make a point I'll bet you $100 Dollars there is a water pump under the hood you can't find."

After a few moments of being encouraged by those around him the person I challenged will confidently take the bet.

The crowd cheers. With the introduction of money, people's interest always seems to be heightened. I make sure he understands the bet. (You always have to make sure educated people understand.) Then I lift the hood. The person I bet with will look under the hood and after a few moments point to the engine's water pump and say, "There's the pump. You better give me the money. I have witnesses!"

"Is that your final answer?" I ask.

"I found the water pump now give me the money. Everyone saw you make the bet!" The crowd around me agrees.

I tell him, "The bet my friend is you *can't* find a water pump under the hood of my car, not that you *can* find one. Sir, so far, you haven't found a water pump just as I bet you. There are two water pumps and you haven't showed me the other one." (My vehicle is exactly as it was from the factory)

Stunned he stands motionless peering into the engine compartment, as I ask, "Did you give up yet?"

After a while I impatiently point to the other water pump and the crowd gasps and then laughs as I request my money. The expert cries fowl and demands he is not going to pay because being an expert he was easily tricked or by virtue of his authority he is not required to honor the bet. I announce to the crowd, "I rest my case." I close my hood and drive off hoping at least some of them understand.

Just as under the hood of my vehicle, The Great Pyramid is a water pump which the expert community currently cannot "find."

It is interesting to note, I have made the same bet (except in a much lower amount) with professional or amateur backyard car mechanics. With them I have never won the bet. They always point at the water pump on the engine. When I say there is another one they simply point at the other one and I hand them the money. It is an enlightening experiment well worth the investment.

As Edward Kunkel noted in his book, Pharaoh's Pump, it is not the soft handed ultra-educated, ivory tower bound intellectuals who are equipped to understand this revolutionary theory. Those who are best suited by their education and experience to understand and embrace this explanation of the construction method of the Great Pyramid are the technically oriented people who build skyscrapers, maintain factories and work in ship yards. These highly competent professionals have a valuable experience and unique understanding of how monumental goals are accomplished involving massive projects in the real world. It is these people who seem most receptive to this research when they become familiar with this theory.

Tolstoy said, "I know that most men, including those at ease with problems of the greatest complexity, can seldom accept even the simplest and most obvious truth if it be such as would oblige them to admit the falsity of conclusions which they have delighted in explaining to colleagues, which they have proudly taught to others, and which they have woven, thread by thread, into the fabric of their lives."

Dear reader, I do not know what conclusions you have, which you delight in explaining to colleagues, which you proudly teach to others, and which have been woven, thread by thread, into the fabric of your life. Although this explanation of the how the Great Pyramid was built is not the simplest and most obvious method, it is what I maintain happened when the Great Pyramid was built by the Original Builders.

Chapter 18
What's next?

The Great Pyramid was built level by level. Watertight casing stones impounded water and buoyancy was used throughout the building process. Water locks were employed to move stones up to the needed height. Specialized methods were used to move the stones to their final resting place.

So what does it matter? What does it mean? Why should anyone care? Can it somehow make a difference now? Can it help anyone?

Through understanding the construction method of the Great Pyramid the remaining physical evidence speaks of a whole host of high technologies. This author contends these technologies were instrumental in the creation of the structure call the Great Pyramid. But most importantly these ancient high technologies when fully understood can be adapted to be used in our present time to help our modern but very troubled world.

Just some of the high technologies associated with the Great Pyramid's construction are as follows:

• Water Locks. This is a high technology used by the Original Builders and it is still the method of choice used in the 21st century to move massive objects. Our best engineers choose water locks now just as the best engineers chose water locks when building the Great Pyramid.

Water locks are not a lost technology in our age. What *is* lost is modern mankind's knowledge that the Original Builders understood the technology of water locks and utilized that technology on a grand scale.

• Precision stone cutting. The direct physical evidence of the Great Pyramid is replete with examples of extreme precision in stone cutting, both in limestone and granite. I am equal to all Egyptologists in that I too, am unable to demonstrate how the Original Builders cut stone with such exacting precision. The nonprofit foundation I founded is currently conducting research in this area. Developing these advanced stone quarrying technologies would be beneficial in today's world.

• Extremely strong bonding agent. There is great debate as to the chemical composition of the bonding agent found between the casing stones. A bonding agent was also used between the stones of the Grand Gallery as well as many other precision cut stones. This bonding agent is legendary for its strength. Adequate research concerning this bonding agent has not been forthcoming from Egyptology. Certainly to redevelop this extremely strong material would be a tremendously valuable product with many applications in today's world.

• Other less known technologies. Besides the previously listed high technologies that were used in the construction of the Great Pyramid there are other technologies that are not so apparent. This is because there is even less physical evidence to analyze. One example comes to mind.

• Communication. How was the vast amount of complex and technical communication required for such a construction project accomplished? To coordinate the daily ongoing activities at the building site, work camps, quarries, water locks, river transportation and suppliers of everything that would be involved in such a project would be a daunting task!

The ability to accomplish the necessary communication would require some form of high technology. Writing on rocks or broken pieces of pottery isn't good enough. Possibly they used the reflection of mirrors visible over great distances or even some form of wireless telegraphy or even radio. As an Amateur Radio Operator this subject intrigues me yet evidence for communication methods is virtually nonexistent.

These examples are but a very short list of the high technology which was involved in the construction of the Great Pyramid. Yet there is another high technology which is pivotal to the construction method. This high technology is so important that all other ancient but advanced technologies pale by comparison. This high technology, the crowning achievement of the geniuses who built the Great Pyramid was their ability to pump water!

Yes, it was the advanced and highly sophisticated water pumping technology which was the most important lost high technology of the Great Pyramid. Certainly all technologies were important but the *water pumping* technology was set apart and of a higher order than all other high technologies of this ancient civilization. For not only did the water pumping technology keep the ever rising construction pond full and supply water to the water locks built into the casing stones, the pumping of water served as the purpose of the Great Pyramid itself!!

The Great Pyramid was not built to house a dead man's body. It was built for the living. The Great Pyramid was built as a functioning machine. The Great Pyramid was infrastructure for the civilization who built it. The Great Pyramid was a water pump! Building the Great Pyramid was not an expense but a wise investment. The Great Pyramid turned desert into farmland, powered machinery and transformed subsistence into prosperity.

This specific ancient lost high technology and purpose of the Great Pyramid is so important that this subject will be the focus of my next book. The quantity of research conducted by the author in conjunction with the nonprofit foundation associated with this research is so vast that it will fill another book or more! There is so much new information resulting from this extensive research authoring another book which is dedicated specifically to the water pumping technology of the Great Pyramid is a necessity.

I know the questions you are asking. How did it pump water? Where did the water enter the Great Pyramid? Where did the water exit the Great Pyramid? Why build the Great Pyramid to be a water pump if the construction pump could already pump water? How was the water delivered to where it was used? What evidence is there for any of this? What was the power source? Where did these ideas come from? What proof is there for these ideas? These questions and others must surely be on your mind. But the most important question you can and should ask is this. Can this ancient lost but highly advanced technology of pumping water help us in the here and now?

This author has founded a 501 (c) 3 nonprofit organization dedicated to answering these questions. This organization's goal is to understand how and why the Great Pyramid was built and to re-develop the Great Pyramid's ancient high technology and adapt it to help our modern but very troubled world. Our web address is www.thepump.org. If you find this book interesting please visit our web site.

All of these questions and so much more will be addressed in my next book. The book in your hands is about *how* the Great Pyramid was built. My next book will be about *why* the Great Pyramid was built. That book will describe the operation of the Great Pyramid water pump in all its glory. It will discuss why the Original Builders went to the massive effort to build their colossal water pump and why it was worth it for them.

Beyond just explaining how and why this water pumping technology helped the Original Builders, my next book will discuss ways in which this ancient high technology will help *our* modern but troubled and hurting civilization. More importantly there will be an impassioned discussion as to why our civilization must have the courage and willpower to *redevelop* this ancient high technology to improve our environment, enhance our standard of living and bring a renewed prosperity to *our* lives in *our* age.

If we as a people are allowed to redevelop this specific ancient but lost highly advanced technology, we too can experience the prosperity provided by the high technology of the Great Pyramid water pump!

Author's Note

Thank you for reading *Lost Technologies of the Great Pyramid.* I hope this explanation of the assembly process used to build the Great Pyramid was thought provoking and informative.

If you liked this book you are sure to be interested in my second book titled, *the Great Pyramid Prosperity Machine.* This book describes why the Great Pyramid was built. *The Great Pyramid Prosperity Machine* explains the manner in which the Great Pyramid's passages and chambers were designed and built to be a massive water pumping system!

The Great Pyramid was a prosperity machine for the civilization which invested the time and effort to built it. In the book, *the Great Pyramid Prosperity Machine,* I describe how the ancient but high technology of the Great Pyramid can be redeveloped to help our modern but troubled world. Find out how this is possible by reading *the Great Pyramid prosperity machine.*

The Great Pyramid Prosperity Machine is available from Amazon.com or any fine bookstore. For more information about myself or the research related to the Great Pyramid water pump please visit www.thepump.org.

Appendix
50,000 Dollar Research Scholarship

When traveling, I always try to visit historical locations. I especially enjoy the locations which bring history to life through the use of real people reenacting the activities of those who once lived in historically significant areas. People remain the same but what is interesting about history is how people of different eras develop different methods of interacting with the world around them. This interface with the world is expressed in various period authentic technologies.

Recently I visited Fort Clatsop in northwestern Oregon. To my delight there were real people reenacting how the Lewis and Clark expedition performed various activities. They showed how candles were made and how salt was extracted from sea water. There were demonstrations on how food was prepared and preserved. They showed period authentic weapons as well as medical devices. Wearing period authentic costumes people of today depicted how members of the Lewis and Clark expedition lived and the way in which they preformed the activities described by historians.

The results of the demonstrations are remarkably similar to the original artifacts from the Lewis and Clark expedition.

In Colonial Williamsburg it is much the same. There you will find reenactments of the activities of the original colonists of that area. The various technologies they used are demonstrated in many significant ways. Real people demonstrated how spinning wheels operated as well as the making of yarn. There are demonstrations of paper making, book binding, sewing, blacksmithing, carpentry, glass blowing, and furniture making, just to name a few.

The results of their demonstrations are remarkably similar to the original artifacts made by the original colonists. The items created in these demonstrations are so much like the original artifacts that everyone agrees these demonstrations show how the original artifacts were made.

Many of the people doing reenactments are either college students working through the summer or people who are keeping traditional crafts alive. Yet, to me, these folks are true scientists in the purest form. They are engaged in demonstrations which prove how historical activities were performed. They have my greatest respect.

There is no centuries long debate as to the validity of these recreations. The reason for this lack of academic debate is that the recreations are like the originals. A Coppersmith or Silversmith of today making an item in a traditional way does not generate much debate. This is because the results of their modern day demonstrations are virtually the same as an original artifact. This is true for a print shop or blacksmith shop in Colonial Williamsburg. The articles they make today using period authentic methods are the same as original artifacts made hundreds of years ago. Again the reason there is no raging debate is because the recreated artifacts are virtually the same as the original artifacts.

These reenactors are using the Scientific Method. That is why I call them scientists.

Yet in stark contrast there is tremendous debate concerning virtually every aspect of the Great Pyramid. There is continuing heated debate among Egyptologists, independent researchers, alternative scholars and authors. This is because of two reasons. The first reason is a total lack of demonstrations which recreate the artifacts or construction procedures necessary to achieve the results evident in the Great Pyramid. The second reason there is ongoing and increasing debate as to how the Great Pyramid was built is that the few demonstrations that have been performed do not recreate similar objects or construction results that the construction of the Great Pyramid required.

I am not suggesting Egyptologists recreate the Great Pyramid. That is not necessary. But to demonstrate a few of the tasks listed below would help substantiate their position. The burden is on their shoulders to scientifically prove what they say is factual.

Has a 15 ton casing stone been quarried to the same accuracy as an original using the primitive tools Egyptologists say were available? No. Has a 15 ton casing stone been moved on or off a barge? No. Has a 15 ton casing stone been moved and set in place with the same precision that the original casing stones? No. The demonstrations of these activities are a litmus test of Egyptologist's cherished theory as to how the Great Pyramid was built.

Traditional Egyptologists the world over are in basic agreement as to how the casing stones of the Great Pyramid were quarried, moved and set in place. They speak of quarrying operations, moving techniques and their descriptions are in amazing agreement. There is universal agreement as to how the above activities were performed but virtually no accompanying demonstrations in the last 200 years to validate these assertions.

To help provide a motivation to create a valid demonstration of these activities the nonprofit organization I have founded is offering the research scholarship described below.

$50,000 Casing Stone Research Scholarship

The Pharaoh's Pump Foundation is offering a $50,000 Research Scholarship. The conditions and requirements of this Research Scholarship are as follows.

Synopsis of $50,000 Research Scholarship

Quarry and move five casing stones to the same precision and size of those remaining at the Great Pyramid. Move and place them in the manner that is described by traditional Egyptologists. Place these five casing stones in the configuration shown in the image below. Whoever is first in completing this task in the manner prescribed below will be awarded $50,000.

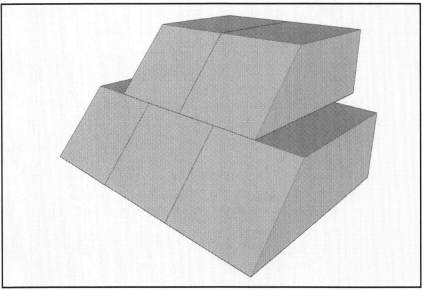

Fig. A.1 This is the configuration of the placement of the five casing stones necessary to complete the conditions of this scholarship.

Purpose of $50,000 Research Scholarship

The purpose of this Research Scholarship is to demonstrate how the Original Builders quarried, moved and placed the casing stones of the Great Pyramid in the manner asserted and maintained by traditional Egyptologists.

Requirements of the $50,000 Scholarship

Quarry 5 casing stones to the size and precision of the originals found at the Great Pyramid. Each of the 5 casing stones must exceed 14 tons in weight. These stones must be from limestone which is available in numerous areas throughout the world.

Move these 5 casing stones from the quarry onto a barge on a river. It is not necessary to use the Nile River. Any fairly large river will do. It is not necessary to use a period authentic loading-dock or to build a barge to the specifications of original barges of ancient Egypt. The loading dock or barge does not have to be recreated to complete this scholarship. The use of a contemporary loading dock and barge are allowed in this research scholarship.

Move the barge at least 2 miles on the river. This could be 1 mile one way and then 1 mile back to the original dock. This movement of the barge is intended to represent the transport of the casing stones accomplished by the Original Builders.

Move the casing stones off the barge and to the site prepared for their placement. This site must be at least 100 yards away from the river. This will allow the demonstration of the movement of the casing stones.

Place the casing stones in the configuration illustrated, with three casing stones in a row and two casing stones placed above the first three. The original casing stones are placed on a series of paving stones. In this demonstration it is not necessary to recreate the paving stones. A poured cement slab will be adequate and acceptable.

Time limit. No longer than 90 days from the start of quarrying actives to the completion of the entire demonstration. A three month period per year is the time traditional Egyptologists say that most of the work on the Great Pyramid took place. Egyptologists say a stone was placed every two minutes so, according to Egyptologists, this $50,000 Scholarship represents ten minutes work! Three months should be an ample amount of time to quarry, move and place 5 casing stones.

To receive the $50,000 the above tasks must be completed in the manner described by traditional Egyptologists, and the results must be of the same precision as the original casing stones. No steel hammers, chisels, or other steel tools can be used. No chains or nylon ropes can be used. No forklifts or heavy power equipment can be used. This scholarship allows only the use of tools and stone moving methods described by traditional Egyptologists. This includes the option to use up to 100,000 slaves or workers if you want to.

Evidence of your having completed the requirements of this scholarship can be submitted in the form of a video and photographs. The Pharaoh's Pump Foundation reserves the right to inspect the casing stones.

To participate in this research project simply Email or FAX the Pharaoh's Pump Foundation (www.thepump.org) and let us know your starting date. If you are the first to complete and provide documentation showing that you have completed the requirements of this scholarship you will receive $50,000.

Frequently Asked Questions about this Scholarship

Who is eligible? Egyptologists, University Departments of Egyptology, students majoring in Egyptology, University Professors, independent researchers, authors, stone masons or anyone else who is interested. This scholarship is open to any University, organization, group or individual, worldwide.

How will the funds be transferred to whoever completes the requirements of the Scholarship? Either by certified check or electronic funds transfer, depending on the preference of the first person or group completing the required tasks.

Is the money available? Yes, to whoever first completes the requirements of this scholarship.

Do I have to do this on the Giza Plateau using the exact same quarries? No. Anywhere on earth is acceptable that is convenient for the completion of the required tasks.

Can I keep the casing stones? Yes, you maintain ownership of the stones you create. They would be a nice display on a University campus and would be of high monetary value.

Can we have the money "up front" to help finance the cost of attempting to perform the required tasks? No, the money is awarded after the completion of all tasks including review and acceptance of submitted proof of completing the requirements of this scholarship.

If you have any questions about this research scholarship please feel free to contact us at: www.thepump.org.

Selected Bibliography

Recently the trend seems to be the greater number of books listed in a bibliography the better. Some books list in their bibliography over thirty pages of books! The use of a copious quantity of footnotes is becoming popular to justify what an author writes. A huge bibliography does not validate what is in a book nor does a short bibliography make a book less reputable or the information in its pages less valid. Multiple hundreds of footnotes are not validation, it is simply excessive. This author has kept the footnotes to a minimum and has provided only a short bibliography.

You can rest assured I have read more than my fair share of books concerning the Great Pyramid and related subjects. Instead of providing a prodigious list of the same books you can find in virtually every current book on the Great Pyramid, I have listed here just a few books to help you on your quest for knowledge and understanding. Many of these books are not usually associated with the Great Pyramid. Including a book in this limited bibliography is by no means an endorsement of everything in that book. There are few books with which I am in full agreement.

The Great Pyramid Prosperity Machine by Steven Myers
This book starts where *Lost Technologies of the Great Pyramid* ends. My second book describes in detail how the Great Pyramid was used as intended by the Original Builders. The Great Pyramid was a prosperity machine! This book describes how the passages and chambers of the Great Pyramid operated as a water pump!

Pharaoh's Pump by Edward Kunkel. As far as I am concerned, this book is one of the most important books written in the last 1,000 years about the Great Pyramid! Although sometimes difficult to follow, Kunkel does his best to tell the construction procedure and original purpose of the infrastructure we call the Great Pyramid.

One Bright Day by Edward Kunkel. This is Kunkel's autobiography. It is a frequently told story of the trials and tribulations of a genius rejected in his own time. Although hampered by a chronic lack of resources and the rejection of so-called experts he describes his life-quest of pursuing his research and his attempts at convincing the world of the importance in redeveloping this ancient high technology.

River and Canal by Edward Boyer. Although this book is for a juvenile reader its text and especially its illustrations are absolutely stupendous in describing the fascinating technology associated with canals and water locks. I highly recommend it.

Complete Pyramid Sourcebook by John DeSalvo

Decoding the Pyramids: Exploring the World's Most Enigmatic Structures by John DeSalvo

Pyramids on Water, Floating Stones: The Role of One of the Ancient Elements by István Sörös. There is much in this book I disagree with but the idea of the "Sun Ships" serving as floating cranes is very well researched.

Below are a couple of books relating to Catastrophism—a theory that the history of the earth has been punctuated by one or more catastrophic events. I have included these books because a number of researchers contend that the precision and high technology associated with the Great Pyramid was beyond the capability of ancient Egypt (and modern Egyptologists) therefore the creation of the Great Pyramid must have been performed by an advanced civilization *before* at least the last catastrophe.

The Path of the Pole: Cataclysmic Poleshift Geology by
Charles H. Hapgood
Maps of the Ancient Sea Kings by Charles H. Hapgood

Although I did not fully develop the idea of the
majority of Egyptian pyramids being an expression of some
sort of Cargo Cult, I have listed below a few books on this
subject. If the construction of the Great Pyramid predated
pharaonic Egypt most of the other pyramids could have
incorporated the basic shape of the Great Pyramid but also
served the purposes of the Ancient Egyptian's civilization.
Hopefully in a later manuscript I can fully address this
fascinating explanation for the construction of these other
pyramid structures.

The Cargo Cult by John Thorpe
Cargo, Cult, and Culture Critique by Holger Jebens
Cargo Cults and Millenarian Movements: Transoceanic
Comparisons by G. W. Trompf
Cargo Cult: Strange Stories of Desire from Melanesia and
Beyond by Lamont Lindstrom

The next two books I found of interest.

The Crystal Sun: Rediscovering a Lost Technology of the
Ancient World by Robert K. G. Temple. Much of the thrust
of this book is that Historians have misinterpreted the
function and purpose of a large number of artifacts that are
actually ancient lenses. This is a similar theme to what I
have written, in that, lost technology of the ancient world is
misinterpreted by Egyptology.

Forbidden History by J. Douglas Kenyon. This book
addresses a number of alternative theories, but my favorite
was Archeology and the Law of Gravity by Will Hart. This

chapter discusses the unworkable aspects of traditional Egyptologist's explanations of how the Great Pyramid was built.

For me it is difficult to recommend books that support the interpretations offered by the "science" of Egyptology. About the only thing I use these types of books for is the measurements of pyramids, passages and chambers. I can trust them to at least measure the direct physical evidence, but I am very suspect of their interpretations of the direct physical evidence. If for some reason you need an enormous bibliography both of the following books will help you out.

Giza: The Truth : The People, Politics, and History Behind the World's Most Famous Archaeological Site by Ian Lawton and Chris Ogilvie-Herald. This book does describe the early Arab writings but for the most part it is a book which follows the "company line" of Egyptology.

The Complete Pyramids by Mark Lehner. This book is authored by one of the most prominent of the high priests of Egyptology. This book, although lavishly illustrated, just rehashes the same undemonstrated hypotheses that so many open-minded researchers acknowledge as impossible. At least this book has pretty drawings to look at. If this book was about the scientific demonstrations provided by Egyptology to prove their stories then it would be filled with blank pages.

This short list of books is intended as a stepping stone on your path to further your research, help answer your questions, and to come to the truth you are seeking.

Index

Made in the USA
Charleston, SC
09 August 2012